For Key Stage 3 Science

Peter Ellis • Phil Godding • Derek McMonagle
Louise Petheram • Lawrie Ryan
David Sang • Jane Taylor

8

Published in 2005 by:
Nelson Thornes Ltd
Delta Place
27 Bath Road
CHELTENHAM
GL53 7TH
United Kingdom

05 06 07 08 09 / 10 9 8 7 6 5 4 3 2 1

A catalogue record for this book is available from the British Library

ISBN 0 7487 7989 2

Illustrations by Mark Draisey, Bede Illustration
Cover illustration by Andy Parker
Page make-up by Wearset Ltd

Printed and bound in China by Midas Printing International Ltd

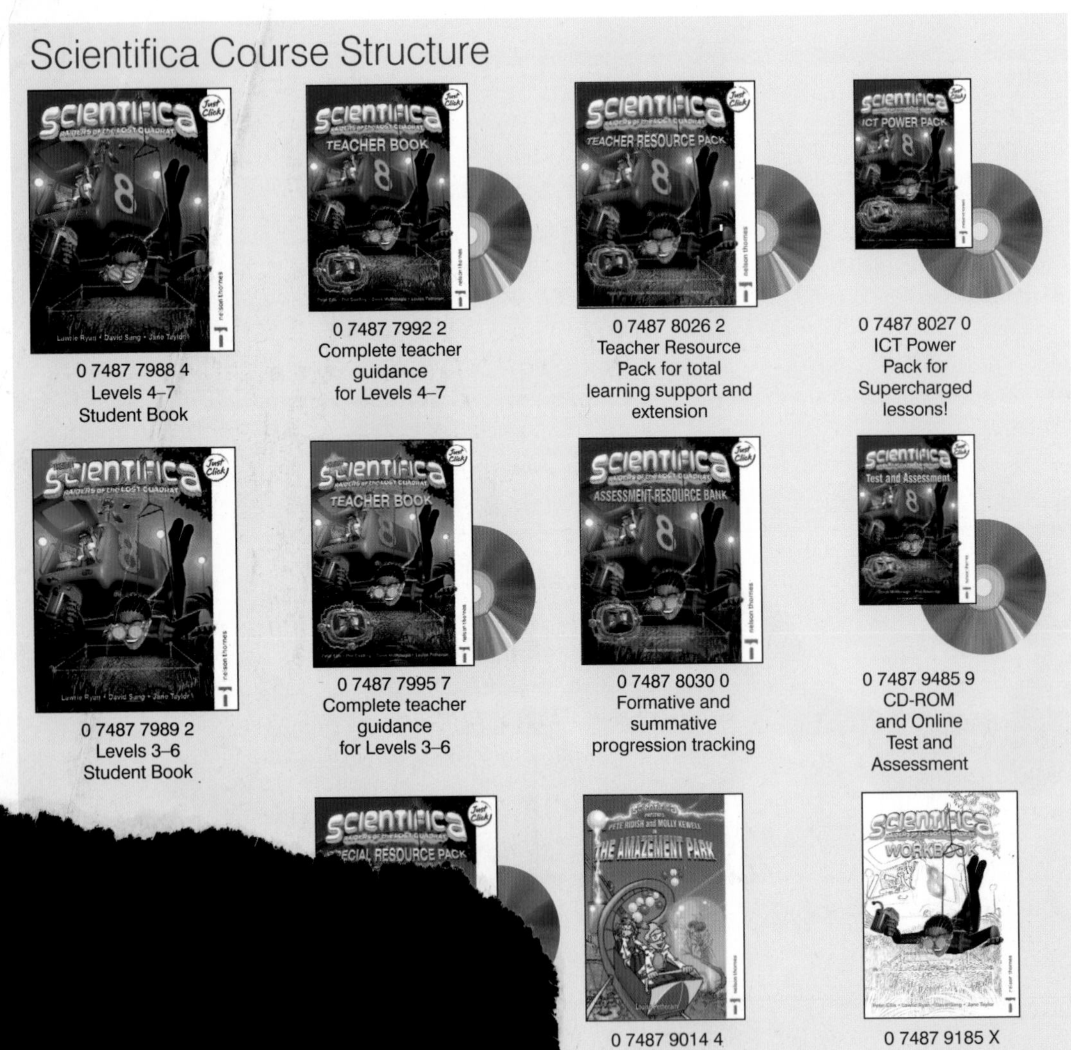

CONTENTS

SCIENTIFICA

See which lesson you are studying

This shows what you should hope to learn in this lesson. If you don't understand these things at the end, read through the pages again, and don't be afraid to ask teacher!

LEARN ABOUT
How Scientifica works

You can use the things you learn in Science in other subjects too. These panels will help you watch out for things that will help you in other lessons like Maths, Geography and Citizenship. Sometimes they will contain handy hints about other sections of the book.

CHALLENGE

It's really important to develop good computer skills at school. These ICT Challenges will provide lots of interesting activities that help you practice.

Welcome to Scientifica

Why should Science textbooks be boring? We think Science is amazing, and that's why we've packed this book full of great ideas. You'll find tons of amazing facts, gruesome details, clever activities and funny cartoons. There's lots of brilliant Science too!

Here are some of the main features in Scientifica. There are lots more to discover if you look…

Get stuck in

Whenever you see a blue-coloured panel, it means it's time to start doing some science activities. This blue panel provides a set of simple instructions you can follow. Your teacher may also have a sheet to help you and for you to write on.

Meet the Scientifica crew!

Throughout the book you may see lots of questions, with four possible answers. Only one is correct. The answers **are in different colours**. If the teacher gives the class coloured cards to vote with, it will be easy to show your vote.

Did you really understand what you just read?

Are you sure?

Won't these questions help you check?

SUMMARY QUESTIONS

At the end of each lesson, there is a set of questions to see if you understood everything.

☆ See those stars at the beginning of each question?

They tell you whether a question is supposed to be Easy (☆), Medium (☆☆) or Hard (☆☆☆).

Freaky insects, expanding bridges, boiling hot super stars... These are the most fantastic facts you can find!

Find out how scientists worked out what we know so far. Don't worry! There's plenty more for the scientists of the future to find out.

Gruesome science

Lethal clouds of poison gas, dead human skin cells, killer electric eels... Sometimes Science can be just plain nasty! Why not learn about that too?

UNIT REVIEW

There are loads of homework questions at the end of each Unit. There are lots of different types too. If you complete all the SAT-style questions, the teacher may be able to tell you what Level you are working at. Do your best to improve as you go along!

DANGER! AVOID THESE COMMON ERRORS

'Er, the Sun goes out like a light-bulb at night, right?' People make mistakes about science all the time. Before you leave the topic, this will help you make sure you're not one of them!

Phenomenal performance

If you do *brilliantly* in the lesson, your *extraordinary* teacher may ask you to turn towards the back of this *fantastic* book. There are lots of *super* activities for you to try in the *Phenomenal Performance* section.

Key words

amazing
brilliant
phenomenal

Keywords are a handy way of remembering a topic. Some might be scrambled up though!

We think you'll enjoy Scientifica, and hopefully Science too. Best of luck with your studies!

The (other) Scientifica crew – *Lawrie, David and Jane*

8A

Food and digestion

Coming soon

What's it all about?

Do you like chicken and gravy, or dhal and spinach, or perhaps groundnut stew? One thing's for sure – people all round the world love their food. Food is vital for life. It gives you energy and the things you need to grow and stay healthy.

In this unit you will find out what food is made of and how much you need. You will learn about the digestive system and how you digest food.

What do you remember?

You already know about:

- the different sorts of foods you need to have a healthy diet.
- why too much fat or sugar is harmful.
- how substances exist as particles that can move around.
- cells and organs.

1 Which of these foods are good for energy?
potatoes salad rice fish

2 Which of these foods are good for growth?
potatoes salad rice fish

3 Which of these foods contain a lot of sugar?
fish biscuits pasta jam

4 Which of these organs is in the digestive system?
lungs brain
small intestine heart

When you have decided, look at the diagram and match the letter to the organ.

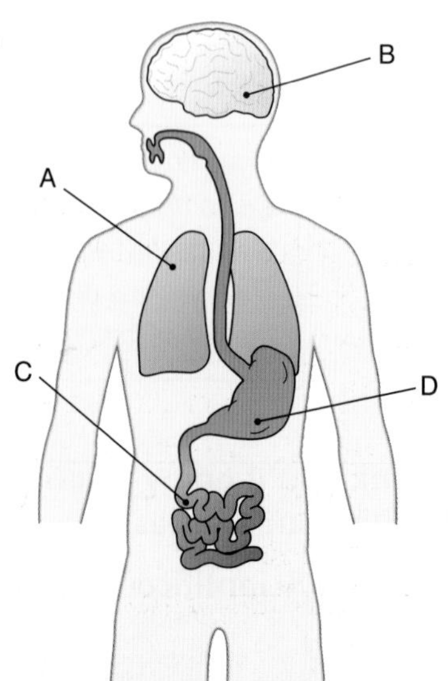

Ideas about food

QUESTIONS

The Scientifica crew likes the food in their canteen.
There's plenty to choose from.

a) Molly is vegetarian. Benson says you can't live without meat. Is Benson right?

b) Why should you eat five portions of food and vegetables every day?

c) Benson and Pete are playing in a match this afternoon. They can't decide whether to have pasta for dinner or wait until after the game. What would you choose? What are your reasons?

d) Is Mike right? Is that where his stomach is?

LEARN ABOUT

- nutrients

Eat your greens

Have you heard that you should eat fish because 'it's good for your brains'? Scientists have discovered that this is true. Fish and other foods contain substances called **nutrients.** Nutrients are essential for our health. Food is a mixture of nutrients. Different foods contain different amounts of them.

Nutrients

We need large amounts of **carbohydrates**, **proteins**, and **fats** every day. You can see some of the foods that provide them in Table 1. **Starch** and **sugars** are types of carbohydrate. They are found in plant foods such as cereal grains, roots and fruits.

Eating lots of different foods gives us all the nutrients we need

We need small amounts of **vitamins** and **minerals** each day. We also need about 1.5 litres of **water** every day.

Plant foods contain **fibre** as well as nutrients. We cannot digest fibre. It is not a nutrient, but we need it to help move food through our digestive system.

What do we use nutrients for?

Protein

We use protein to make new cells to repair damage and heal wounds. We also need protein to grow. Our nails, hair and skin cells all contain protein.

Fats and oils

Some people think fats and oils are unhealthy, but we must eat them to be healthy. Fat is an excellent energy store. We also need fat to make cells, such as nerve and brain cells.

The layer of fat under your skin reduces the amount of body heat you lose. It is an insulation layer.

Hair, even when it is turned into a quill, is mainly protein

Carbohydrates

We use carbohydrates to supply us with energy for everyday activities. Starchy foods contain other nutrients as well so they are healthier for us than sugary foods. They give us a steady supply of energy.

Table 1 The major nutrients

Nutrient	What we use it for	Good sources
carbohydrate	supplies energy for life processes	potatoes, pasta, rice, bread, sugar, cereals
protein	making new cells, growth,	meat, fish, nuts, cheese, eggs, beans, peas, lentils
fat	energy source, making cells and hormones, heat insulation	butter, nuts, sunflower oil, red meat, salmon, cheese, margarine, ice cream

CHALLENGE

Use a spreadsheet to work out which foods are 'best buys' for protein. You need to know how much each food costs, how much there is in the packet, and how much protein there is in the food.

An average 70 kg man contains about 47 litres of water – nearly 5 bucketfuls!

Testing foods

- Do some tests to find out if there is any starch, sugar, protein or fat in the samples of food you have been given.
- Be a detective! Use food tests to decide whether the mixture you have been given is chicken soup or a malted milk drink. Write down your test results and explain your decision.
- Food packets show how much of each nutrient is in the food. It is written as grams of nutrient per 100 g of food. Look at food labels to find three foods that are high in **a)** fat **b)** protein **c)** sugar.

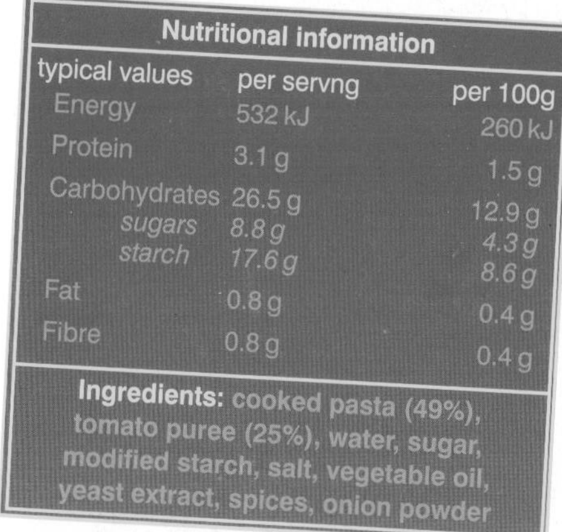

Nutritional information

typical values	per servng	per 100g
Energy	532 kJ	260 kJ
Protein	3.1 g	1.5 g
Carbohydrates	26.5 g	12.9 g
sugars	*8.8 g*	*4.3 g*
starch	*17.6 g*	*8.6 g*
Fat	0.8 g	0.4 g
Fibre	0.8 g	0.4 g

Ingredients: cooked pasta (49%), tomato puree (25%), water, sugar, modified starch, salt, vegetable oil, yeast extract, spices, onion powder

Can you guess what food this is?

SUMMARY QUESTIONS

1 ☆ Which nutrients provide energy?

2 ☆ Write out the six important substances in food.

3 ☆ List three foods that are a good source of a) protein b) starch.

4 ☆ Why do we need to eat protein?

Key words

carbohydrate
fat
fibre
nutrient
protein
starch
sugar

8A2 Vitamins and minerals

LEARN ABOUT
- vitamins
- minerals

We limey sailors are never scurvy dogs
LIMES

Scurvy

Five hundred years ago European sailors went on voyages that took them a long way from land and fresh food. They usually ate old salted meat and ship's biscuit for months at a time. Many sailors developed an illness called scurvy and died. Plenty of remedies were tried but there was no cure.

Sailors did not get scurvy when they had fresh fruit and vegetables. James Lind, a surgeon in the British navy, carefully tested an idea that fruits such as oranges and lemons kept away scurvy. His idea was correct. The Royal Navy gave sailors lemon or lime juice to stop them getting scurvy.

Q1 James Lind was testing an idea he had. Was his idea:

an hypothesis? an evaluation?
a prediction? a suggestion?

Vitamins

Lind did not know how citrus fruits protected sailors. Citrus fruits contain **vitamin C**. There are several vitamins. We need them in small amounts every day. If we do not have enough vitamins we develop a **deficiency disease.** Scurvy is a deficiency disease. You can find out about vitamins in Table 1.

You can store some vitamins in your body when you eat more than you are using. Humans cannot store vitamin C so we must eat fresh fruit and vegetables containing vitamin C every day. The amount of a vitamin that you need each day is your **RDA** – **R**ecommended **D**aily **A**mount.

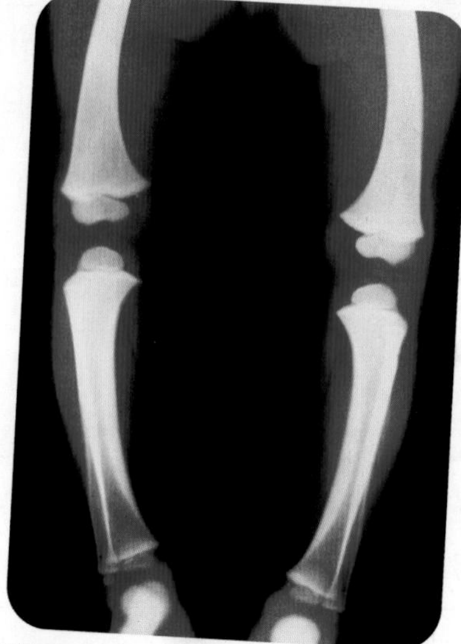

Without vitamin D your bones are too soft to support your weight

AMAZING SCIENCE!

If you added together the RDA of all the vitamins you need it would be about 0.1 g each day.

ICT CHALLENGE

Research folic acid. Why is it important for pregnant women?

Table 1 Vitamins and minerals

Nutrient	Use	Deficiency disease	Good food sources
vitamin A	eyesight, healthy skin	night-blindness	dairy products, oily fish, carrots, dark green vegetables
vitamin B1	healthy nerves, releasing energy	beri-beri	wholegrain cereal, yeast, eggs, nuts, liver, peas and beans
vitamin C	protects cells, absorbing iron	scurvy	oranges, lemons, tomatoes, blackcurrants, salad greens
vitamin D	absorbing calcium, strong bones	rickets	oily fish, milk, butter, eggs, made in the skin in sunshine
calcium	in bones and teeth, nerve cells	soft bones, rickets	cheese, milk, sardines, chocolate, bread, spinach
iron	making red blood cells, releasing energy	anaemia	liver, meat, eggs, cereals, apricots, spinach, cocoa

Minerals

We need small amounts of **minerals**. You need **calcium** to make strong bones. **Iron** is needed to make red blood cells.

Finding out about vitamins

Sir Frederick Gowland Hopkins showed that milk contains important vitamins. Six rats were fed on an artificial diet. Another six were fed on the artificial diet plus 2 cm^3 milk each day. By the 27th day, five of the rats on just the artificial diet had died. You can see the results in the graph.

In another experiment two groups of rats were used, but their diets were swapped after 18 days.

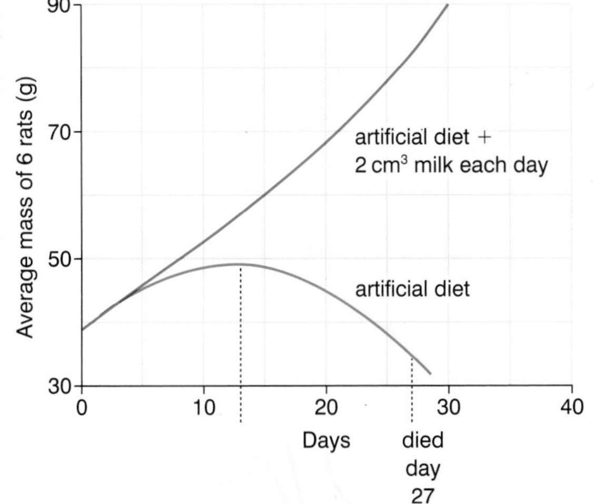

Q2 On which day did these rats stop growing?

Q3 What do you predict would happen to these rats?

Research vitamins

- Compare the vitamin C content of two fruit juices. Compare one that has been open for a few days with a fresh juice.
- Write a magazine article about why it's good to eat fruit.

SUMMARY QUESTIONS

1 ☆ Why do we need calcium?
2 ☆ Think of three foods that contain vitamin C. Why do we have to have vitamin C every day?
3 ☆☆ Why do teenage girls need more iron than boys?

Key words

calcium
deficiency disease
iron
mineral
vitamin

Learn about

- energy in food
- balanced diet

So if you eat your greens you should be healthy – right? Not quite. To be healthy you must have:

- the right amounts of carbohydrates, proteins and fats in your food,
- enough vitamins and minerals,
- enough energy to live and grow.

If you have all of these, and not too much of anything else, you have a **balanced diet**.

A traditional Christmas dinner contains over 4500 kJ. It's a good job you only eat it once a year.

Energy needs

	Daily energy need (kJ/day)
baby	4200
child	6800
boy	9600
girl	9200
woman	9500
man	11 500
pregnant woman	10 000

Energy and food

Food is the fuel that keeps us going. It gives us **energy**. Carbohydrates are our main source of energy in a healthy diet. We also use fat.

Q1 Which units do we use for energy?

kJ Nm kg km

We use energy:

- for the processes that keep us alive, such as breathing,
- to keep warm,
- to grow,
- for pregnancy,
- to replace or repair damaged tissues,
- to move about.

How much energy?

Different people need different amounts of energy. Year 8 students need lots of energy. This is because you are growing and do physical activities such as sports and walking to school.

A checkout cashier does not use as much energy as a classroom assistant because the cashier is sitting down most of the time. They are both working hard, but the cashier is not as physically active.

Men are larger than women. They need more energy to maintain their bodies. A builder will use more energy than a cashier or classroom assistant because building is physically demanding. Heavy work like this may use 1000 kJ per hour.

The more active you are the more energy you need

Malnourishment

Malnourished people do not have a balanced diet. When you do not have enough to eat, your body does not grow as much as it should.

Some people have enough energy in their food but not enough of one particular nutrient. Many people in the UK do not have enough vitamin C or D, or iron in their food.

Q2 Why does a young baby need nearly as much energy as an active child?

Many people get too much of their energy from fat. We should get 65% of our energy from starchy foods and just 25% from fat, but often the proportions are the other way round.

Not enough protein leads to kwashiorkor – a swollen belly is a symptom

Obesity

When we take in more energy than we need the extra is stored in body fat. Everyone needs some body fat to stay healthy. If we have too much body fat we may become **obese**. This puts a strain on our systems, such as the heart and joints.

In Unit 7I you found out how to measure the energy in food.

How balanced are you?

- Keep a food and energy diary for one ordinary school day. Record everything you eat and everything you do. Use data tables to find out how much energy you take in and how much energy you use.
  Are you in balance?
- Make a poster about your perfect meal. Write down what would be in it. Use tables of nutrients to find out about the nutrients in it. Draw bar charts of the nutrients.

CHALLENGE

Use a spreadsheet to calculate your energy input and energy output.

SUMMARY QUESTIONS

1. ☆ Why does a 13-year-old girl need more energy than her bank cashier mother?
2. ☆ Why is eating too many chips and drinking lots of soft drinks bad for you?
3. ☆ Give *two* reasons why a male footballer needs more energy than a female writer.

Key words

diet
energy
malnutrition
obese

8A4 The digestive system

Learn about

- your digestive system

Digestion

The digestive system is the group of organs that you use to digest food. You chew your food into small pieces in your mouth and swallow it. It passes along a long tube that extends from your mouth to your anus. It is mixed with digestive juices that digest food as it passes through. You absorb any useful nutrients on the way.

Why do we digest food?

Starch, fat and protein molecules are too large to absorb. They have to be broken down into smaller molecules that can be absorbed. We can absorb vitamins and minerals without digesting them.

The digestive system

Digestion starts when you chew food. You grind it into smaller particles with your teeth and mix it with **saliva**. Saliva helps you to swallow and it starts to break down starch.

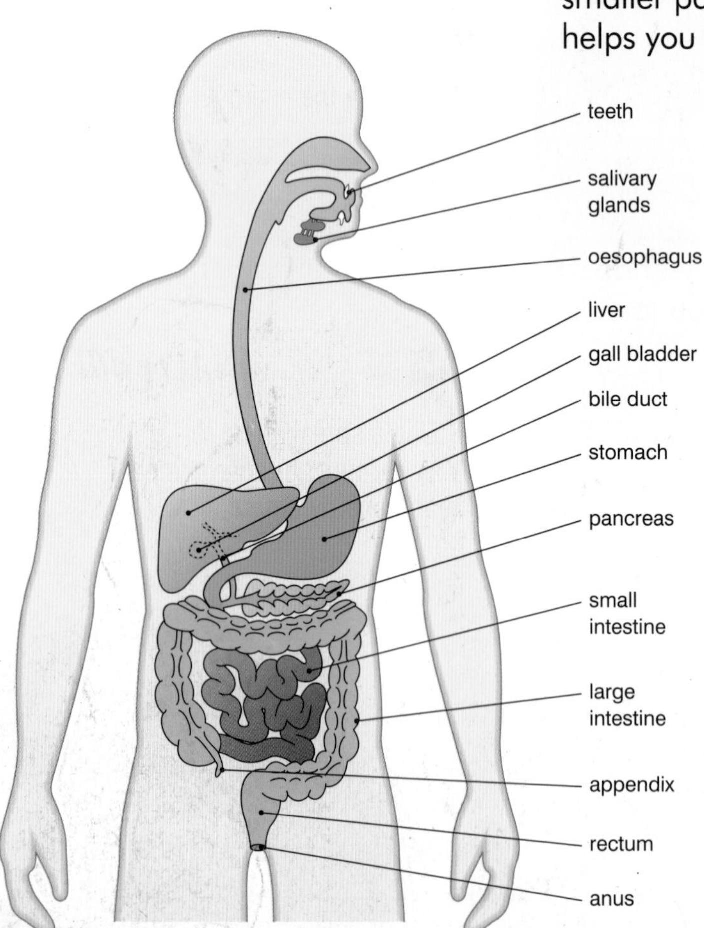

The digestive system

Food passes to your stomach through your **oesophagus**. As you swallow you can feel its muscles contract to push food along. Your food is pushed in this way all the way along to your anus.

Food in your **stomach** is pounded into a fine paste by muscles in your stomach wall. Digestive juices made in your stomach start to digest protein in your food.

You also make **hydrochloric acid** in your stomach. This kills bacteria in food and helps you to digest it. A thick layer of mucus protects your stomach wall from these digestive juices.

Q1 Is chewing your food a physical or chemical change?

This partly digested food enters your **small intestine**. A digestive juice from your **pancreas** is mixed with it. This finishes digesting starch, protein and fats. Your liver makes bile, which travels along the bile duct into your small intestine. Bile helps you digest fats.

Absorbing food

Your small intestine has millions of very small finger-like villi lining the inside. These form a very large surface. Digested food molecules pass into the villi, then into tiny blood vessels inside them. They are circulated round your body.

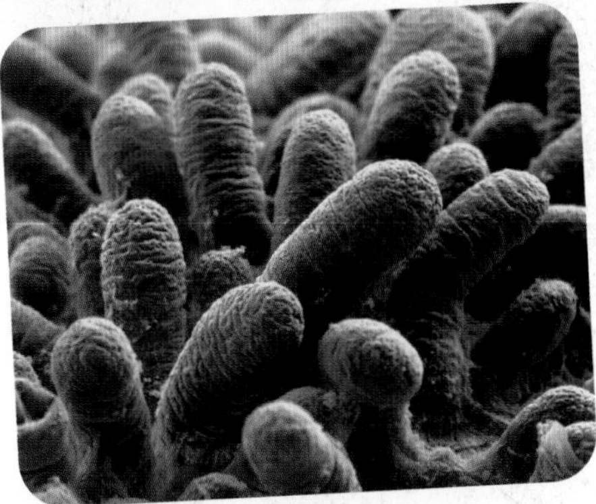

Villi make the surface of the intestine larger

Wastes

There are some things we cannot digest, like fibre in plant foods. These substances pass into the **large intestine**. We absorb water from what's left.

Indigestible material, fibre and bacteria from your large intestine form **faeces**. Faeces are stored in your rectum until they are pushed out through your anus.

Modelling intestines

Visking tubing is a membrane tube that is porous. Use Visking tubing to make a model intestine.

- Fill a length of tubing with a mixture of starch and glucose dissolved in water. Put it in a large test tube of warm water and keep it warm.
- After 20 minutes find out if starch or glucose has passed from inside the tubing into the water.
- What do you predict will happen?
- How will you detect starch or glucose?

The tubing is a model intestine, the starch and sugar is model food. What is the warm water round the tube a model of?

- Make a 'lift the flap' model of your digestive system.

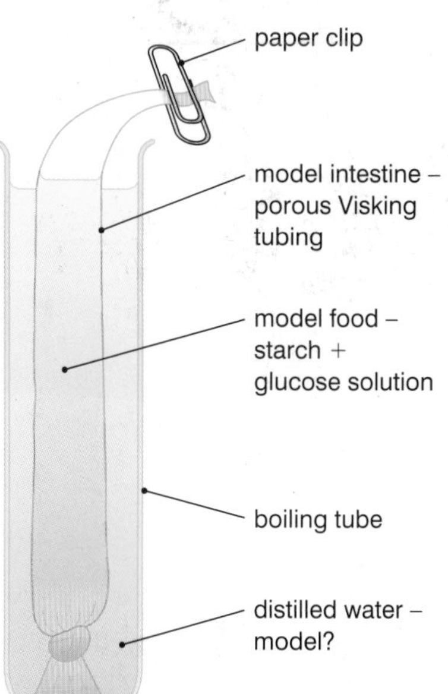

You can learn more about molecules in Unit 8E.

SUMMARY QUESTIONS

1 ☆ Match each part of the gut with its function:

stomach	absorbs water
small intestine	makes bile
liver	churns food to a paste
large intestine	absorbs digested food

2 ☆ Name two parts of the body where food is digested.

3 ☆☆ Some people make too much stomach acid. This gives them indigestion. Indigestion remedies often contain sodium hydrogencarbonate. Can you explain why this might relieve indigestion?

Key words

faeces
hydrochloric acid
intestine
pancreas
saliva
stomach

Digesting food

LEARN ABOUT
- how food is digested
- products of digestion

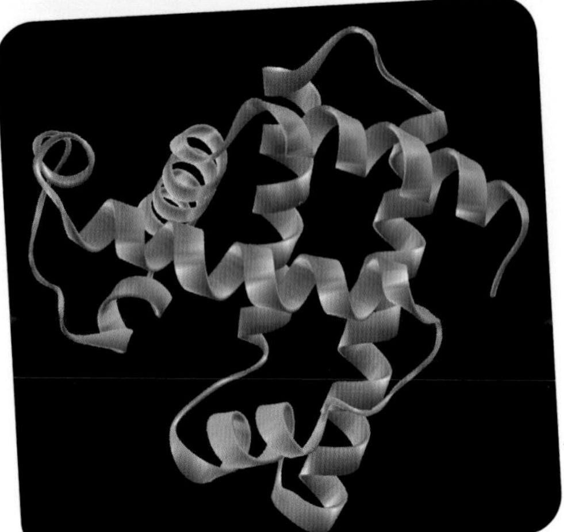

A 3-D model of a muscle protein

Large molecules

Protein and starch are very large molecules. They are made of smaller molecules linked together in long chains. When they are digested the chain is broken up.

Starch molecules are long chains of **glucose** units. When starch is digested glucose is made.

Protein molecules are long chains of molecules called **amino acids**. When they are digested amino acids are released. There are 20 different amino acids.

Different proteins contain different combinations of amino acids. We have to eat a variety of foods to get all the amino acids we need.

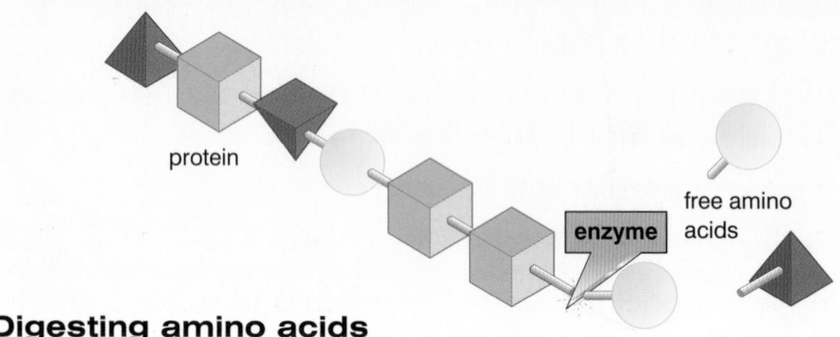

Digesting amino acids

Q1 Is digesting protein a physical or chemical change?

Digesting with enzymes

We use **enzymes** to break down starch, protein and fat.

Digestive juices contain a mixture of enzymes. Saliva contains **amylase** enzyme that breaks down starch to glucose in your mouth. In your stomach gastric juice contains a **protease** enzyme that digests protein.

In your small intestine the mixture of enzymes includes **lipase** to digest fats. Other enzymes finish digesting starch and protein.

The molecules made during digestion are:

- amino acids from protein
- glucose from starch
- **fatty acids** and **glycerol** from fat.

Gruesome science

Bile carries red and green substances that come from breaking down proteins from old red blood cells. They colour the contents of your intestines.

What happens to food after it has been digested?

Digested nutrients pass from your intestine into your blood stream. They are dissolved in your blood and carried to the liver.

You store iron and vitamin B in your liver. You also store some glucose in your liver and muscles. Glucose is converted to a substance called **glycogen**. This is your 'front-line' energy store. You use it to supply your cells with glucose for their energy needs.

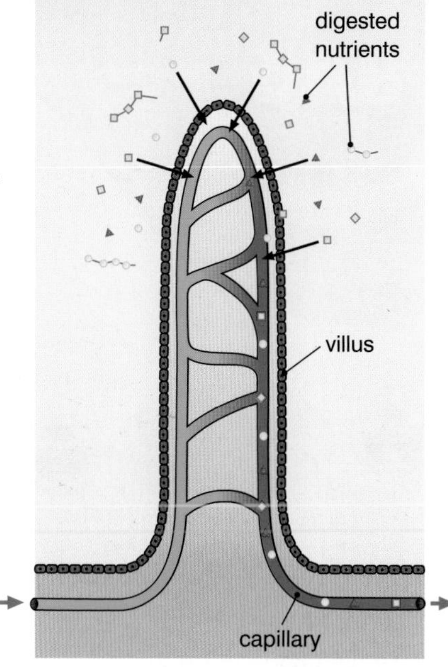

Absorbing nutrients

Digesting starch

Investigate how amylase breaks down starch to glucose.

- Warm a solution of starch and a solution of amylase enzyme separately to 37°C.
- Add a small quantity of enzyme to the starch solution.
- Test the mixture with iodine solution regularly to see if the starch has been completely broken down.
- When the starch has been broken down, test the mixture to see if there is any glucose present.

You learned in Unit 7E that we cannot make essential amino acids, so we have to have them in our food.

SUMMARY QUESTIONS

1 ☆ What is made when protein, carbohydrate and fats are digested?

2 ☆ What is an enzyme?

3 ☆ How do we store glucose?

4 ☆☆ Match the food with the type of enzyme digesting it:

butter	protease
beef	amylase
cornflakes	lipase

Key words

amino acid
amylase
enzyme
fatty acid
glucose
lipase
protease

Enzymes

LEARN ABOUT

- factors that affect how enzymes work

People go to the hairdresser to change their hair. People with curly hair have it chemically straightened. People with straight hair have it permanently curled. Hairdressers can do this because hair is made of protein. Chemicals and heat alter the shape of a protein.

An enzyme molecule can work on over 1000 molecules each minute.

Hair strands take on a different shape when their proteins are altered by hairdressing chemicals

Denaturing enzymes

The **enzymes** we use to break down food molecules are made of protein. Chemicals and heat affect them too.

Enzymes are permanently changed when they are heated to high **temperatures**. If they are heated above normal body temperature they become **denatured**. They cannot break down food molecules when they are denatured and so digestion stops.

Enzymes in the human digestive system work best at 37°C. In cool temperatures they work more slowly, but at higher temperatures they stop working altogether.

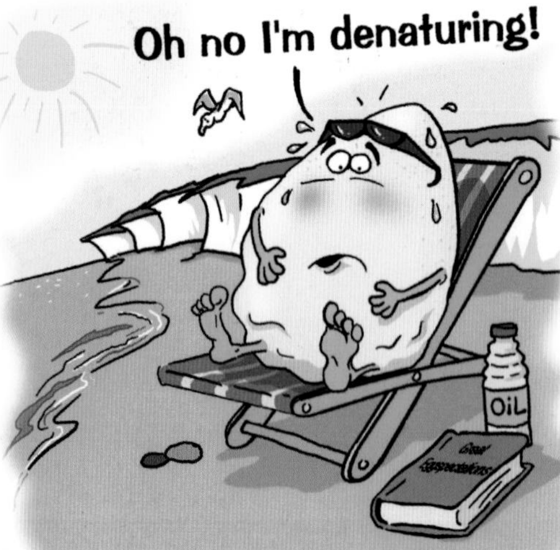

Egg white is a protein called albumen. It changes from runny and clear to white and hard as it denatures.

Acids, alkalis and enzymes

We measure the acidity or alkalinity of a solution by its **pH.** Each of our digestive enzymes works best at a particular pH. Our digestive system is arranged to give them the correct pH for their action.

Saliva makes your food slightly alkaline. This is the best pH for the enzyme in saliva. Chewing mixes the enzyme into food. It starts to work on starch in the food particles.

Your stomach enzyme needs acid conditions. Hydrochloric acid in your stomach produces a pH of 2–3. This is too acid for the enzyme in saliva and it stops working soon after food reaches your stomach.

When your food reaches the small intestine it passes into an alkaline environment again. The enzymes here will now work on finishing digestion.

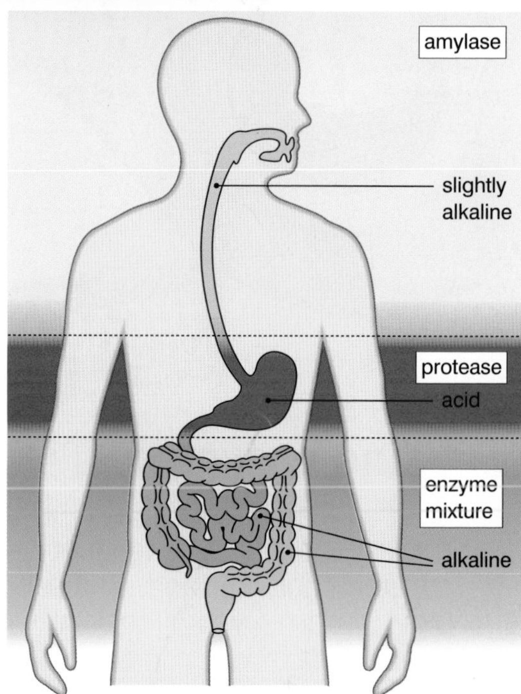

Different regions of the digestive system have a different pH

How temperature affects enzymes

- Plan and carry out an investigation to find out how quickly amylase breaks down starch at different temperatures.
- What procedure can you use to show that amylase breaks down starch? You will need to think about how you will know when starch has been broken down.
- What variables could affect how quickly the reaction will happen?
- What quantities of material and equipment will you need? Think about what you have learned from previous experiments with amylase

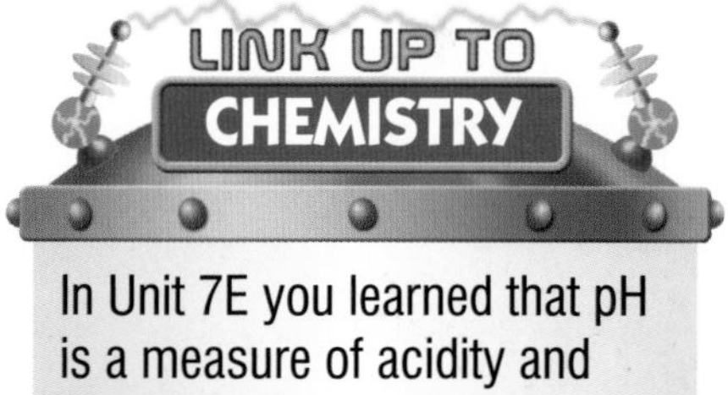

In Unit 7E you learned that pH is a measure of acidity and alkalinity.

SUMMARY QUESTIONS

1 ☆ Why do we have an acid in the stomach?

2 ☆ How does high temperature affect enzymes?

3 ☆☆ In experiments with digestive enzymes we usually keep the food and enzyme mixture at 37°C. Explain why.

Key words

enzyme
denatured
pH
temperature

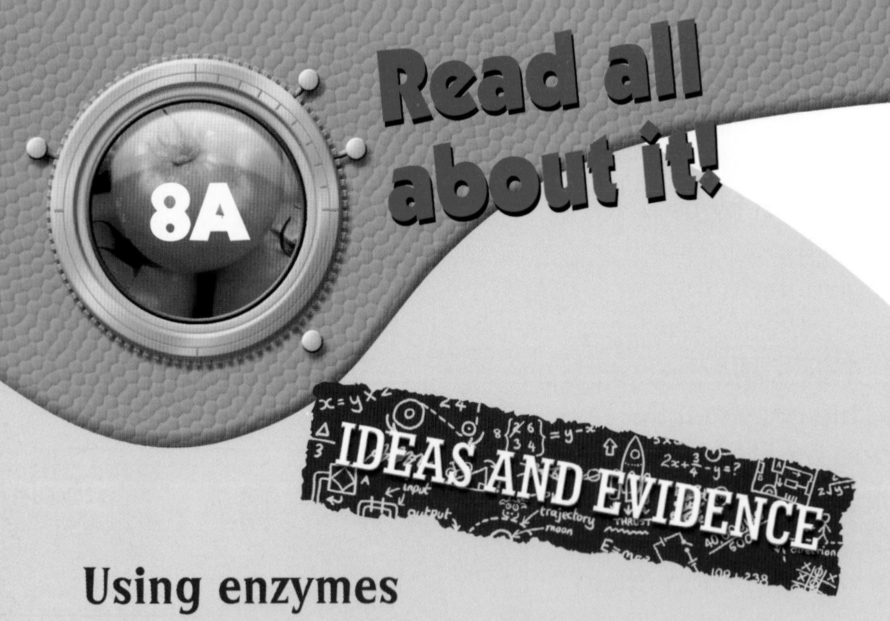

Using enzymes

After a meal there is always the clearing up. You have to clear the table and wash up. Your plates are covered in bits of food. The pans have crispy burnt bits. Swoosh – you fill the sink with hot water and a good squirt of washing-up liquid. The hot water loosens food particles so they can be washed away. **Detergent** breaks up fatty food traces into smaller particles.

Or, if you're lucky, all you have to do is load the dishwasher. Dishwater tablets and powder contain **enzymes** that digest food traces sticking to pots and pans. Large dried-on molecules are soaked and broken down to smaller soluble molecules that can be lifted off by the detergent. A dishwasher uses a spray jet of water hotter than your hands could cope with to wash these food traces off the crockery.

Dishwashing enzymes are not human digestive enzymes. Our enzymes would be denatured at washing temperatures of 60°C. These enzymes are from bacteria that are adapted to live in hot springs in volcanic areas.

SCIENTIFIC PEOPLE

Dieticians know about food and how we digest it. They give diet advice to people who have health worries.

Pregnant women are given advice on healthy eating to keep their iron and vitamin levels high enough for their baby's needs. Overweight people may need advice to help them lose weight and stay thinner.

A large part of a dietician's work is linked to specific health problems. People with **diabetes** struggle to control the amount of glucose in their blood and may not have enough energy stores for their needs. They need advice on how to control their carbohydrate input.

Other people react badly to substances in food. Many people cannot tolerate gluten, a protein found in wheat products such as bread, or lactose the sugar found in milk. A dietician can help them plan a balanced diet that avoids the foods they cannot eat.

The gluten in this bread could make some people sick

Use the Internet to find out about lactose and gluten intolerance.

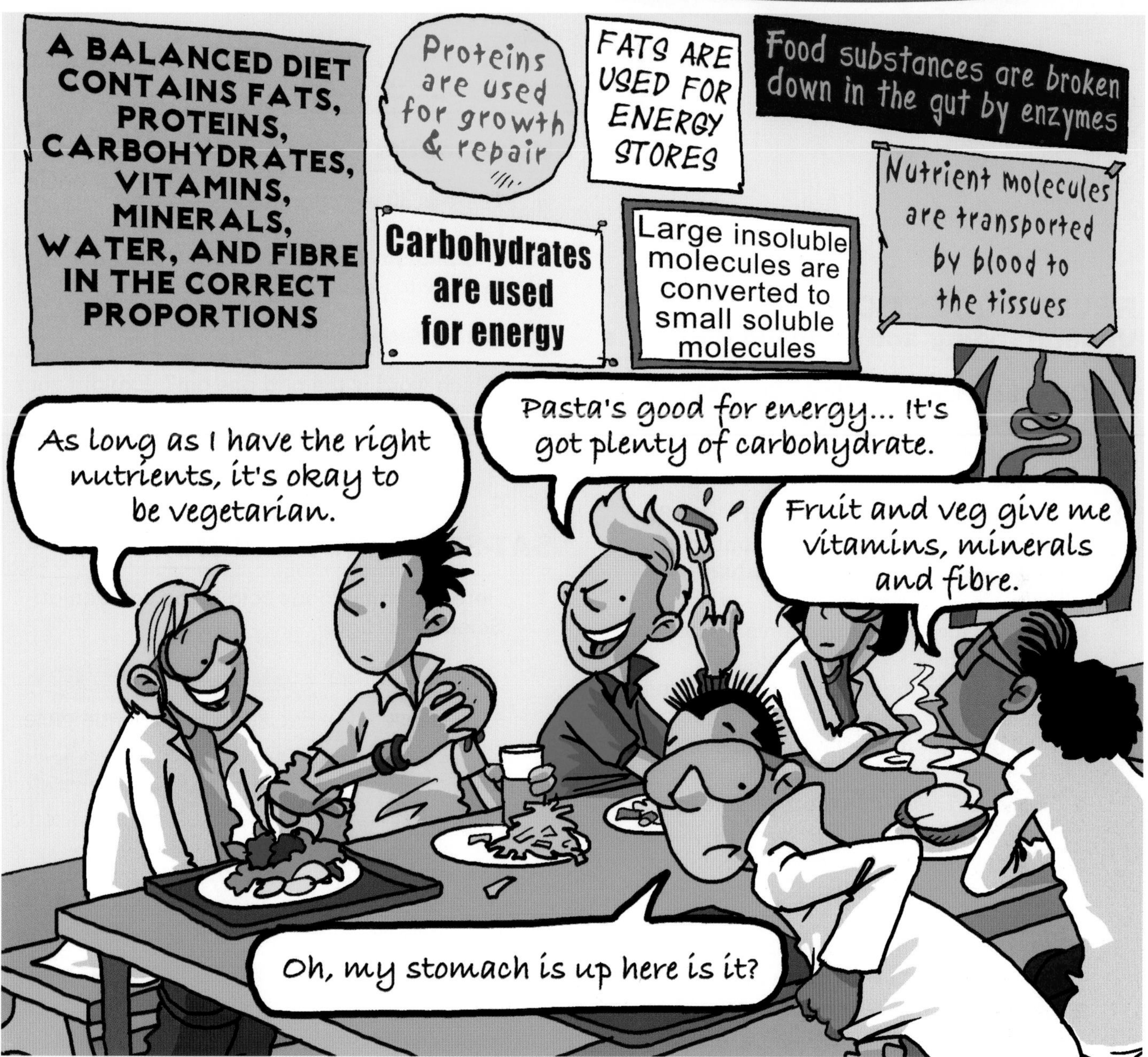

A BALANCED DIET CONTAINS FATS, PROTEINS, CARBOHYDRATES, VITAMINS, MINERALS, WATER, AND FIBRE IN THE CORRECT PROPORTIONS
Proteins are used for growth & repair
FATS ARE USED FOR ENERGY STORES
Food substances are broken down in the gut by enzymes
Carbohydrates are used for energy
Large insoluble molecules are converted to small soluble molecules
Nutrient molecules are transported by blood to the tissues
As long as I have the right nutrients, it's okay to be vegetarian.
Pasta's good for energy... It's got plenty of carbohydrate.
Fruit and veg give me vitamins, minerals and fibre.
Oh, my stomach is up here is it?

DANGER! AVOID THESE COMMON ERRORS

You use carbohydrate and fat to give you the energy you need for your activities. You do not use protein for energy.

Fibre is not a nutrient. You cannot digest and absorb it. Fibre is important in your diet because it helps to keep food moving through your intestines.

Physical activity takes more energy because it involves more physical effort, not because the person is working harder. When the Scientifica crew are doing their homework they may not be making much physical effort but they are working hard.

Key words

detergent
diabetes
enzyme

UNIT REVIEW

REVIEW QUESTIONS

Understanding and applying concepts

1 Copy the sentences. Choose words from the list below to fill in the gaps. You will have three words left over when you have completed the sentences.

glucose starch fat villi enzymes nutrients amino acids digest vitamins absorbed minerals

a ... are the food components we need to be healthy.

b We need carbohydrates, proteins and ... in large amounts.

c We also need smaller amounts of ... and minerals.

d Food is digested in the digestive system using ...

e Digestion is the process of breaking down large molecules to smaller molecules that can be ...

f Starches are broken down into ...
Proteins are broken down into ... ...

g Digested food is absorbed through ..., which are small finger-like structures in the small intestine.

2 Give one reason why we need each of these in our diet:

protein fat vitamin C fibre iron

3 Which one of the following do you need for strong bones and teeth?

iodine copper calcium iron

4 Explain why a professional footballer needs a higher energy diet than a call centre operator.

Using maths

5 There is 30 mg vitamin C per 100 cm^3 orange juice. Your RDA is 75 mg.
Calculate how much orange juice you need to drink to get your RDA of vitamin C.

Thinking skills

6 Which word is the odd one out? Explain your choice.

a starch, fat, vitamin

b protein, fibre, iron

c glucose, amino acid, fat

SAT-STYLE QUESTIONS

1 Here are some foods sold in the canteen at Scientifica High.

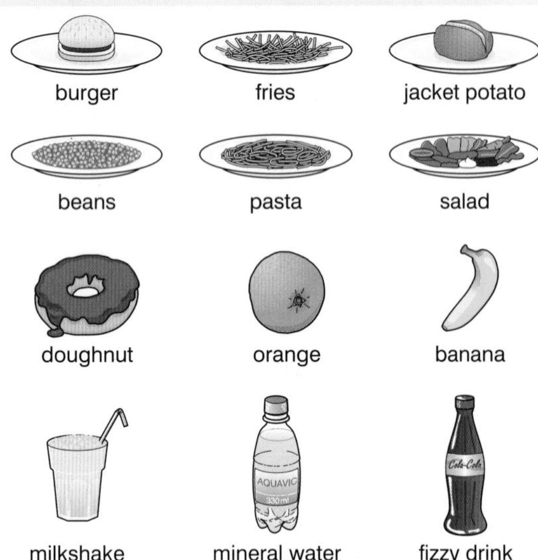

a Mike chose a 'meal deal' of burger, chips and a fizzy drink for his lunch. Reese thought it wasn't a healthy choice. Give one reason why Mike's meal was not very healthy. (1)

b Change one food to make his meal healthier.
Explain why this makes it healthier. (2)

c Reese chose pasta and an orange. Name a nutrient that is in Reese's meal but not in Mike's. (1)

d Choose one food from the foods in the picture that is rich in:
i) protein **ii)** vitamin C **iii)** fibre (3)

2 The diagram shows a villus. Villi line the small intestine, covering the surface.

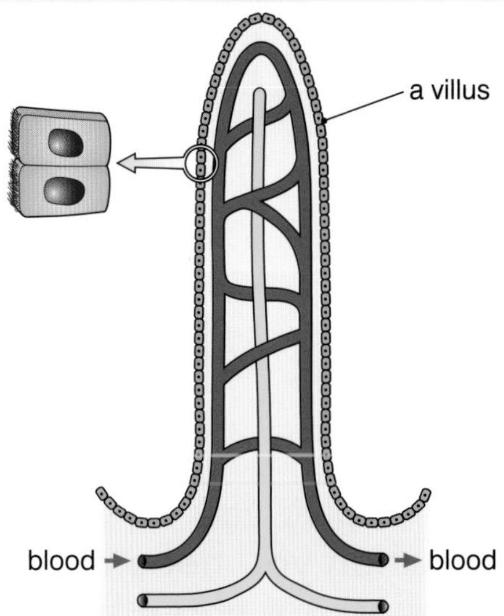

a What is the function of villi? (1)

b **i)** Which of these foods are digested in the small intestine?

starch **protein** **fat** (2)

ii) Name one substance that is not digested in the small intestine. (1)

c What is absorbed in the large intestine? (1)

3 Pete and Benson were investigating how amylase affects starch. Pete predicted that starch would only break down into glucose if amylase was present.

They put their bottles of starch solution, distilled water and amylase in a water bath at 37°C to warm up.

a What is amylase? (1)

They took two lengths of Visking tubing and put 15 cm^3 starch solution inside each. They rinsed the outside of the tubing.

Pete added 0.5 cm^3 amylase to one of the tubes as Benson started the stopwatch.

Pete closed the tubing, mixed the contents, and put them into boiling tubes of distilled water. You can see their experiment in the diagram.

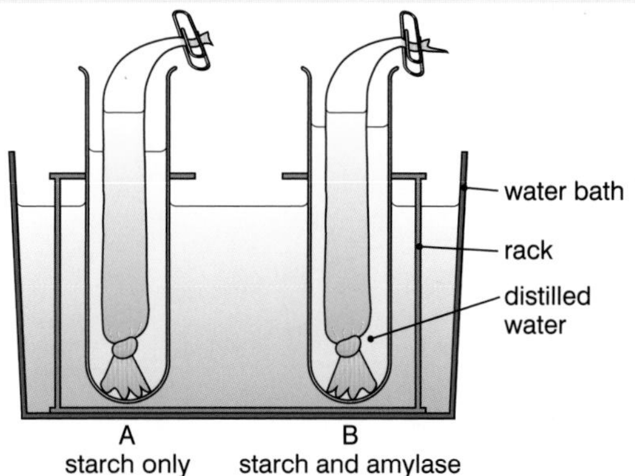

b What is the purpose of the tube with just starch? (1)

Pete and Benson timed for 20 minutes. They took samples of the distilled water round each piece of Visking tubing. They also sampled the solution inside each tube. They tested each sample for starch and glucose.

c What could Pete and Benson use to detect **i)** starch? **ii)** glucose? (2)

Their results are in the table.

	Starch test		Glucose test	
	colour	present	colour	present
inside tubing with starch only	black	yes	blue	no
inside tubing with starch and amylase	yellow-brown	no	orange	yes
water round starch only	yellow-brown	no	blue	no
water round starch and amylase mix	yellow-brown	no	orange	yes

d Do the results support Pete's prediction? (1)

Pete and Benson wanted reliable results.

e **i)** Why were they careful to warm everything to 37°C? (1)

ii) Give one other thing they did to make their results reliable. (1)

f Explain why there was glucose in tube B. How did it get into the water outside the tubing? (2)

Key words

Unscramble these:

harry dabcote
o sing tide
ise in tent
miccaul
vain tim

8B

Respiration

Coming soon

I haven't the energy for this!
20
20

What's it all about?

Have you seen adverts for high-energy drinks that give you an extra burst of energy when you need it? In this unit you will find out about how energy in foods ends up as energy that keeps your legs moving.

You will learn how your blood takes nutrients from digested food to all parts of your body. Blood is part of your circulatory system. You might be surprised to find out that we need a good pair of lungs to get energy from food as well. To find out more, read on.

What do you remember?

You already know about:

- how we need oxygen from the air to live.
- how gas molecules diffuse through air.
- how your heart pumps blood through arteries and veins.
- how starch is digested into glucose.

1 Which of these gases would you expect to find in air?

oxygen carbon dioxide
nitrogen argon

2 What is diffusion?

3 Which of these is *not* a part of the circulatory system?

heart artery capillary liver

4 Three of these are produced from digested food. One isn't. Which?

fatty acids
amino acids
cellulose
glucose

5 Make a list of as many ways as you can think of in which we use our energy.

Ideas about energy

Yeeeees, I won!

SCIENTIFICA HIGH

My heart's pounding.

Phew, what an effort!

Wait till I get my breath back.

QUESTIONS

It's sports day at Scientifica High. Year 8 have been training hard for their races. Mike and Molly had a good meal of pasta yesterday to prepare for the day's energy demands.

a) Where does the energy for running the race come from?

b) How would a plate of pasta the night before help Mike or Molly?

c) How is Reese's heart rate and breathing rate different from usual after a race?
Why do you think they are different?

Respiration

Learn about
- how energy is released from food

Life and energy
What have you, your hamster and a geranium plant got in common? You are all alive. You carry out life processes such as growing. You need energy to carry out life processes. Every living cell needs **energy**.

About 80% of the energy we take in is used to keep warm.

Cells and energy
Cells use **glucose** as their energy source. Glucose comes from the food we have digested.

Q1 Which type of food releases glucose?

protein starch fats vitamins

Respiration
Cells use a process called **respiration** to release energy. Respiration takes place inside cells. It uses glucose and oxygen.

Carbon dioxide and water are waste products from respiration.

We can show respiration as a word equation:

glucose + oxygen → carbon dioxide + water + energy

Respiration that uses oxygen to release energy from nutrients is called **aerobic** respiration.

Water polo uses energy to contract muscles

What do we use the energy for?
We use energy for many different purposes. You can see the main uses in the table.

Use	How we use energy
growth	to make new cells, replace cells, grow babies
chemical energy	to make substances we need, e.g. protein, enzymes
energy stores	animals store fat, plants store starch and oils we make fat stores when we have more energy than we are using
keep a steady body temperature	warm-blooded animals use energy to keep warm – we keep our body at 37°C
movement	to move muscles, for example, running, breathing and heart beat
transport	cells use energy to take in and push out chemicals

Detecting respiration

- How can we tell if cells are respiring? We look for evidence of carbon dioxide being made.
  Look for yeast making carbon dioxide.
  Mix yeast with sugar solution. Use a delivery tube to pass any gas made through lime water.
  What does this tell you about the gas produced?
  What would be a suitable control activity that showed the gas came from yeast not the sugar solution?

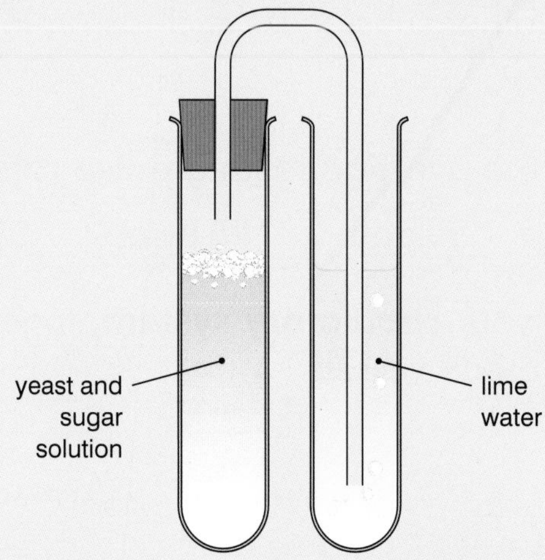

- Measure the temperature of the air in your laboratory. Measure your own temperature. Explain why you are warmer than the air. Use the word 'respiration' in your answer.
- Use what you learned about burning fuels to find out which of these foods releases the most energy
  a plain crisp a bread crouton
  a piece of breakfast cereal a rice cracker

In Unit 7I you learned that burning fuels releases energy and carbon dioxide.

CHALLENGE

Set up a vacuum flask with germinating peas. Use a data logger to find out whether they release energy as heat during the next three days.

SUMMARY QUESTIONS

1 ☆ List two things used up in respiration, and two substances that are released.

2 ☆ Write out a word equation for respiration.

3 ☆☆ Space probes to Mars have looked for carbon dioxide production in Martian soil samples. Why could this be a sign of life?

Key words

aerobic
carbon dioxide
energy
glucose
oxygen
respiration

The heart and circulation

LEARN ABOUT
- how blood circulates round your body
- the heart

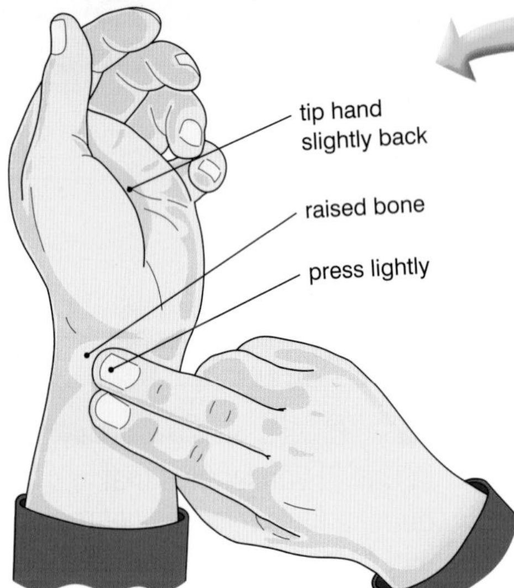

Circulation

When you take your pulse at your wrist you can feel your blood being pumped to your hand. The cells in your hand need a steady supply of glucose and oxygen for respiration. Blood brings them and takes away the wastes cells make. They also need other substances such as amino acids to carry out their jobs.

Q1 What is the average resting pulse rate?

35 bpm   50 bpm   75 bpm   95 bpm

Blood is part of your **circulatory system,** together with your heart and your blood vessels.

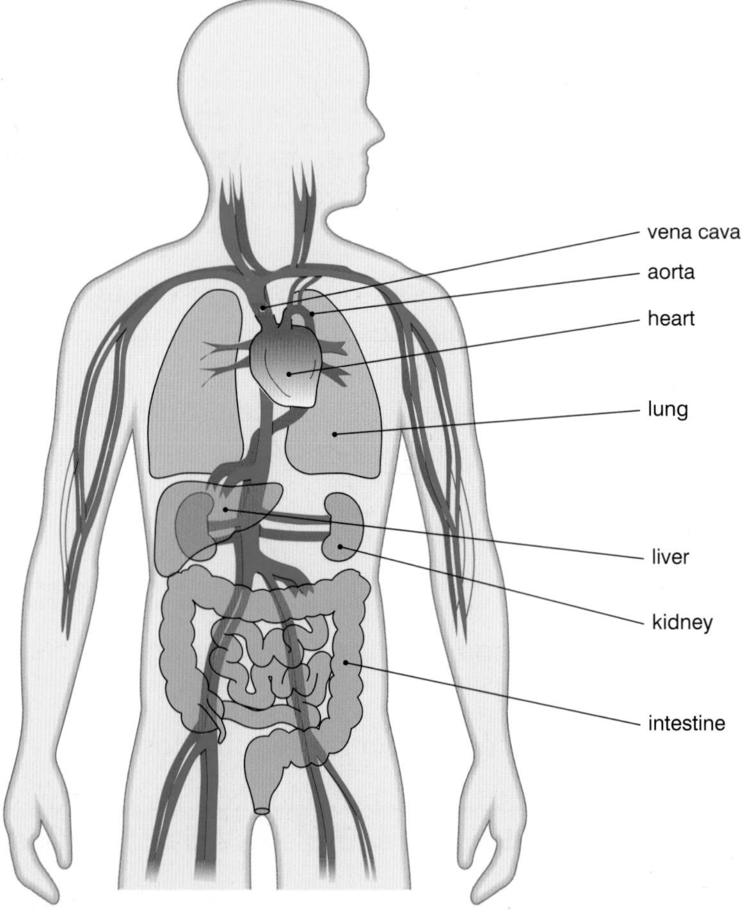

Your heart beats at least 40 million times every year.

Heart

Your **heart** pumps your blood round your body. It is a muscle that contracts, or beats, regularly. When it beats it pumps blood into your main blood vessels.

The right side of your heart receives blood that has been round your body and pumps it to your lungs. In your lungs blood picks up oxygen and loses carbon dioxide. Blood returns from the lungs to the left-hand side of your heart. The left side of your heart pumps blood to the organs of your body.

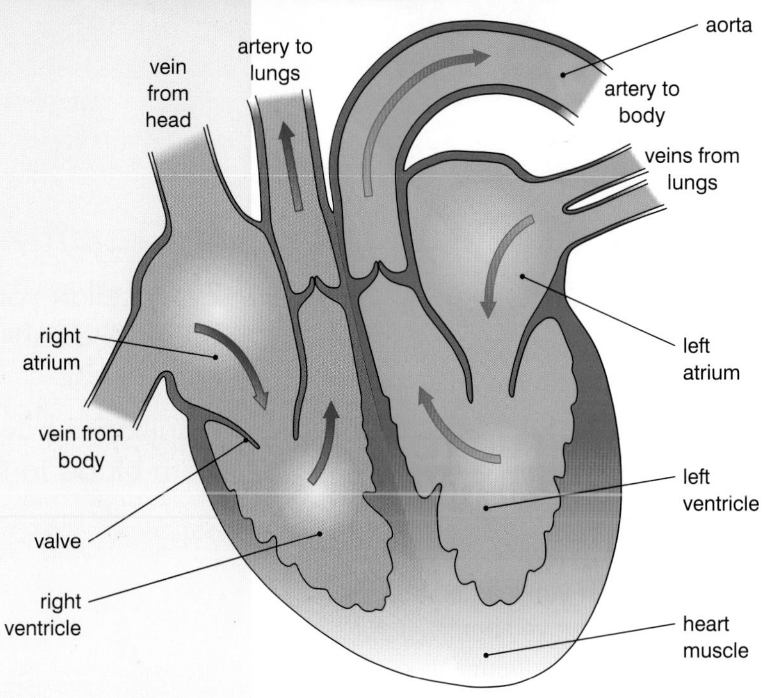

The heart

Blood vessels

Arteries: Blood leaving your heart passes through arteries to reach your organs. Arteries branch into smaller and smaller blood vessels inside your organs taking blood to every part.

Capillaries: The smallest blood vessels are capillaries. These take blood to every cell in an organ. Capillaries have very thin walls so that substances can pass through them to and from the cells.

Veins: These take blood from an organ back to your heart.

Measuring your pulse

- Measure your pulse. First sit quietly for a few minutes, then take your pulse. This is your resting pulse rate. Does everyone have the same resting pulse rate?
  Collect data from your class and display it in a suitable graph or chart.
  Exercise on the spot for one minute. Retake your pulse. How has it changed? Do other people's pulses change in the same way?
  Why do you think your pulse rate changes?
- Draw arrows on an outline drawing of the heart to show the path blood follows as it passes through the heart.

ICT CHALLENGE

Use a pulse monitor to see how your pulse changes when you change from sitting to standing then from standing to jogging.

SUMMARY QUESTIONS

1 ☆ What is the job of **a)** an artery? **b)** a vein? **c)** a capillary?

2 ☆ What is the pulse?

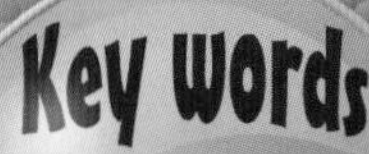

Key words

artery
capillary
circulatory system
heart
vein

Supplying cells

LEARN ABOUT
- giving cells what they need

Capillaries

Every cell in your body has a capillary close by. Cells obtain the substances they need from blood flowing in these capillaries.

Capillaries have very thin walls. Substances pass easily from blood to the cells, or from cells into blood.

In Unit 7H you learned that particles move about without having to mix them.

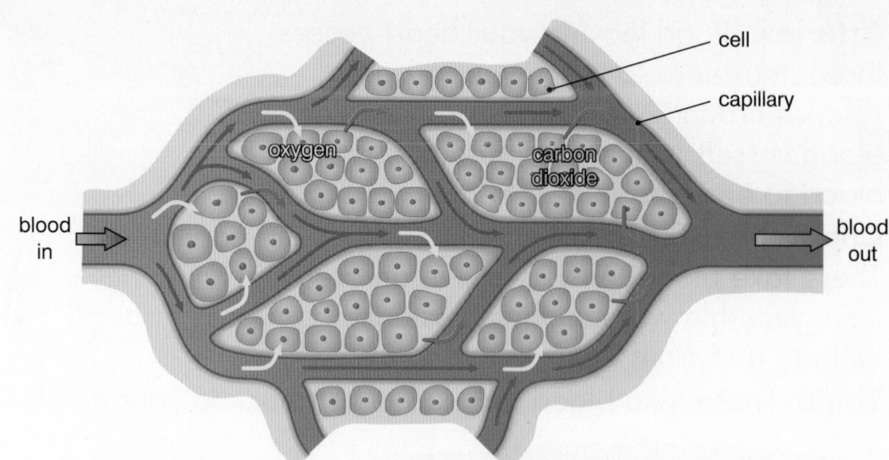

Cells have several capillaries passing close by. Even if one capillary is damaged another can supply nearby cells.

Supplying the cells

Oxygen is transported by **red blood cells**. Red blood cells contain **haemoglobin**. Oxygen bonds to haemoglobin. Red blood cells release oxygen when they pass through tissues that need it.

Glucose and other nutrients from digested food are dissolved in blood. They can also pass through the capillary wall to the cells that need them.

Carbon dioxide is made in respiration. It passes in the opposite direction, from cells into blood.

All these substances move from blood to the cells, or from cells to blood by **diffusion**.

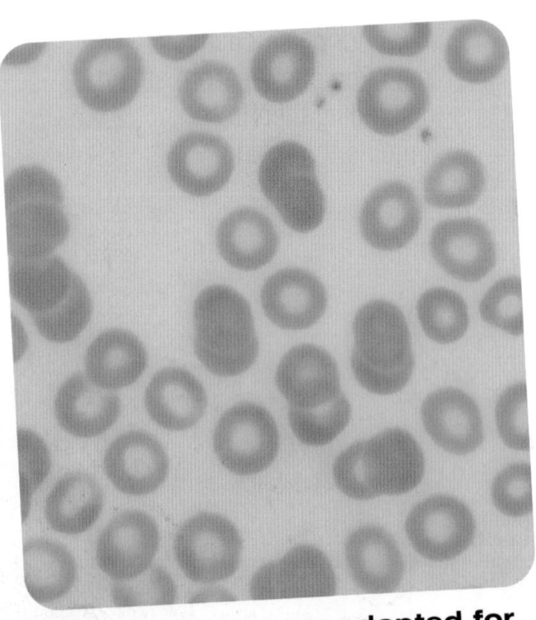

Red blood cells are adapted for transporting oxygen

Anaerobic respiration

A champion sprinter runs 100 metres in around 10 seconds. The sprinter cannot take many breaths. How can she or he release enough energy to run so fast without breathing?

We can use **anaerobic respiration** in our muscles for a short time. Our cells partly break down glucose without using oxygen. This releases a smaller amount of energy.

Glucose is made into **lactic acid** in this process. When lactic acid builds up it affects muscle cells. We develop cramp. Once the action is over we take deep breaths to get enough oxygen to get rid of lactic acid.

Barcelona '92
402

Yeast uses anaerobic respiration when there isn't much oxygen. Yeast breaks down glucose to ethanol, not lactic acid. This is how yeast ferments sugary fruit juices to wine.

Energy without oxygen

- Use the apparatus in the diagram to show that yeast can respire glucose without oxygen.

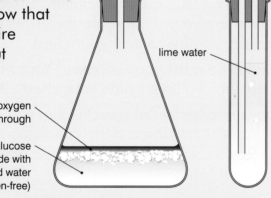

lime water

oil to stop oxygen passing through

yeast and glucose solution made with boiled water (oxygen-free)

- Make a flow chart of the route oxygen takes from the lungs to reach a leg muscle cell.
  Make another to show the route carbon dioxide takes from a leg muscle cell to the lungs.

Oxygen, someone bring me oxygen.

SUMMARY QUESTIONS

1 ☆ Which substance do red blood cells contain that carries oxygen?

2 ☆ How do substances move from blood to cells?

3 ☆ Name one substance that passes into the blood from the tissues. Name one substance that passes from the blood into the tissues.

Key words

carbon dioxide
diffusion
haemoglobin
lactic acid
oxygen
red blood cell

LEARN ABOUT
- how we breathe
- lungs

Breathing

Put your hands on your chest and breathe in and out slowly a couple of times. What do you feel? Your hands move up and out slightly as you breathe in. Breathing in is called **inhaling**. Your hands drop down again as you breathe out, or **exhale**.

When you breathe you move air in and out of your lungs. This is **ventilation**.

Ventilation

You use muscles to move your chest. Muscles running over your **ribcage** contract to lift it up and outwards. At the same time your **diaphragm** contracts. Your diaphragm is a muscle that runs across the bottom of your ribcage. When it contracts it becomes flatter. Lifting your ribcage and flattening your diaphragm increases the volume inside your chest. Air then enters your chest.

To exhale you relax your muscles. Your ribcage drops. This decreases the volume inside your chest. Air is pushed out.

You have another set of muscles that you use when you cough, sneeze or blow out the candles on your birthday cake. These contract to pull the chest down quickly and push air out fast.

How we breathe

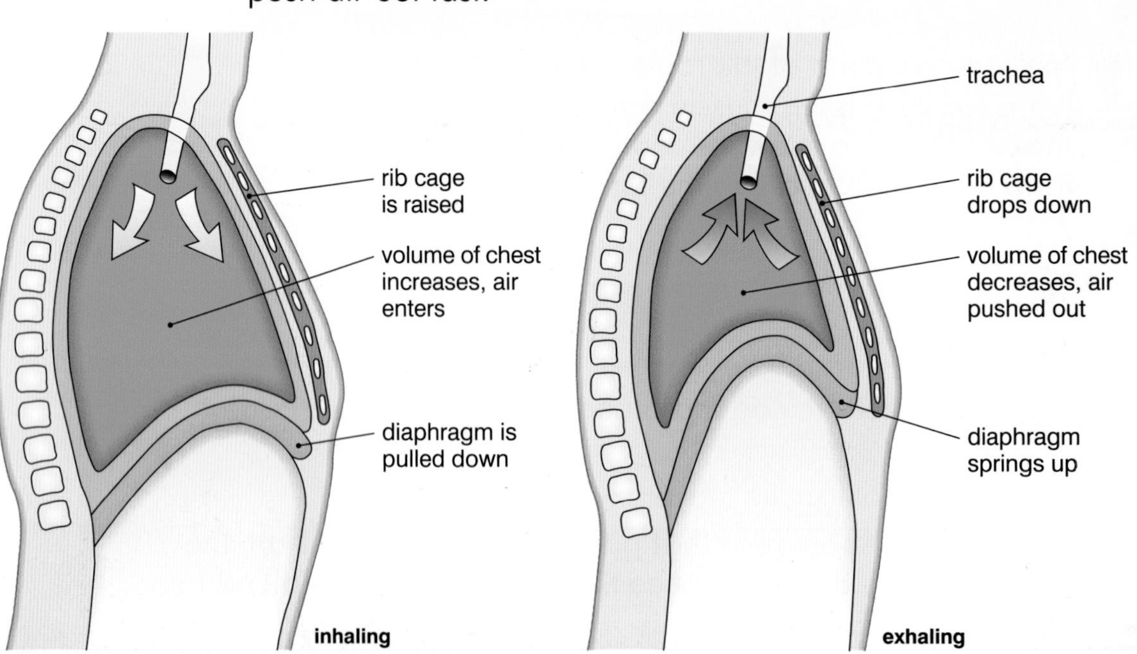

Lungs

Your **lungs** are inside your ribcage surrounding your heart. You have two lungs, left and right.

The **trachea**, or windpipe, connects your throat to your lungs. Air passes through your **larynx**, or voice box, at the top. The trachea is held open by rings of **cartilage**.

At the bottom the trachea divides into two **bronchi** that direct air into your right and left lung. The bronchi branch several times into bronchioles. Bronchioles end in a cluster of several air sacs, or **alveoli**.

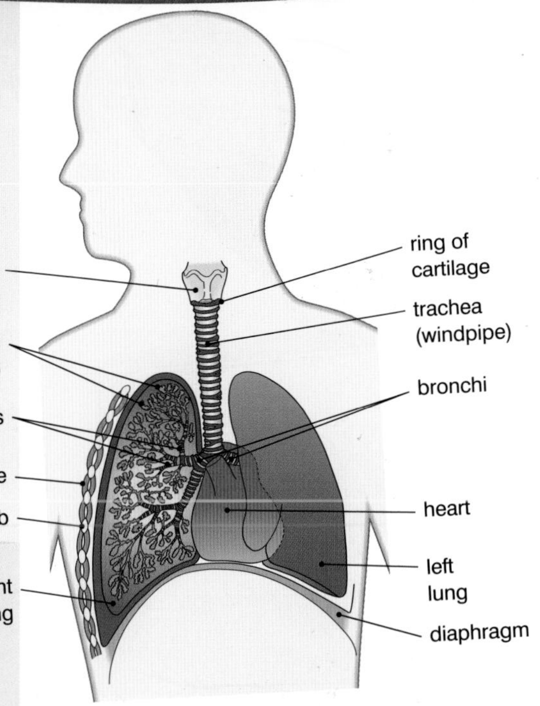

Lung structure

Lung capacity

- Use a model chest to see how ventilation works.
- Examine a set of animal lungs. Identify the trachea, rings of cartilage, larynx, left and right lungs, and bronchi. Use tubing to partially inflate a lung.
- Measure your lung volume using the equipment provided. Plan an investigation to find out why people who play brass musical instruments have a larger lung volume.

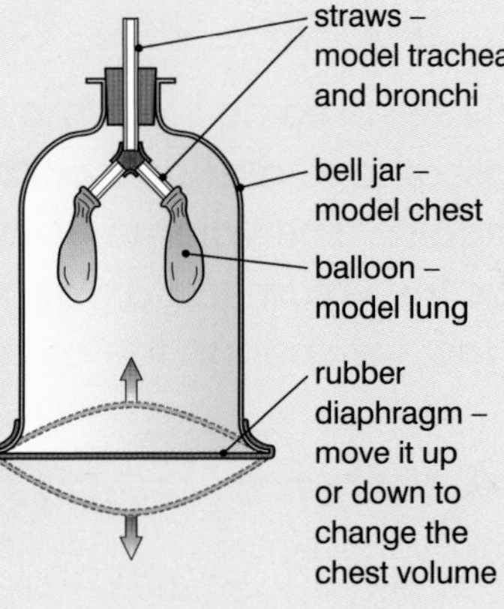

A model chest

ICT CHALLENGE

Use a graphing facility to display the range of lung volumes in your class.

SUMMARY QUESTIONS

1 ☆ Match the parts of the lungs with the correct label on the diagram.

diaphragm **trachea** **alveolus** **bronchus** **rib**

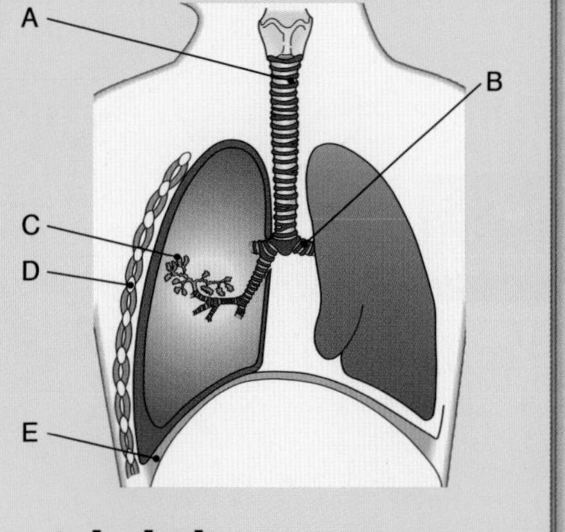

2 ☆ What do the rings of cartilage round your trachea do?

3 ☆☆ Explain in your own words how we breathe. Use these words in your answer:

ventilate **trachea** **exhaled** **inhaled**

Key words

bronchus
diaphragm
inhale
lung
ribcage
trachea
ventilation

8B5 What happens in your lungs

LEARN ABOUT
- what happens in your lungs?
- alveoli

Air

Do you remember writing your name on steamed-up windows on the bus? The windows are steamed up because moisture from the air has condensed on the cold windows.

Where does the moisture come from? It comes from people on the bus. They breathe out water vapour in their breath. On a frosty morning you can see water vapour in your breath condensing as you breathe out.

Q1 What other gases are present in air?

Moisture in the whale's breath condenses in cold air

What happens to the air when we breathe?

As we breathe we remove some **oxygen** from the air we breathe in and add **carbon dioxide** before we breathe it out again. The volume of carbon dioxide we release is the same as the volume of oxygen we take in. In the table, you can see how we change the composition of the air as we breathe.

Gas	% of inhaled air	% of exhaled air
oxygen	21	17
carbon dioxide	0.04	4
nitrogen	78	78
noble gases	1	1
water vapour	varies	saturated

What happens in the alveoli?

We take in oxygen and release carbon dioxide in **alveoli**. Alveoli are tiny air sacs clustered around the end of a bronchiole.

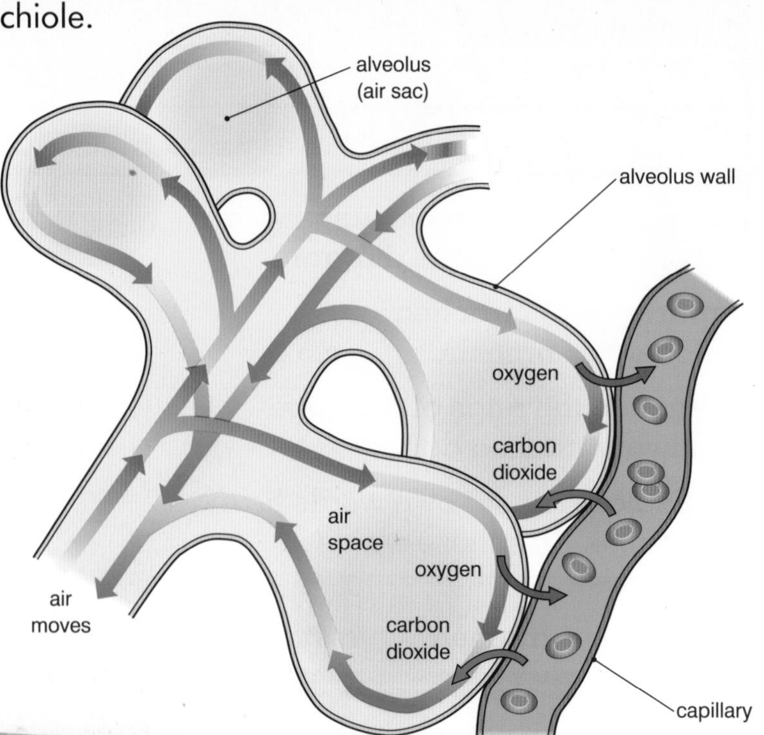

Alveoli are specialised for taking in oxygen and releasing carbon dioxide. Each alveolus has very thin walls and a large surface. This surface is very easily damaged.

Capillaries surround each alveolus. Blood arrives with a lot of carbon dioxide and just a small amount of oxygen. Oxygen **diffuses** from the air space in the alveolus into the blood. It is picked up by red blood cells. Carbon dioxide leaves the blood and diffuses into the air space. It leaves the body with the next breath.

Our lungs have about 300 million alveoli. They have a surface area about as big as a tennis court.

How do you change air when you breathe?

- Collect samples of inhaled and exhaled air. Compare the amount of carbon dioxide and oxygen in each sample.
- Breathe onto a cold mirror. Test the condensation on the mirror with cobalt chloride paper. What is the liquid?
- Investigate whether other living things release carbon dioxide using the apparatus in the diagram.
  How could you use this experiment to compare the amount of carbon dioxide produced by maggots and germinating peas?
  Write a plan for your investigation.

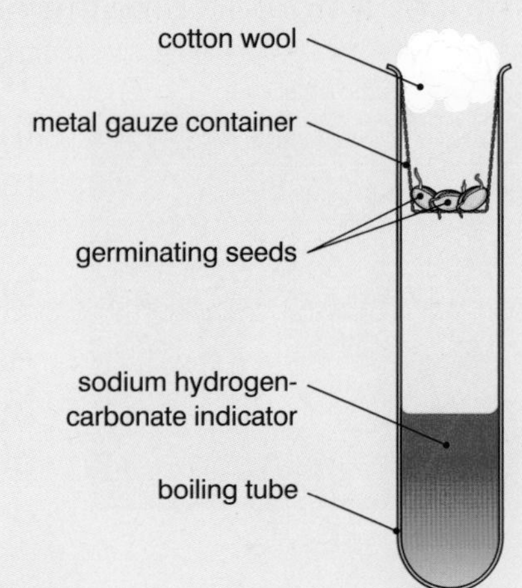

Air is a mixture of gases. Carbon dioxide in air makes rain acidic. (You will find out more about these in Unit 8F.)

SUMMARY QUESTIONS

1 ☆ Which gas passes from the air in an alveolus to the blood? Which gas passes from the blood into the alveoli?

2 ☆ How would you detect carbon dioxide in a sample of air?

3 ☆ Think of three differences between air that Pip breathes in and the air she breathes out.

Key words

alveolus
carbon dioxide
diffusion
oxygen

8B6 Lung damage

LEARN ABOUT

- factors that harm your breathing

Dust and your lungs

Babies take a breath as soon as they are born. This breath inflates their lungs. The first breath is usually followed by a yell showing the new-born baby has a healthy pair of lungs. Most of us have healthy lungs but some people are not so lucky. They have problems breathing.

Asthma

More and more children suffer with **asthma**. No-one is sure what causes asthma, or why more children have it. In an asthma attack the muscles round the airways tighten. The lining swells inside the airways. They can get clogged with thick mucus. The airways become narrower which makes it hard to breathe out.

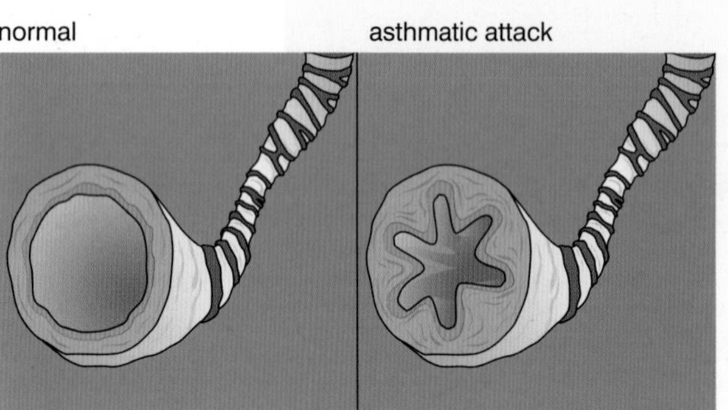

The drugs in inhalers make the muscles round the airways relax. They can also reduce the swelling and make it easier to breathe.

Asthma attacks can be triggered by many factors, including allergies, chest infections, exercise and cigarette smoke.

Cystic fibrosis

People with **cystic fibrosis** have inherited a problem through their genes. They make thicker and stickier mucus than usual. This clogs their lungs and traps bacteria. They are more likely to catch infections and find it harder to breathe.

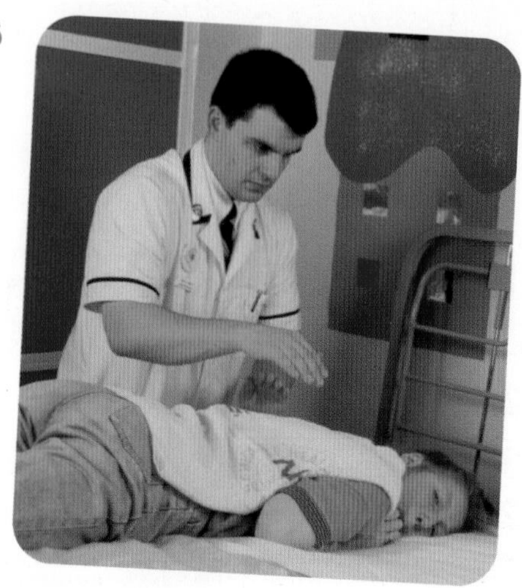

Work and your lungs

Some people work in dusty places, such as flour mills, quarries and timber yards. These industries produce fine powdery dusts. The dust damages the delicate alveoli when it is breathed in. Thick scar tissue grows over the damaged parts. This reduces the area that we have for absorbing oxygen. Workers should wear face masks to filter the air they breathe.

Tiny stone particles damage the alveoli

Looking at breathing

- Look at the photograph of alveoli damaged by dust and compare it to the photograph of healthy lung tissue.
  Describe any differences you can see in the alveoli. How will this affect the surface for absorbing? How could this affect a person with lungs damaged in this way?
- Look at the material that collects in a smoking machine. Cigarette smoke contains hot gases, ash and tar. Explain why hot gases and a coating of tar could affect the alveoli.

SUMMARY QUESTIONS

1 ☆ Why do people working in flour mills and quarries wear masks?

2 ☆ How does asthma affect someone's breathing?

Key words

asthma
cystic fibrosis
lung damage

IDEAS AND EVIDENCE

William Harvey and solving the circulation problem

It seems obvious to us that blood flows round the body – but it took centuries of observations and deductions to work out how.

The ancient Greeks saw heart valves and described veins and arteries. They thought that arteries were full of air. This was because the arteries in the corpses they dissected were always empty. They thought that blood that came from wounds must have come from veins to replace escaping air.

Mistaken ideas like this set people on the wrong track, even though they knew all the facts needed to understand blood **circulation**.

In Roman times, Galen, a physician, showed that arteries carried blood. He developed a theory. He thought that new blood was constantly forming in the body and then at every pulse it passed through the heart and was reabsorbed. He thought that blood was enriched with 'vital spirit' in the lungs.

Galen's ideas lasted until Shakespeare's time. At the University of Padua in Italy another doctor, Vesalius, found mistakes in Galen's work. New theories were developed but they still weren't right. People thought that valves slowed the blood down so it could enter small blood vessels. Leonardo Da Vinci recognised that the heart was muscle – but not that it pumped blood.

William Harvey

William Harvey (1578–1657) studied at Padua. He put together known facts with his own observations. He correctly worked out what heart muscle, arteries and veins did, how blood passed through the heart, and what caused the pulse. He thought blood circulated round the body but didn't know how it got from arteries to veins. He **inferred** that tiny blood vessels must link them.

Then at last Professor Malpighi spotted capillaries with the newly discovered microscope.

- But why hadn't anyone seen capillaries before?
- Why do you think the arteries in dissected corpses were empty?
- What do you think 'vital spirit' might be?

- We use our lungs to obtain oxygen. They also get rid of carbon dioxide.
- Oxygen passes from the air in an air sac into the blood. Carbon dioxide passes in the opposite direction.
- Oxygen is carried around the body by red blood cells.
- Oxygen passes to cells that need it from blood. Carbon dioxide made by cells passes into blood.
- Respiration releases energy from glucose, using oxygen.
- Glucose + oxygen → carbon dioxide + water, energy is released.
- The cells of all living things, including plants and bacteria, respire.

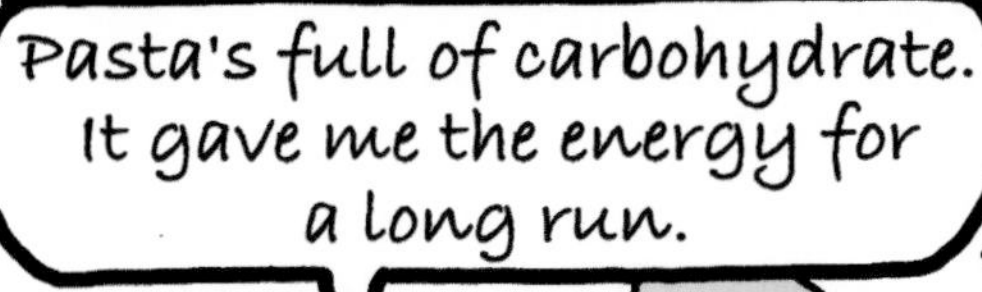

Pasta's full of carbohydrate. It gave me the energy for a long run.

I must be fit because it didn't take long to get back to 74bpm.

So respiration isn't breathing, it's releasing energy from food!

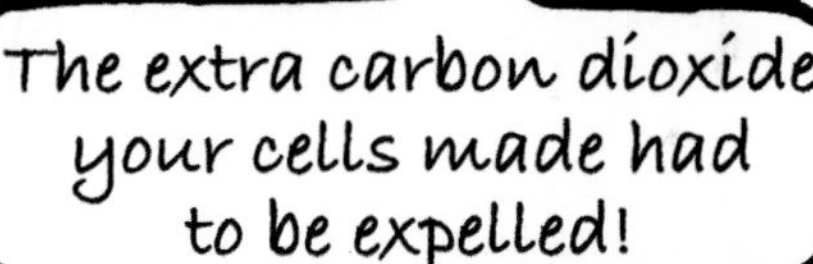

The extra carbon dioxide your cells made had to be expelled!

DANGER! AVOID THESE COMMON ERRORS

Cartilage in the trachea holds it open – it does not protect it.

When people take in more energy than they use, they store the extra as glycogen in muscles, or as fat. They do not become hotter or more active. But if they are more active they will use more energy, and become hotter.

People use more energy when they do more active things that take more physical effort. They may not be working harder than some one who is sitting down.

Key words

circulation
infer
William Harvey

UNIT REVIEW

REVIEW QUESTIONS
Understanding and applying concepts

1 Copy the following sentences. Complete them by filling in the gaps.
   a Respiration releases . . . from food. It takes place in . . . In respiration . . . and oxygen produce . . . . . . and water.
   b The heart pumps . . . round the body. We can feel its action by the . . . at the wrist. The left side of the heart supplies blood to the . . . The right side of the heart sends blood to the . . .
   Blood travels round the body through arteries, . . . and . . .
   c When we breathe we use muscles that move the ribcage . . . The diaphragm becomes . . . This . . . the volume inside your chest, and air enters.
   Oxygen and carbon dioxide are exchanged in small structures in the lungs called . . .

2 List three differences between the air we breathe in and the air we breathe out.

3 What is the job of an alveolus (air sac)?

4 How can working in a dusty place affect alveoli?

5 Make a flow chart of how the carbon dioxide produced by a cell is eventually passed out by the lungs.

6 When you are active you need more energy. Your pulse increases. How can increasing your pulse rate help you release more energy?

7 Write out the word equation for respiration.

8 Make a concept map that includes the terms:

respiration alveolus capillary gas exchange energy

SAT-STYLE QUESTIONS

1 a What useful gas do we take from the air in our lungs? (1)
   b There is less air at the top of mountains than at sea level. People who live in high mountains have more red blood cells in their blood than people who live at sea level.
   How can having extra red blood cells help people who live at high altitude? (2)

2 Organise the following substances into two lists with the headings:

Move from blood to cells
Move from cells to blood

oxygen glucose carbon dioxide vitamins amino acids (5)

3 Pip and Reese investigated respiration in yeast cells. They carried out the following steps:

They filled a test tube with glucose solution.
They added some yeast and mixed it together.
They fastened a balloon over the test tube.
They put the test tube in a water bath set at 30°C.
Soon small bubbles of gas formed in the solution and rose to the top. One hour later the balloon had inflated.

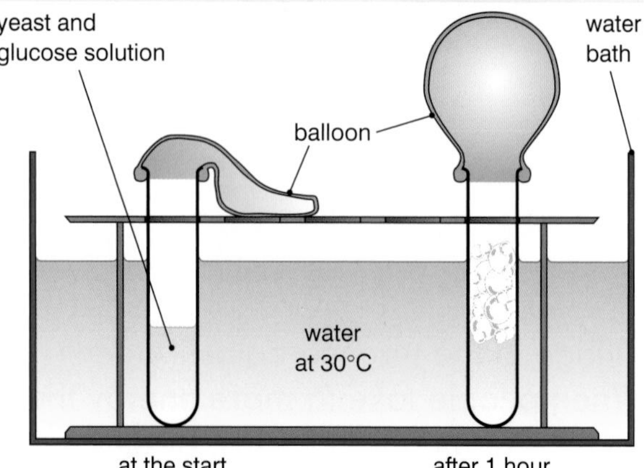

   a What is the gas that formed in the mixture? (1)
   b What is the process which produced the gas? (1)
   c Write a word equation for this process. (2)

Pip decided to find out if temperature made a difference to the process. She repeated the investigation at two different temperatures.

d Suggest *two* things she should do to make the investigation fair. (2)

e Draw the apparatus as you would expect to see it after 1 hour if it had been kept at 15°C. (1)
Explain your drawing. (1)

4 Benson and Mike wanted to investigate respiration. They decided to use peas. Mike soaked some peas and let them germinate. Then he boiled half of the peas and left them to go cold.

Benson put four spoonfuls of the ordinary peas into a vacuum flask. Then he put the same number of spoonfuls of boiled peas into another flask.

Mike said they should have measured the peas so that they could be sure they had the same mass in each flask.

a Why is it important that they have the same mass? (1)

b What could they use to measure the peas more accurately? (1)

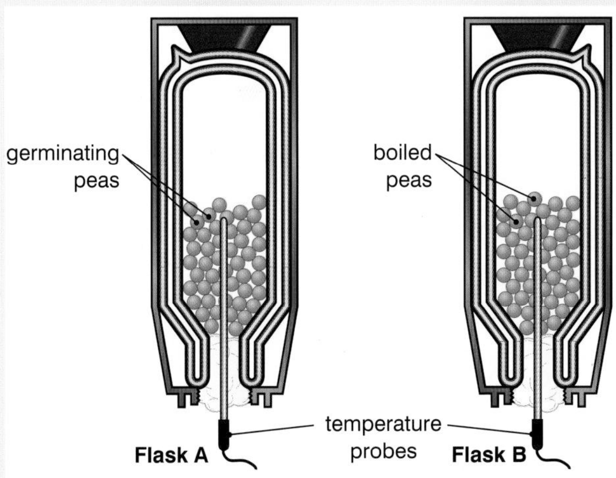

They used a data logger to record the temperature inside the vacuum flasks for the next five days. The table shows their results.

		Flask A (°C)	Flask B (°C)
Day 1	11 am	18	18
	11 pm	18	15
Day 2	11 am	18	17
	11 pm	18.5	15
Day 3	11 am	18.5	16
	11 pm	19	14
Day 4	11 am	19	16
	11 pm	19.5	14
Day 5	11 am	19.5	17
	11 pm	20	15

c i) Draw a graph of how the temperature changed in flask A with the ordinary peas.
Include the correct units. (5)

ii) Describe what happened to the temperature in flask A. (1)

Mike predicted that the temperature wouldn't change in flask B because the peas had been boiled.

d i) Does the data in the table support Mike's prediction? (1)

ii) Why would boiled peas be different to the peas in flask A? (1)

e Explain why the temperature changed in flask A. (2)

Key words

Unscramble these:
shrub con
socugle
perrise
lotte in vain
biorace

8C Microbes and disease

Coming soon

What's it all about?

'Atishoo – oh no – another cold! Molly Kewel sneezed all day Monday and has been off school since. Benson and Pip are off today. This cold is going round the class.'

Do you know how colds spread from one person to another? In this unit you will find out about viruses (which cause colds) and other micro-organisms. You will learn about how infections spread and how your body defends itself against infections.

Micro-organisms aren't all bad news. You will also find out how micro-organisms make food and other useful things.

What do you remember?

You already know about:

- how micro-organisms make things rot.
- micro-organisms called bacteria, viruses and fungi.
- how micro-organisms can cause some diseases.
- how micro-organisms are used to make some foods.
- living things using glucose for energy.

1 What sort of living thing is this?

bacteria virus
fungus
flowering plant

2 What caused Molly Kewel's cold?

getting wet
not enough sleep
not enough vitamins
a virus

3 What is respiration?

making food using light
treating people who have nearly drowned
releasing energy from food
breathing in air

Ideas about microbes

Ring a ring o'roses,
Pocket full of posies,
Atishoo, atishoo,
We all fall down!

You can't eat that now,
it's full of germs!

TOWN
PARK

QUESTIONS

Look at the cartoon. With your partner decide if these are true or false.

a) The nursery rhyme 'Ring a ring o' roses' is about the Black Death, the time that thousands of people died of plague. True or false?

b) Micro-organisms are used to make cheese. True or false?

c) You can catch diseases by eating dirty food. True or false?

d) Bacteria are always harmful. True or false?

Micro-organisms

LEARN ABOUT
- different sorts of micro-organisms

What is the tiniest living thing you can think of? Probably a **bacterium**. Bacteria are a sort of micro-organism. Micro-organisms are so small we need a microscope to see most of them.

There are several groups of micro-organism. Some of them have common names – like 'flu virus or mould – but we use scientific names for most of them.

Fungi

Fungi are the biggest micro-organisms. They usually live as fine white threads growing in soil, and animal or plant remains. They cause decay as they digest dead material and take in nutrients. Some fungi reproduce by making mushrooms and toadstools.

Toadstools make spores. They release them into the air.

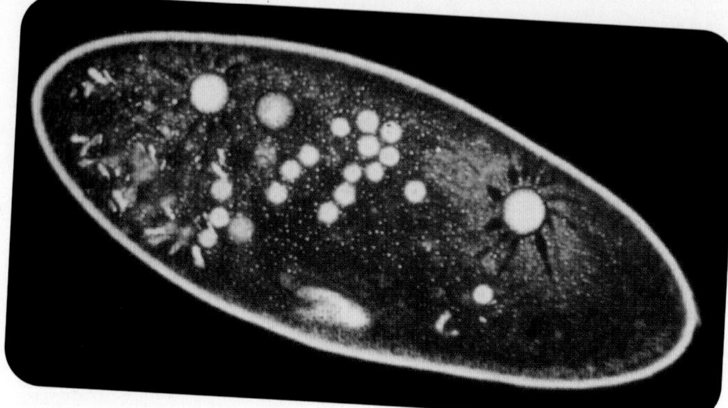

Protozoa

Protozoa are single-celled animals. They live in ponds, soil and damp places. They feed on bacteria and minute particles of plant and animal remains.

Bacteria

Bacteria have just one very small cell. They are found everywhere, in soil, water, and even inside animals. Bacteria in the soil feed on dead leaves and animal matter, causing decay.

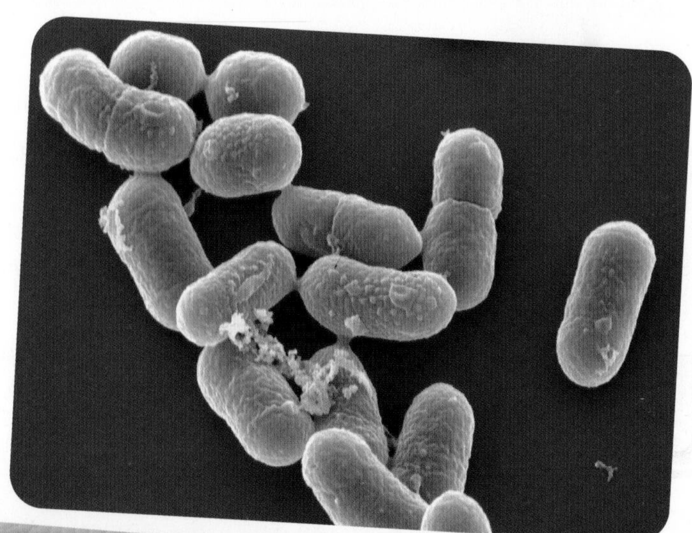

The 'waistline' shows where a bacterium is dividing into two

Virus

Viruses are different from other living things. They are the smallest organisms. They cannot grow and reproduce by themselves. They must infect other cells to reproduce. They are made of an outer coat enclosing a few genes.

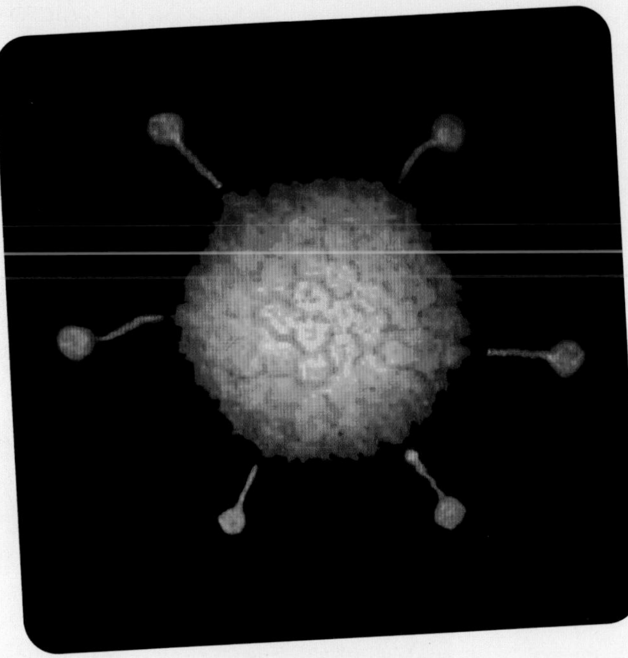

This virus uses its spikes to attach itself to a cell

The largest living thing is a fungus that grows over 1 kilometre of forest floor in the USA.

ICT CHALLENGE

Make a presentation about micro-organisms.

Finding out about micro-organisms

- Look at the examples of micro-organisms that you have been given.
  Look at their activity. Describe what you can see and what it tells you about each micro-organism. You should include things such as how big they are. Also why they are important.

In 7A5 you learned that bacteria reproduce by binary fission.

SUMMARY QUESTIONS

1 ☆ Arrange these micro-organisms by size, largest first:

bacteria **fungi** **virus** **protozoa**

2 ☆ Which micro-organisms break down dead animal and plant matter?

3 ☆ How are viruses different from other micro-organisms?

Key words

bacterium
fungus
virus

8C2

Growing micro-organisms

Learn about
- growing micro-organisms

Hmm, I think something's escaped from the Biology lab!

Sometimes you find a dusty green and white mould, or fungus, growing on lemons in your fruit bowl. The dust is spores that the fungus makes to reproduce itself. Spores are spread in air currents. If you leave any food out long enough, bacteria or fungi will grow on it. Scientists grow micro-organisms more carefully – especially if they are infectious.

Keeping things clean

Scientists grow bacteria using specialised equipment. They have to take care not to let wild bacteria contaminate their work. Their work area and their equipment are **sterilised** before they are used to kill any micro-organisms. They are careful not to let any of the bacteria they are growing escape. Everything they have used is sterilised afterwards.

Growing bacteria in a factory to make medicine

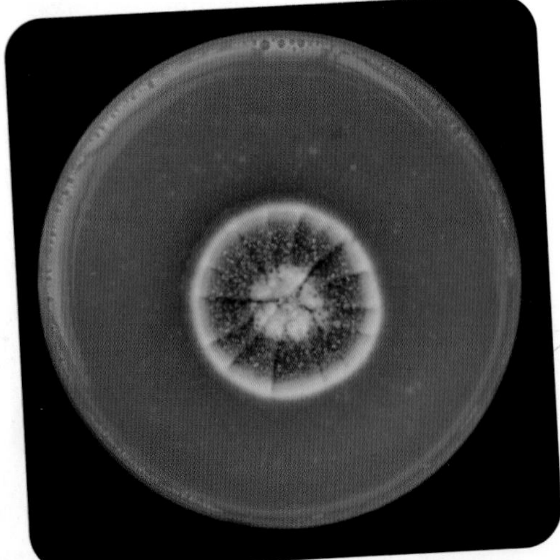

A fungus grown on nutrient jelly. The 'fur' is spores ready to spread through the air.

Growing bacteria

Scientists growing bacteria in a laboratory grow them in a broth or on a jelly containing a mixture of nutrients. In the photo you can see bacteria growing on a layer of **nutrient agar jelly** in a **petri dish**.

A sample of bacteria is spread onto the surface of the jelly. The dish is kept in an **incubator** to grow for a few days. The bacteria form clusters, or **colonies**, as they grow and reproduce on the dish of jelly.

Using science

Scientists sample our drinking water and food supplies to check the hygiene. They spread the sample on nutrient agar jelly and count the number of bacteria that grow. If there are too many, or the wrong sort, there could be trouble.

Growing microbes

It is important that you follow *all* your safety instructions when working with micro-organisms.

- Spread bacteria on two petri dishes of nutrient agar jelly.
- Put one in an incubator to grow. Put the other in a cool place. Don't forget to measure the temperature.
- After a few days compare the colonies on each dish.
- How has the temperature affected how the bacteria grew?

There are more than a hundred million bacteria in a gram of soil.

SUMMARY QUESTIONS

1 ☆ How do we grow bacteria in a laboratory?

2 ☆☆ Write three sentences using these words:

sterile **colony** **nutrient jelly**

3 ☆☆ Why is it important to use sterile equipment and materials when growing bacteria?

Key words

colony
incubator
nutrient agar jelly
petri dish
sterilise

Microbe factories

LEARN ABOUT
- making useful products

Do you like cheese sandwiches? What about a Chinese take-away meal? Did you know that we use micro-organisms to make bread, cheese and soy sauce? We use micro-organisms to make other useful things too. It would be hard to go for a whole day without using something made with microbes.

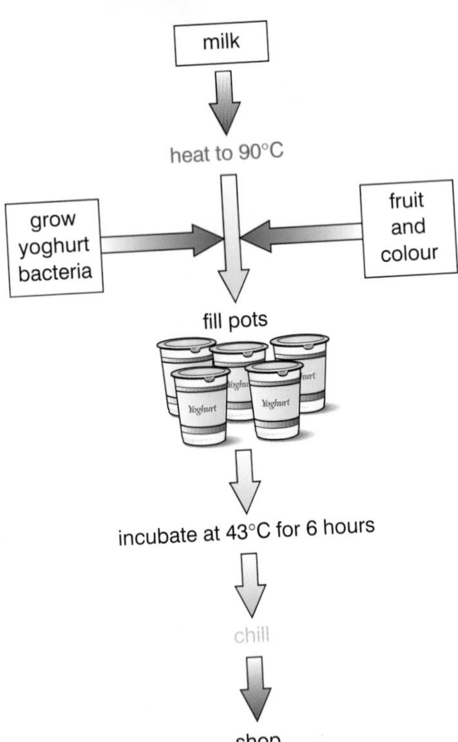

Making yoghurt

What do micro-organisms make?

Micro-organisms make **enzymes** to digest their food. We use their enzymes to do jobs for us. For example, microbial enzymes in biological washing powders help get our clothes clean. Enzymes in dishwasher powder clean our plates.

Microbial enzymes help to make waste carbohydrate into a sugary syrup for soft drinks and sweets. They change flour to make crisper biscuits and better bread.

Fungi even make medicines, such as **antibiotics**. Penicillin is an antibiotic made by a fungus. The doctor might give you a penicillin-based medicine to treat an ear or throat infection.

Yeast

We use **yeast** to make bread, beer, wine, savoury spreads and vitamins. Yeast is a fungus. It grows on sugary substances and releases carbon dioxide from respiration.

To make bread we mix yeast with flour and water to make dough. Yeast cells release carbon dioxide that collects into bubbles and makes the bread dough rise.

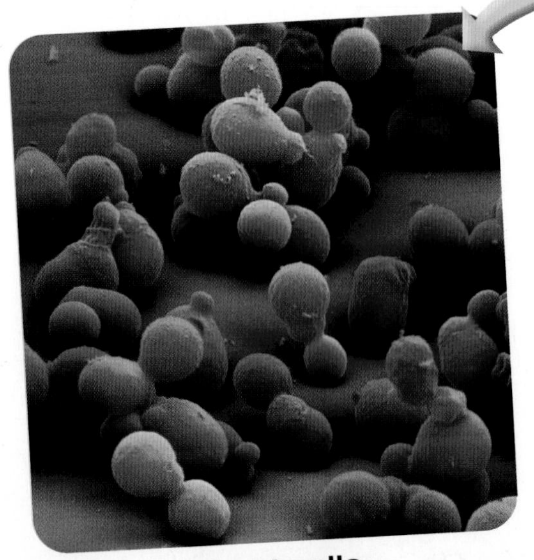

Yeast cells

Brewers grow yeast in a sugary solution of fruit juice, or mashed germinating barley grains. There is not enough oxygen for aerobic respiration. Instead yeast breaks down sugar to carbon dioxide and ethanol. This process is called **fermentation**. When it is finished we can extract vitamins from the left-over yeast or make savoury spreads.

Penicillin is the most commonly prescribed medicine in the world.

Making dough

Make model bread to find out how temperature affects yeast respiration.

- Mix together yeast, sugar, flour and warm water to make a sloppy dough.
- Pour 30 cm^3 of this dough into a measuring cylinder. Repeat with two more measuring cylinders.
- Put one measuring cylinder in a water bath at 50°C, one at 30°C, and leave one at room temperature.
- After 30 minutes, measure how far the bread dough has risen.
- Draw a graph of the increase in volume at each temperature.

Your 'dough' has risen because yeast makes carbon dioxide. How could you show that your mixture is releasing carbon dioxide?

- Plan an investigation to find out how changing the amount of sugar affects your dough.

ICT CHALLENGE

Find out about making yoghurt or cheese.

In 8B1 you saw that respiration is the process of releasing energy from glucose.

SUMMARY QUESTIONS

1 ☆ Yeast is a micro-organism. Which group does it belong to?

2 ☆ Name one important product made by fungi. Give one use for microbial enzymes.

3 ☆☆ Benson tried making bread at home. He made dough with flour, water and yeast, then left it on the table to rise. When he came back 30 minutes later it had hardly increased in size at all. Give *two* possible reasons why Benson's dough had not risen.

Key words

antibiotic
enzyme
fermentation
yeast

8C4

Harmful micro-organisms

Learn about

- how infectious micro-organisms are passed on

If you cut yourself, you wash the cut and cover it with a plaster to stop an infection. You are trying to stop bacteria getting into the wound.

Although most bacteria just cause decay, some can grow inside your body and cause an **infection**.

Pathogens

A micro-organism that can grow inside your body and cause an illness is called a **pathogen**. You can see some of the illnesses they cause in Table 1.

Table 1 Some of the illnesses caused by micro-organisms

Micro-organisms	Diseases caused
bacteria	food-poisoning, TB, tetanus, bacterial meningitis
virus	measles, chickenpox, colds, viral meningitis
fungus	ringworm, athlete's foot
protozoa	food-poisoning, malaria

Infectious diseases are caused by pathogens that can spread from one person to another. There are many different ways in which micro-organisms spread. Table 2 shows you the most common ways.

Table 2 How micro-organisms are passed from one person to another

	Method of transmission	Examples
droplet	We breathe in air carrying tiny moisture droplets full of micro-organisms. These have been exhaled by people with infections.	common cold, 'flu, TB
oral	We eat food contaminated by micro-organisms. We eat food that has traces of faeces from unhygienic caterers.	salmonella and other food poisonings, listeriosis
water	We drink water contaminated with micro-organisms that infect the digestive system. These micro-organisms are found in faeces and get into water with untreated sewage.	cholera, dysentery, typhoid, food-poisoning
touch	We touch something the micro-organism is on, or a part of an infected person's body	impetigo, ringworm, conjunctivitis
insect bites	Insects carry micro-organisms that enter the body when they bite you	malaria, sleeping sickness, yellow fever
wounds	Micro-organisms enter with dirt, blood or tooth marks	tetanus, rabies, HIV

Stopping the spread

Good hygiene is the best way to stop infectious micro-organisms passing from one person to another. We treat waste water from houses and factories to kill harmful micro-organisms before it goes into rivers. Drinking water contains chlorine to kill micro-organisms. Supermarkets and restaurants follow regulations designed to reduce the chances of bacteria getting into food.

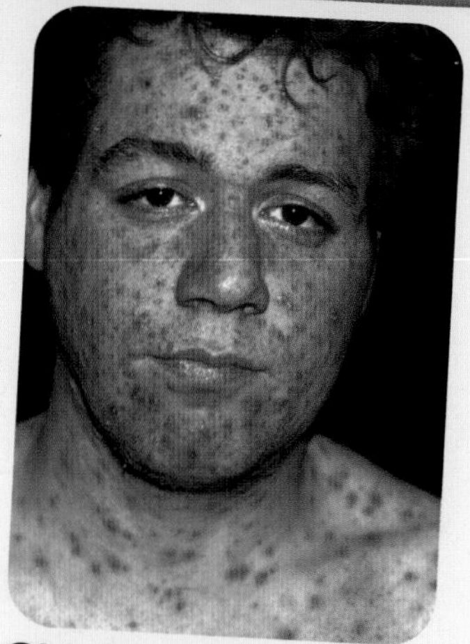

Chickenpox virus reproduces in the skin. It easily passes to a new victim.

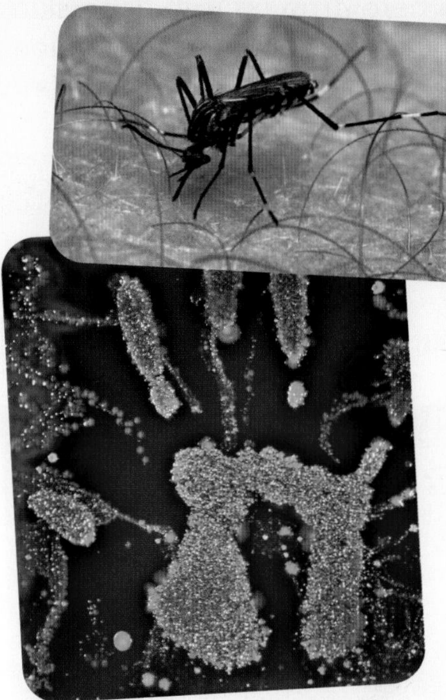

Malaria microbes are injected into your blood by infected mosquitoes

Bacteria on your hands – that's why you have to wash them

Viruses in a sneeze travel at over 45 metres per second from your nose. They spread for up to 4 metres around you.

Food-poisoning

- Some people have their holidays spoilt when they are infected by a **food-poisoning** bacterium. It causes vomiting and diarrhoea. Find out about salmonella and other food-poisoning micro-organisms. Produce a leaflet that will help holidaymakers avoid such an infection.
- People in the food industry study for a certificate in basic food handling hygiene. Find out about some of the rules for handling meat in a butcher's shop, or prepared foods in a delicatessen.

ICT CHALLENGE

Use the Internet to find out about Dr John Snow. He found how cholera spread in London in the 19th century.

SUMMARY QUESTIONS

1 ☆ Explain how colds pass from person to person in a class.

2 ☆☆ Pip made sandwiches for her lunch with some leftover cooked chicken. She left her lunch in her desk in the warm classroom. She was on last sitting for lunch that day so she couldn't eat it until very late.
a) Explain why she was at risk of food-poisoning.
b) Suggest one way she could reduce the risk.

Key words

food-poisoning
infection
infectious
pathogen

8C5 Defending your body

LEARN ABOUT
- how skin protects us
- white blood cells and antibodies

If you are surrounded by millions of micro-organisms in soil, water and air, why aren't you ill more often? You catch so few infections because your body is very well defended.

chemicals in tears protect your eyes
chemicals in saliva protect your mouth
mucus traps microbes in your airways
chemicals in oils on the skin slow microbial growth
acid in your stomach kills microbes
skin is too hard and dry for microbes to grow
chemicals in mucus protect delicate membranes

Protecting your body

Keeping microbes out

Skin is good at keeping bacteria out. The outer layer of your skin is hard, dry and constantly flaking off. Bacteria or fungi growing here drop off with dead skin cells. When you cut yourself, blood quickly clots in the wound and seals it. The scab that forms stops bacteria getting in through the cut.

Your eyes, nose, sweat glands and other entrances to your body are warm, moist and have plenty of nutrients. This would make them ideal places for micro-organisms to grow. They are protected by anti-microbial substances in the moisture.

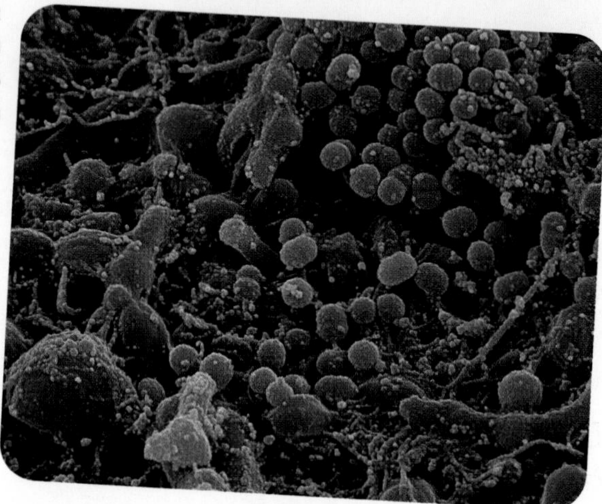

Bacteria growing on food traces round teeth

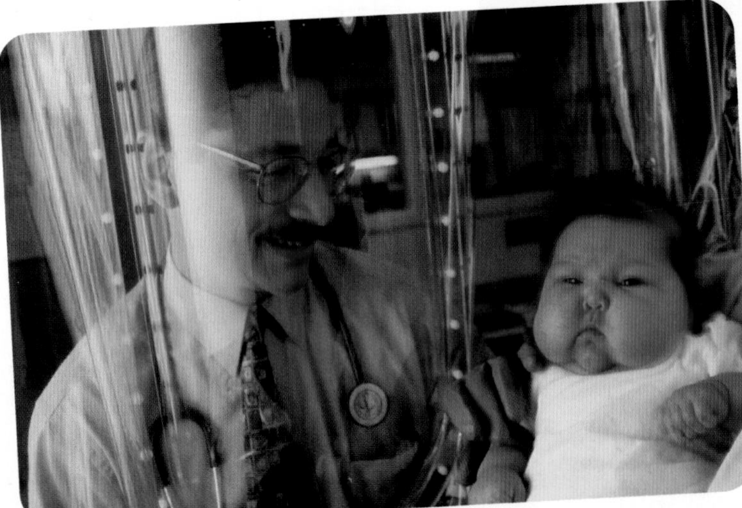

This baby must live in sterile surroundings because he cannot make white blood cells

The immune system

Your **immune system** protects you from harmful micro-organisms that manage to get inside your body, through a wound for example. **White blood cells** are an important part of your immune system.

What do white blood cells do?

Micro-organisms carry chemical markers on their surface called **antigens.** White blood cells take in and destroy any cells with these antigens. Infections are usually mopped up by white blood cells before they can start an infection.

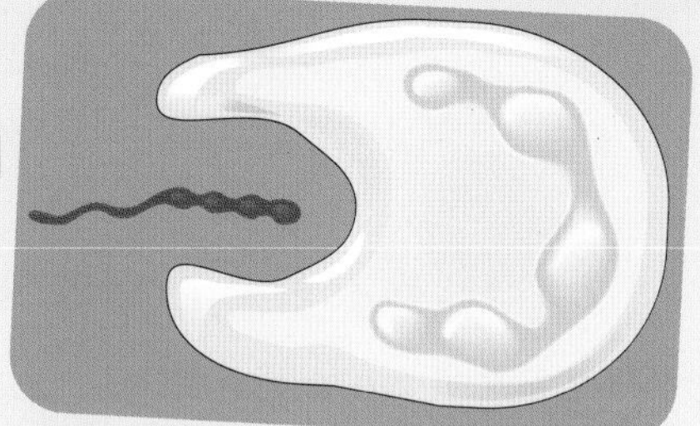

White blood cells take in and break down bacteria

Antibodies

We have special glands round the body that make a different kind of white blood cell called a lymphocyte. Lymphocytes make **antibodies**. Antibodies match and stick to the antigens on infecting micro-organisms. It sticks them together, neutralises toxic chemicals they make and stops them infecting our tissues.

Q1 What is the link between antigens and antibodies?

Mothers who breast-feed their babies pass antibodies on in breast milk. This protects new-born babies from infections.

Remembering infections

These special glands remember the antigens on infecting micro-organisms. If one gets into the body again, even years later, it is recognised. We make fresh lymphocytes very quickly and the antibody they make soon deals with the infection.

Different micro-organisms have different antigens, so we have to make a different antibody for every new micro-organism we meet.

Defending the body

- Use an outline of the human body. Label the places where micro-organisms can enter the body. By each one, write one defence mechanism.
- Find out why tuberculosis (TB) is such a difficult infection to recover from.

Gruesome science

The black buboes found on bubonic plague victims were swollen inflamed glands.

SUMMARY QUESTIONS

1 ☆ Give *two* ways in which white blood cells defend us against bacteria.

2 ☆ Why is it difficult for bacteria to infect through your skin?

Key words

antibody
antigen
immune system
white blood cell

8C6

LEARN ABOUT
- immunisation
- vaccines

Being immune

When you were small you probably caught chickenpox and had a week off nursery. Once you have had chickenpox you do not usually catch it again. You are **immune**. Being immune means that you are resistant to a disease and the micro-organism cannot infect you again.

Immunisation

Your body can remember antigens on the micro-organisms that you have met. Your body makes antibodies against them each time they try to infect again. We can mimic this process to make you immune to infections that you have not met before.

When you are **immunised** you are given a **vaccination**. **Vaccines** are harmless preparations of micro-organisms that contain their antigens. The vaccine cannot cause an infection.

Your body makes antibody against the antigens in the vaccine. You make a memory of them at the same time. You will be ready for this micro-organism if it ever infects you.

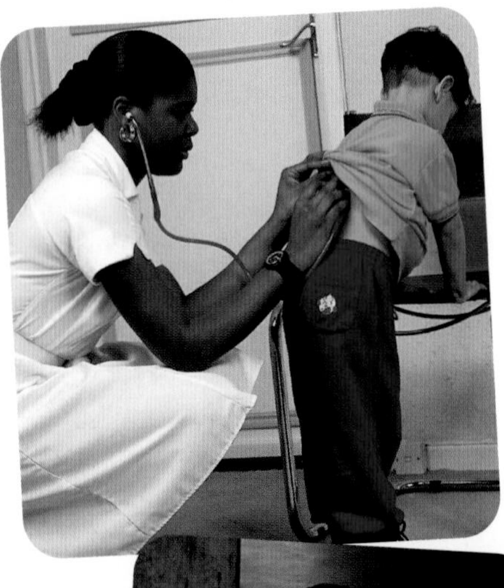

Having a polio vaccination

What is in the vaccine?

Vaccines are made from killed micro-organisms, or from fragments of their cells. The polio vaccine is different because it contains a weakened virus. It protects against the normal virus.

Babies are given their first vaccinations when they are two months old. They are protected from diseases such as tetanus and diphtheria. These killer diseases are rare in developed countries but more common in countries where it is hard to get vaccinated.

Two diseases, smallpox and polio, have been almost wiped out through vaccination. Measles is next on the 'hit' list.

Q1 Which vaccine do you get in Year 8 or Year 9 in secondary school?

Hib   measles   TB   athlete's foot

How do we protect our children?

- Find out which immunisations children are given in their first two years. Which did you have before you started school?
- From the data in the table, draw a graph of the number of cases of measles between 1989 and 2002. Round the numbers before plotting them.
- The MMR vaccine protects children from measles infections. On your graph mark :
  a) when you think the MMR vaccine was introduced.
  b) when parents read a health scare about the vaccine.

Year	Number of cases
1989	26 222
1990	13 302
1991	9680
1992	10 268
1993	9612
1994	16 375
1995	7447
1996	5614
1997	3962
1998	3728
1999	2438
2000	2378
2001	2250
2002	3187

Scientists can find out which infections you have had from the antibodies in your blood.

CHALLENGE

Visit the World Health Organisation website. Find out how the campaign to eradicate polio is progressing.

SUMMARY QUESTIONS

1 ☆ What does immune mean?

2 ☆ What is in a vaccine?

3 ☆☆ Why do you think the whooping cough vaccine does not protect you from chickenpox?

Key words

immune
immunisation
vaccination
vaccine

8C7 Preventing infections

LEARN ABOUT
- antibiotics
- disinfectants
- antiseptics

If you do catch an infection your doctor might prescribe a medicine to help you get better.

If you have a bacterial infection, like an ear infection and throat infection, you might be given an **antibiotic.** **Penicillin** is an antibiotic. Antibiotics made from penicillin are used to treat bacterial ear infections.

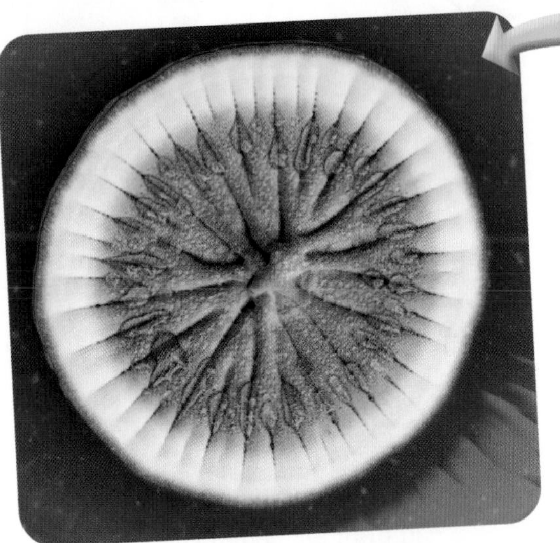

Penicillium fungus makes penicillin. Its effects were first noticed by Sir Alexander Fleming.

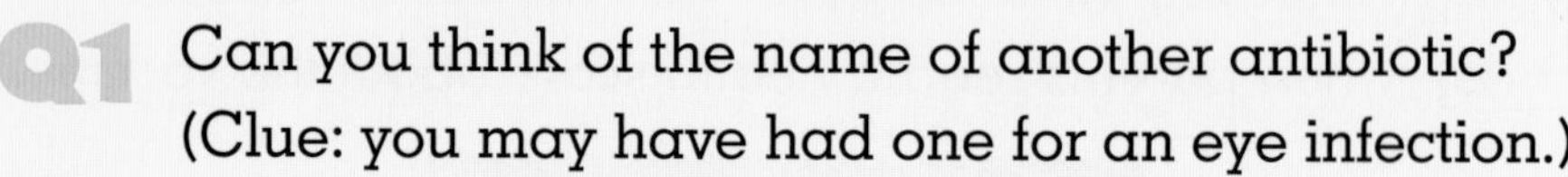

Q1 Can you think of the name of another antibiotic? (Clue: you may have had one for an eye infection.)

Antibiotics stop young bacteria growing and reproducing. They do not affect viruses at all because viruses grow and reproduce in a different way. So if you have a cold, caused by a virus, you will just have to get better on your own.

You have to take antibiotics for several days to completely stop the infection. If you stop too soon, some bacteria will still be alive and will quickly grow again.

Disinfectants and antiseptics

Disinfectants are chemicals that kill micro-organisms. We use disinfectants on surfaces, in bathrooms, in kitchens, babies' bottles and anywhere there are harmful micro-organisms.

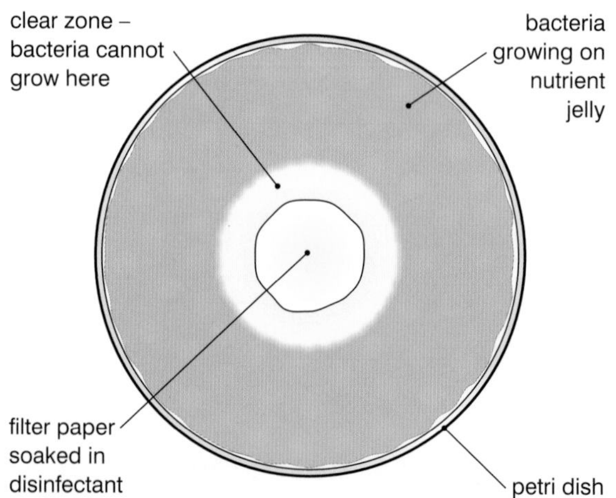

Disinfectant diffuses into the jelly and stops bacteria growing

Bleach is a disinfectant that releases **chlorine**. Chlorine kills micro-organisms.

Disinfectants also damage human cells. We have to use milder **antiseptics** to deal with micro-organisms in spots, cuts and in your mouth. Antiseptics slow down microbial growth.

ICT CHALLENGE

Penicillin was first observed by Alexander Fleming and developed by Florey and Chain. Write a magazine page about the story of penicillin.

How effective is your disinfectant?

Always follow *all* safety rules when working with microbes.

- Soak discs of filter paper in household anti-microbial chemicals. You could try disinfectant, toothpaste, deodorant, antiseptic solution, sterilising solution, mouthwash. You could also cut a small square of an anti-microbial wipe to try.
- Using forceps, place your discs on nutrient agar jelly that has been seeded with bacteria. Incubate them for a few days.
  - **a)** Where have bacteria grown? If an anti-microbial substance has stopped bacteria from growing, there will be a clear area round its disc. Draw what you see.
  - **b)** Which substance seems to be the most effective against the bacteria you were growing?
- Look around your house for products you use to keep clean. Read the labels and make a list of the disinfectant or antiseptic chemicals they contain.

SUMMARY QUESTIONS

1 ☆ Why doesn't the doctor give you antibiotics when you have a cold or chickenpox?

2 ☆ Match the chemical with the job it is used for.

clean up in the kitchen	antiseptic
clean a graze	antibiotic
treat an eye infection	disinfectant

3 ☆☆ Swimming pool water contains chlorine to keep it clean. Explain why adding chlorine keeps the water safer for swimmers.

antibiotic
antiseptic
chlorine
disinfectant
penicillin

IDEAS AND EVIDENCE

Louis Pasteur

Louis Pasteur (1822–1895) was one of the first scientists to discover that bacteria cause diseases.

He had trained as a chemist. An alcohol manufacturer asked him to look at a problem. This problem, and the new ideas it led to, kept Pasteur busy for many years.

Everyone knew that fermenting sugar into alcohol was linked to brewer's yeast, but they weren't sure how. They did not know that yeast was alive.

Some of the manufacturer's brews made lactic acid instead of alcohol. Pasteur examined the fermenting mixes with a microscope. He saw that normal fermentations contained minute rounded bodies. Fermentations that would make lactic acid had long bodies in them. From this he was able to **predict** which brews would be useless.

Pasteur thought that there must be two different processes going on. He extracted a substance a bit like yeast from vats containing the lactic acid. He found that lactic acid was only made if this yeast-like substance was present.

Milk is pasteurised straight after it leaves the cow

Pasteur wondered what it was and how it had got into the vats – perhaps from the air. This eventually led him into work on how bacteria are spread.

Pasteur concluded that these bodies which made the lactic acid were bacteria. He also showed that brewer's **yeast** was alive and **observed** it reproduce. Others thought that fermentation was the result of brewer's yeast decomposing. By using carefully controlled experiments, Pasteur showed that live yeast cells were needed for **fermentation**. During his investigations into fermentations he discovered bacteria that did not need oxygen – the first such organisms ever found.

Pasteur developed a method of treating wine so that vinegar-producing bacteria did not make it sour. This process became known as **pasteurisation**. We use it today to treat milk, beer and fruit juices so they keep better.

Pasteur went on to make vitally important discoveries – what can you find out about him?

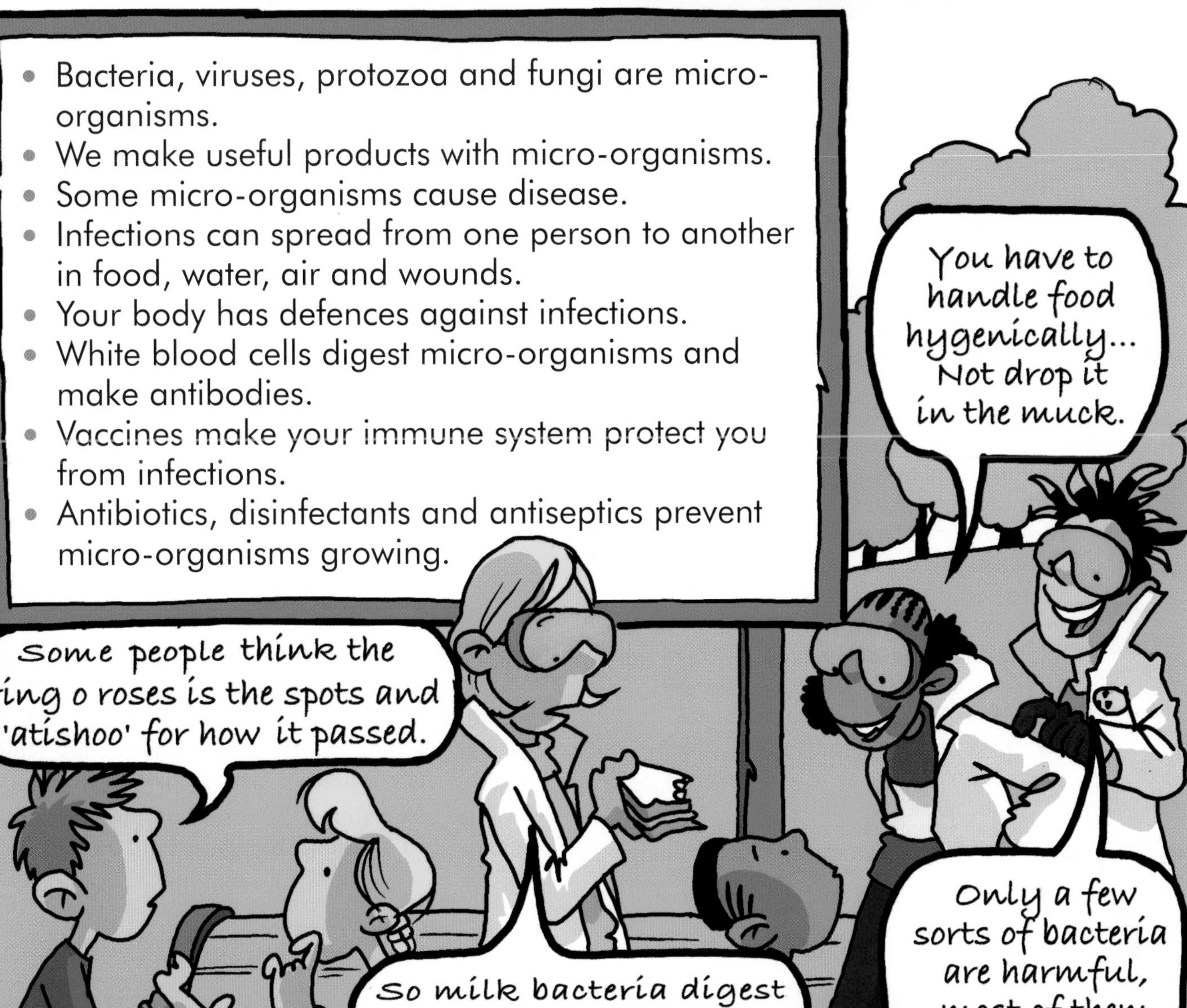

- Bacteria, viruses, protozoa and fungi are micro-organisms.
- We make useful products with micro-organisms.
- Some micro-organisms cause disease.
- Infections can spread from one person to another in food, water, air and wounds.
- Your body has defences against infections.
- White blood cells digest micro-organisms and make antibodies.
- Vaccines make your immune system protect you from infections.
- Antibiotics, disinfectants and antiseptics prevent micro-organisms growing.

You have to handle food hygenically... Not drop it in the muck.
Some people think the ring o roses is the spots and 'atishoo' for how it passed.
So milk bacteria digest milk sugar, and turn milk into cheese.
Only a few sorts of bacteria are harmful, most of them don't affect us at all.

DANGER! AVOID THESE COMMON ERRORS

A *disinfectant* is a very powerful substance that kills micro-organisms. It is used on surfaces such as worktops and sinks.

An *antiseptic* is much more dilute so it can be used on delicate human tissue. It will kill some micro-organisms and stop others growing without harming the skin.

Antibiotics are medicines prescribed by a doctor to kill bacteria. They do not kill viruses so we do not take them to cure a cold.

Key words

fermentation
observe
pasteurisation
predict
yeast

UNIT REVIEW

REVIEW QUESTIONS
Understanding and applying concepts

1 Copy the sentences and fill in the missing words.
   a Micro-organisms . . . the remains of dead animals and plants.
   b There are four types of micro-organisms. They are protozoa, . . ., . . . and . . .
   c Micro-organisms make . . . used in washing powder and dishwasher tablets.
   d Food-poisoning is caused by . . . that get into your food. Colds are caused by . . . that spread in . . . when you sneeze.
   e We are protected from harmful micro-organisms by . . . ., which are part of our immune system.

2 What food do we use to grow bacteria?

3 Name *two* products we make using yeast.

4 Copy and complete the following table.

Micro-organism	Infection	How it is transmitted
bacterium	food-poisoning	
bacterium		droplets from lungs
	common cold	
virus		
protozoan	malaria	
fungus		contact

5 a White blood cells are part of a system. Which is it?

   digestive reproductive immune

   b Describe *two* ways that white blood cells protect us from infections.

6 In the past many children and young people died of diseases such as tetanus and diphtheria. Explain why children do not catch these diseases today.

7 Write definitions of the following words:

   vaccinate sterile incubate

Thinking skills

8 Draw a spider diagram of micro-organisms. Include the following words:

   pathogen yoghurt white blood cell decay immunity virus antiseptic insect

SAT-STYLE QUESTIONS

1 Hib vaccination protects against infections by a bacterium, *Haemophilus influenzae*. This bacterium causes a form of meningitis.

The graph shows the number of infections reported in the UK between 1990 and 2001.

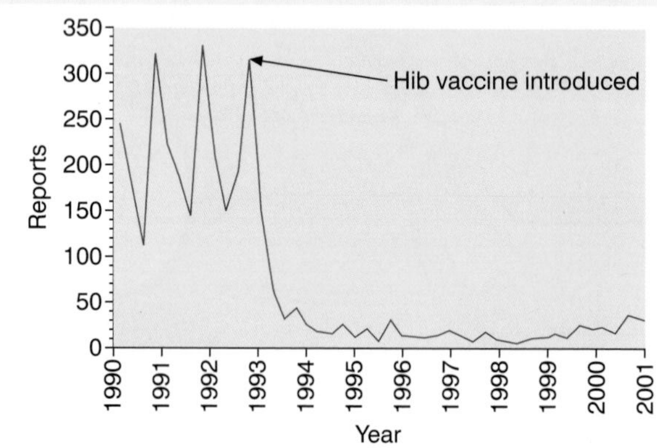

a i) In which year were the largest number of infections reported? (1)
   ii) When did the number of infections fall the most? (1)

The arrow shows when the vaccination programme began.

b Predict what will happen if parents do not have their children vaccinated. (1)

c The bacterium is passed in coughs. What type of spread is this? Choose from:

   blood oral droplet by touch (1)

2 White blood cells are found in blood. Look at the diagram of a white blood cell.

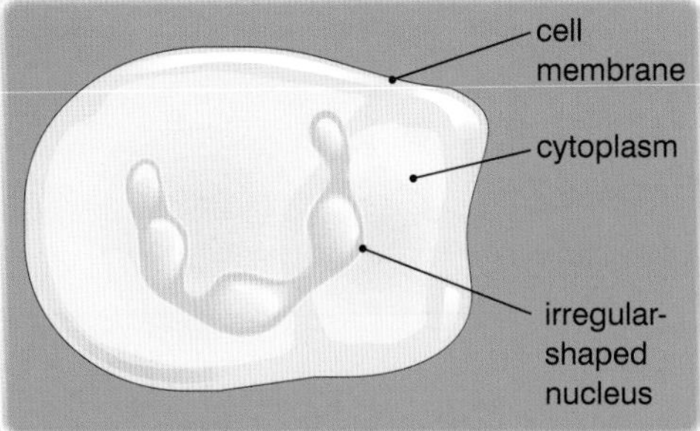

Blood also contains red blood cells. The structure of white blood cells is different to the structure of red blood cells.

a Write down one way in which a white blood cell is different to a red blood cell. (1)

b Give one function of a white blood cell. (1)

Some viruses, such as 'flu, change the composition of their outer layer. This changes their antigens.

c Explain why a vaccine to the old 'flu will not work very well against the new strain. (2)

3 Pip decided to make some bread. She put 250 cm^3 warm water in a jug and stirred in 5 g sugar and 15 g dried yeast. She rested the jug on the radiator. After 15 minutes the mixture was bubbling and there was a froth on the top of the yeast mixture.

a What sort of micro-organism is yeast? (1)

b i) Why did she add sugar to the yeast mixture? (1)

ii) How could Pip accurately measure how much sugar or yeast she added? (1)

c Why was the mixture frothy? (2)

Pip mixed the frothy liquid with 500 g plain flour in a mixing bowl. She kneaded the dough. Then she left it above a warm radiator to 'prove'. Two hours later the ball of dough was twice as big.

d What is the name of the process in yeast cells that has caused the dough to increase in size? (1)

4 Reese and Pete investigated how some household chemicals affected bacteria.

Reese predicted that anti-bacterial spray would be most effective at preventing bacterial growth.

They cut circles from filter paper. Reese used sterile forceps to dip them into the solutions. They placed them on a petri dish in which bacteria were growing. The dishes of bacteria were incubated.

Reese and Pete knew they had to work carefully.

a i) Why did Reese use sterile forceps to handle the discs of filter paper? (1)

ii) Suggest *two* other safety precautions they should take working with micro-organisms. (2)

After three days incubation the petri dishes looked like this:

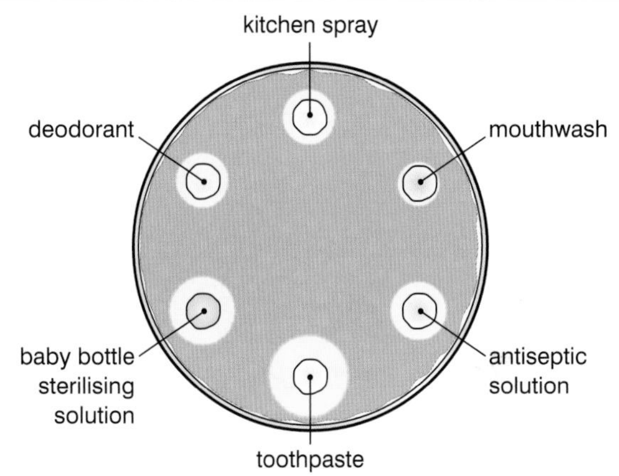

b What should Reese and Pete measure to find out about the effect of the anti-microbial substances? (1)

c Do the results support the prediction? (1)

Key words

Unscramble these:
dintaboy
catabire
tripe hids
unmime

8D Ecological relationships

Coming soon

What's it all about?

Animals and plants live in communities. Many different species live in the same habitat. They are linked together. One kind of link is made when one organism feeds on another. Another sort of link is made when one species provides something that another species needs. For example, grass benefits from a dollop of cow dung occasionally.

In this unit you will find out more about some of these links. You will also learn about how energy from the Sun is transferred through the animals and plants of a community.

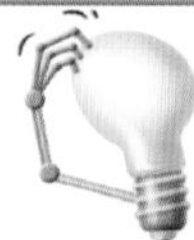

What do you remember?

You already know about:

- sorting plants and animals into groups.
- food chains.
- physical factors in the environment.
- how animals and plants are adapted to their environment.

1 Three of these things are important physical factors in the environment of animals and plants. Which is the odd one out?

amount of light rainfall
highest and lowest temperature each day atmospheric pressure

2 Choose a predator, a primary consumer, and a producer from the list:

lettuce cheetah greenfly slug owl rose bush

3 Match the animal to the group it belongs to

snail frog ladybird woodlouse

crustacean amphibian mollusc insect

Ideas about investigating habitats

I wonder if there is anything in this bush?

I can't tell what sort of bird it is.

I'm not touching that till I've got my gloves on.

QUESTIONS

The Scientifica crew are investigating two different parts of the school grounds.

a) They are comparing a wild area by the sports pitch with the rose garden. They want to know if the communities of animals and plants in the two areas are different.

b) Are there any scientific reasons why the animals and plants might be different in the two places?

c) What sorts of animals and plants would you expect to find in the area by the sports pitch?

d) What items of equipment would help Pip identify the bird?

e) What advice would you give them for working safely outside?

8D1

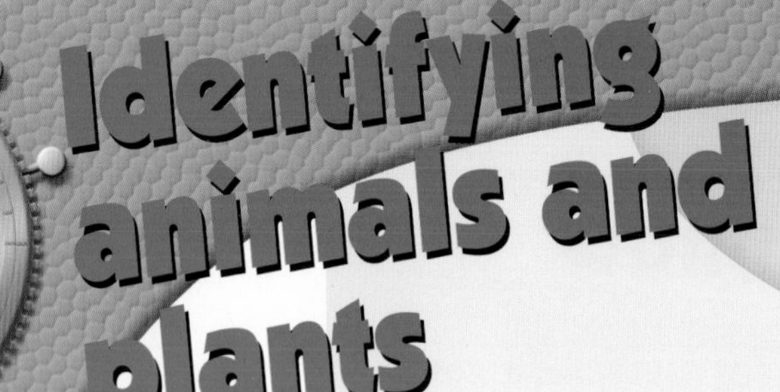

Identifying animals and plants

LEARN ABOUT
- classifying animals and plants
- arthropods

If you went to the seaside what wildlife would you expect to see? Seabirds, seaweed, mussels and a crab perhaps. The seashore always seems packed with life.

There may not seem to be as much wildlife in your school grounds. In fact there are thousands of small animals living among the plants and dead leaves close to the ground. There are also dozens of different plants in the grass of the lawn.

Q1 Where would be a good place to look for animals and plants round the school? What species are you likely to find?

What will you find?

You may not have seen these small plants and animals before. You will have to use a key and your knowledge of the **classification** groups to find out what they are.

Most of the animals living in grassy places, among leaf litter and under shrubs are **invertebrates**. You will find plenty of **arthropods** but also some **molluscs** and **segmented worms**.

Arthropods have a hard outer skeleton and distinct segments to their body. They move about using jointed legs. Arthropods pass through stages as they grow, and the young may look quite different to the adults.

You can see the classification of some of the species you are likely to find in the classification diagram opposite.

Decomposers

Many of the creatures you find are likely to eat debris. **Decomposers** such as fungi feed on dead plant and animal materials. They break up large items like dead leaves into smaller fragments. They recycle nutrients in the community.

Peacock butterflies look very different from their young

Classification key

Invertebrates
- no internal backbone

Segmented worms
- body in many similar segments
- no distinct head
- some bristles

e.g. earthworm

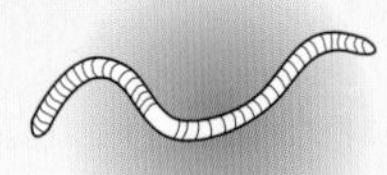

earthworm

Arthropods
- exoskeleton
- moults to allow growth
- jointed limbs

Molluscs
- muscular foot
- no segments
- usually a shell

e.g. slugs, snails

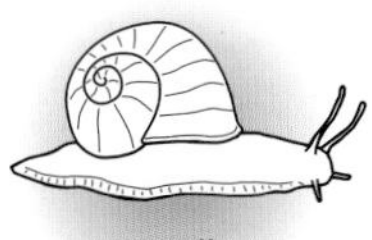

snail

Insects
- body in 3 parts
- 3 pairs of legs
- 1 or 2 pairs of wings

e.g. fungus gnat, beetle, aphid

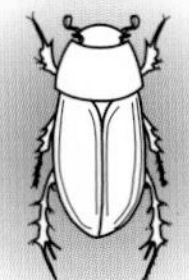

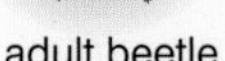

adult beetle

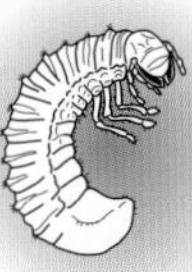

larval beetle

Myriapods
- head and many body segments with legs
- no wings

e.g. centipede, millipede

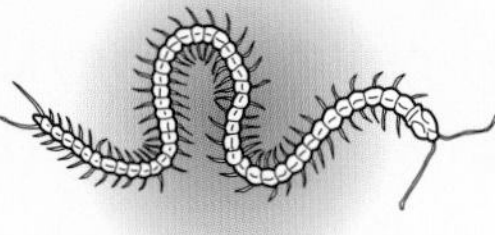

centipede

Arachnids
- body in 2 parts
- 4 pairs of legs
- no antennae

e.g. spider, harvestman, mite

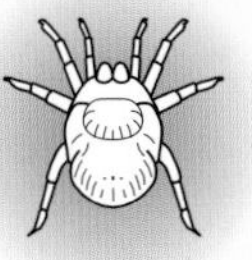

mite

Crustaceans
- body in 2 parts
- many pairs of walking legs
- gills
- 2 pairs of antennae

e.g. woodlouse

woodlouse

Classify

- Practise using a key to identify the specimens you have been given.
- Say what group each of the organisms below belongs to. Do you know what they are?

(a)

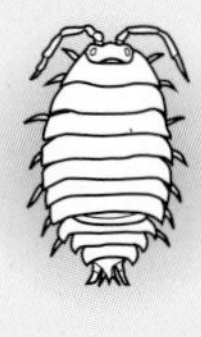

(b)

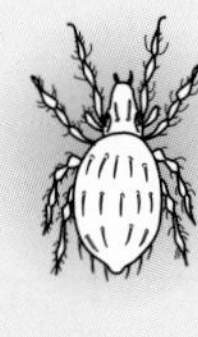

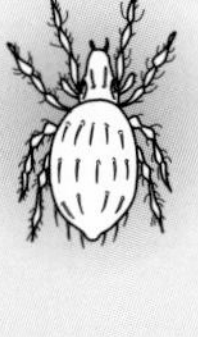

(c)

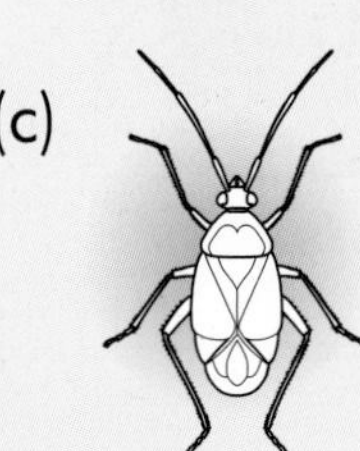

(d)

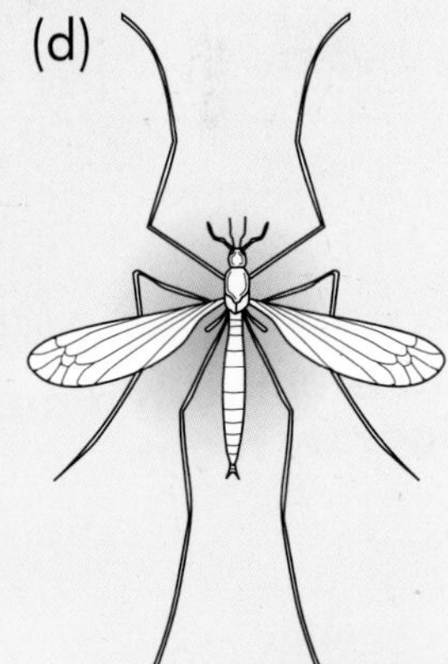

(e)

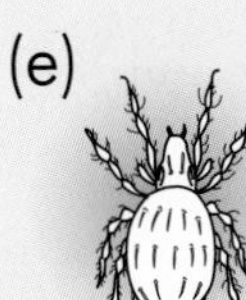

(f)

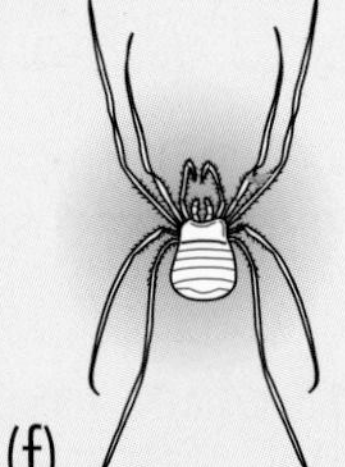

(g)

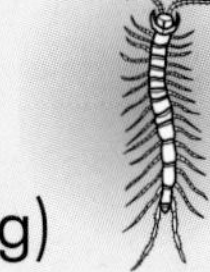

SUMMARY QUESTIONS

1 ☆ Describe the features of an arthropod.

2 ☆ Give *two* differences between an insect and a spider.

3 ☆ What is a decomposer?

Key words

arthropod
classification
decomposer
invertebrate
mollusc

Sampling animals

LEARN ABOUT

- counting animals in a small habitat

How would you find out how many elephants there are in a game reserve? Drive round in a jeep and count? Fly over in a helicopter filming? We need to be ingenious to find and count animals because they don't stick around.

Catching and counting

We can **observe** large animals and birds by sitting quietly in a hidden place (called a hide) using binoculars. Very shy or nocturnal animals can be recorded using a video camera or infra-red camera.

Small mammals are caught in a humane trap. Small birds are caught in mist netting. They are identified and weighed and measured before being released.

Small invertebrates living among the vegetation are caught in a **pitfall trap.** Those feeding or resting in bushes are caught by **tree-beating**.

Caught on infra-red camera – a badger by night

Investigating animals

Choose an area to investigate.

- Find, identify and record as many species of animals as possible in your site.
- Use a pitfall trap to investigate small invertebrates living on the ground.
- Investigate insects and other invertebrates living in shrubs and bushes by tree-beating.
- Investigate a sample of leaf litter to find and identify small invertebrates. Try to estimate how many there are in your sample.

Small invertebrates are very fragile. Do not pick them up with fingers. Always use a paint brush to handle them.

- Research the species you have identified. Include what it eats and its major predators.

CHALLENGE

Pool your information with other groups working in the same area. Then construct a database of information.

How many live here?

We want to know how many individuals there are in a community. This is **quantitative data**. We have to count the number per unit area. We take a sample, examine the wildlife carefully and replace it.

For example, if we wanted to estimate the number of animals living in leaf litter we would mark out a square, 30 cm by 30 cm, on the surface. Then we would use a trowel to dig up the top10 cm of leaf and soil debris to take back to the lab.

Many of the leaf litter animals are too small to see their details clearly. A hand lens and binocular microscope show details of the smallest organisms.

They don't stand still so a **pooter** is very useful for catching them as they try to hide.

There are 36 000 soil mites in a 30 centimetre square layer of leaf litter from a forest.

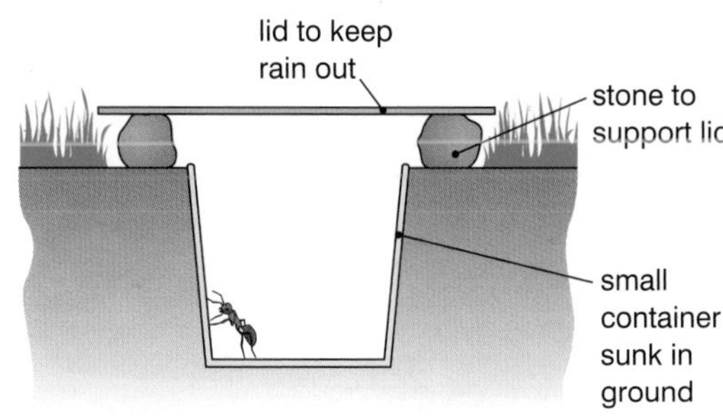

A pitfall trap

SUMMARY QUESTIONS

1 How would you find out how many of the following there are in a community?
   a) ground beetles **b)** aphids (greenfly)

2 Give an example of quantitative data that you have collected in science activities.

Key words

observe
pitfall trap
pooter
quantitative data
tree-beating

Sampling plants

Learn about

- estimating numbers of plants

We notice dandelions and gorse bushes because they have bright and colourful flowers. When we are asked what we saw, these are the ones we remember. We don't notice small and plain plants. Ecologists collect data in a scientific way so that they do not overlook species.

Our eyes are drawn to vivid flowers and we ignore the rest

Sampling

Ideally we should identify and count every single plant in an area. However, it is too difficult and time consuming to count every plant in a forest or across a county.

Scientists take **samples** instead. They investigate small areas within the larger area very thoroughly. They assume that the rest is like the samples they have investigated.

Random sampling

It is important that the samples represent all parts of the area. Scientists take **random samples** – they do not look around for a nice patch with plenty of pretty flowers.

Q1 Try to think why each of these actions could give us biased data:

avoiding the soggy part of a field
going round a clump of bushes

A **transect** is a long line running across an area.
You sample the plants at regular intervals along that line.

Transects are useful when the habitat changes, for example, through a patch of bushes or across a well-used path. You can find out how the plant population changes with different physical conditions.

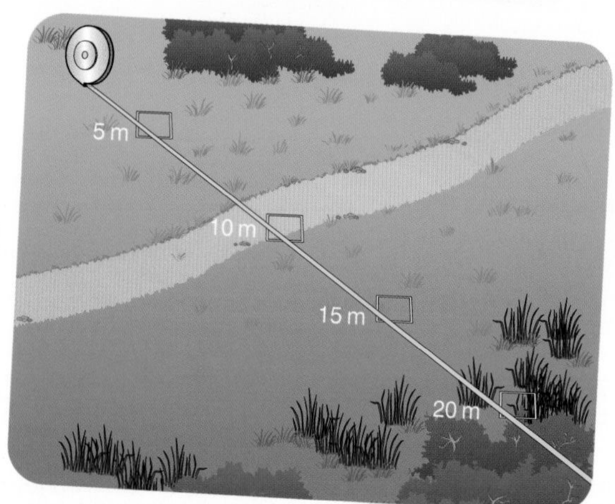

Only the toughest plants can survive being trampled at the path

Quadrats

Each sample must cover exactly the same area. You use a **quadrat** to define the area. You can use it to **estimate** the number of a species per square metre (m^2).

Quadrat data can tell us:

- whether a plant is present or not,
- how many plants per m^2,
- what percentage of the ground is covered by a species.

Percentage cover is useful for plants that make clumps, like rye grass and daisies.

A quadrat

Using quadrats

- Identify the plants growing in two different areas. Use quadrats to estimate the percentage cover for each species.
- Measure the physical factors in both areas.
- Construct a database of the species you have identified.

Mike's phone number ends in 5827. The group has used it to select a random sample site.

SUMMARY QUESTIONS

1 Reese and Pip used a 0.5 m × 0.5 m quadrat to sample the number of ribwort plantain plants in an area behind the school.

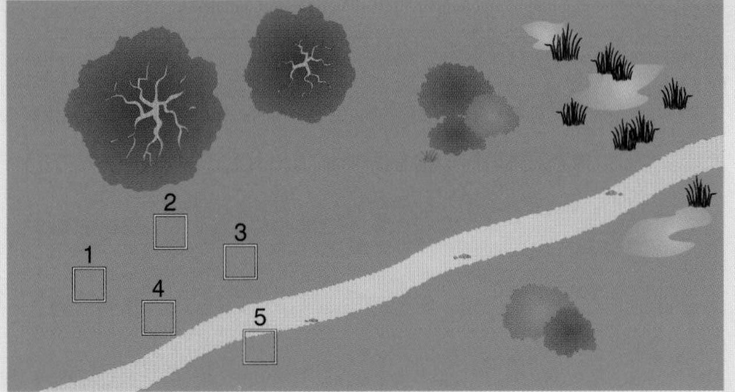

You can see where they sampled in the diagram. Their results are shown in the table.

Ribwort plantain

Square	1	2	3	4	5
Number of ribwort plantain	3	5	6	3	7

a) Using Reese and Pip's data, estimate how many ribwort plantain plants there are in the whole area.

b) Reese and Pip's results may be not be reliable – why not?

c) How could Reese and Pip make their investigation more reliable?

Key words

estimate
percentage cover
quadrat
random sample
sampling
transect

Food webs

8D4

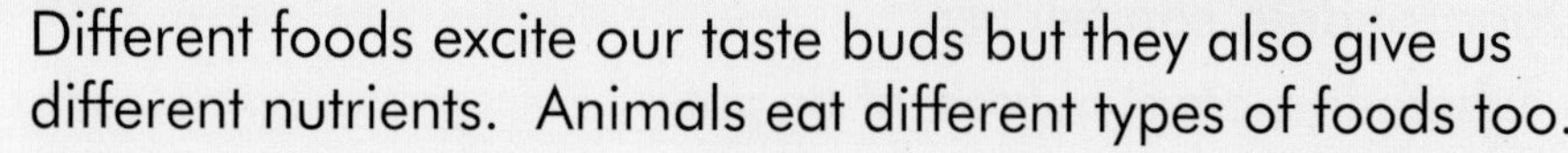

LEARN ABOUT

- more about food webs

Different foods excite our taste buds but they also give us different nutrients. Animals eat different types of foods too.

Some animals change the foods that they eat during the year. Garden birds might eat aphids in the spring, raspberries in the summer, but seeds and nuts in the autumn.

Many animals change their diet as they grow. Newly-hatched tadpoles eat microscopic algae growing on water weeds. When they grow larger they eat small water organisms. As adult frogs they eat flies and worms.

Q1 How do butterflies change their diet during their life?

Make a food web

- Use the database you made in 8D3 to construct food chains for your areas. Try to link the food chains into a food web.
- Make a poster to display a food web in your environment.

Food webs

A **food web** shows the food sources that animals use.

At the base of a food web, **producers** (the plants) convert light energy into chemical energy. The materials they make are the source of energy for the **consumers** in the rest of the food web.

When plants and animals die, they are food for **decomposers**. Decomposers feed from all levels of a food web. They are consumers.

Competition

Organisms on the same level in a food web **compete** for the same food resources. This limits how many animals can live together on one level.

The numbers of any animal species depends on:

- how much food there is
- how much competition there is for the food
- how many are killed by predators.

For example, the number of red squirrels is linked to how much tree seed there is. Red squirrels bring up fewer young in years when there is less seed available.

Red squirrels thrive best in mixed woodlands with conifers

Q2 Can you think of any factors that might result in trees making less seed than usual?

Q3 Pick out two animals in the moorland food web that are in competition for a food source.

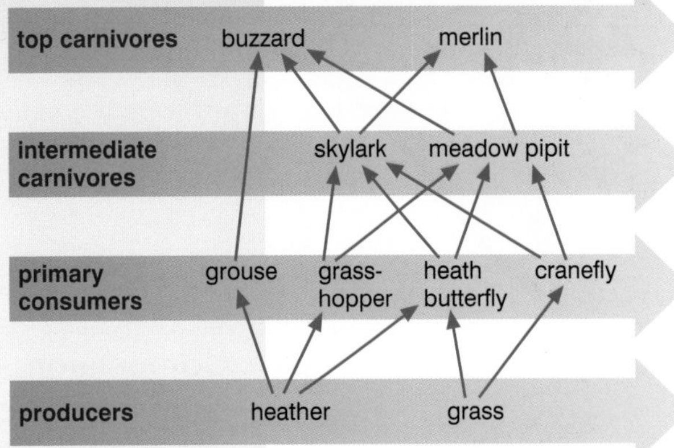

A moorland food web

Changes in the web

Anything that changes the numbers of one animal or plant in a food web will also affect the other species.

For example, the small tortoiseshell butterfly feeds on nectar from many flowers. Their caterpillars eat nettles. If nettles are cleared from an area there are no food plants for the adult to lay eggs on. There will be no caterpillars, and in time no adults.

Farming has affected food webs. Plants are lost when farmers

- flail hedges instead of cutting them
- mow more often
- cultivate soil right to the edges of fields.

If there are fewer flowers there will be fewer butterflies, bees and other nectar feeders. In turn there will be fewer of the animals that feed on them.

Grey squirrels were introduced in 1876. By 1937 they had become such a nuisance in woodlands that laws were passed about releasing them.

Alien invaders

Alien species are animals and plants brought to this country by international trade. Sometimes they escape and join native animal and plant communities. They upset food webs. Many compete well with native species. Chinese mitten crabs and grey squirrels make better use of food resources than native crayfish and red squirrels. Alien plants, such as the sitka spruce, are not as good a food source for native animals.

ICT CHALLENGE

Find out about an alien species such as grey squirrels, muntjac deer, mink, Himalayan balsam or sycamore.

SUMMARY QUESTIONS

1 ☆ Write out a food chain from the moorland food web above.

2 ☆ Give *three* factors that can change the size of an animal population.

3 ☆☆ Red squirrels live and seek food in the treetops. Grey squirrels seek food on the ground. Explain how this could help grey squirrels compete for food.

Key words

alien species
compete
consumer
decomposer
food web
producer

- how the environment affects populations
- links between predators and their prey

Competition – the word brings to mind races and championships. It's hard to think of plants being in competition. Plants compete for space, for water, for **minerals** from the soil, and for **light**.

Q1 Estimate the surface area of a leaf in the sun and one in the shade.

Plants in competition

Plants adapt to different amounts of light. Plants that are shaded by trees or bushes grow larger leaves. With larger leaves they can collect as much light as possible. Plants growing in lighter places do not need such large leaves. Ivy clinging to a tree trunk will have larger leaves on the shady side than the sunny side.

Other plants grow taller when others shade them. By doing this they get their leaves above those of their competitors.

growing in a shaded area

growing in full sun

The periwinkle plant growing in the shaded area needs larger leaves to collect as much light as stems from the same plant growing in the sun

Predators and prey

In some years we have swarms of ladybirds that get everywhere. This **population boom** happens after there have been lots of aphids (greenfly) on plants. Adult and larval ladybirds eat aphids.

When there are plenty of aphids, ladybird larva survive to become adults and the population booms. Aphids become scarce as more and more ladybirds are hunting them.

Populations of **predators** and their **prey** are linked. Predators depend on catching enough prey to stay alive. They also need food to reproduce successfully. If there isn't enough food the predators cannot breed very well. Their numbers go down.

Similarly, the numbers of prey animals are affected by how many predators eat them. When there are many predators the prey population goes down. If there are few predators more prey survive to breed, so their population increases.

Over time we can see the populations changing together, the boom in predator numbers always follows a boom in prey numbers.

Q2 What do you think a larva is?

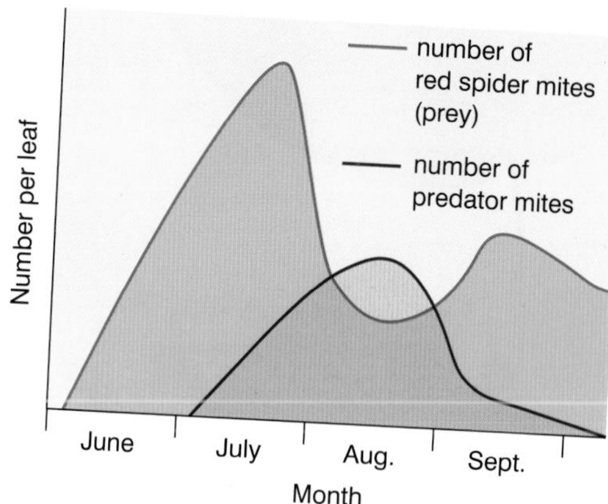

Changing populations of apple red spider mite and its predator

Reporting findings

Use the information you have gathered about the two areas you have investigated and the animals and plants living there.

- Write a report comparing the two communities. Include in your report any factors you have identified that may affect the size of the populations.

ICT CHALLENGE

Prepare a PowerPoint or similar presentation comparing the two sites you have investigated.

SUMMARY QUESTIONS

1 In the diagram you can see dandelion plants. They come from two different areas. One is growing by a sports pitch. The other is from unmown grass:

☆ **a)** Which physical factor could have caused them to grow differently?

☆☆ **b)** How would this factor be different in the two areas?

☆☆ **c)** Explain how human activity could also have resulted in this difference.

2 ☆ Look at the graph above showing the population of red spider mites. What would happen to the numbers of red spider mites if there were fewer predatory mites?

Key words

light
minerals
population boom
predator
prey

Pyramids and energy flow

LEARN ABOUT
- pyramids of numbers
- how energy is lost from a food chain

Pyramids

A food chain tells us what eats what – humans eat tomatoes for example. Ecologists also use **quantitative data,** such as how many organisms are in a food chain.

We display this data in a **pyramid of numbers**. Each step in the pyramid shows how many organisms there are at that level. You can see some pyramids in the diagram below.

- The base is usually the broadest. It shows how many plants there are in the chain. The more plants there are, the wider the step.
- The next step shows the number of herbivores – the primary consumers. It is usually much narrower than the first step because each herbivore needs lots of plants to feed on.
- The third step is the predatory animal that eats the herbivore. This step is narrower than the second step because each predator needs lots of prey herbivores to survive.
- The last step is the top carnivore. This is the narrowest step of all.

As you can see one predator at the top of the food chain relies on the food produced by thousands of plants at the bottom.

The pyramid looks different when a food chain starts with one large producer, such as an oak tree. The bottom step is very narrow. The oak tree will support lots of small herbivores, such as aphids and caterpillars.

LINK UP TO BIOLOGY

Living things use energy from respiration to maintain tissues, for activities and for growth and reproduction (see 8B1).

Q1 Choose the term from the list that best describes the plants:

producer
primary consumer
secondary consumer
decomposer

top carnivores
intermediate carnivores
herbivores
producers

an inverted pyramid

top carnivores
intermediate carnivores
herbivores
producers

Pyramids of numbers

Food chains and energy

Energy passes along a food chain. When an animal eats a plant, the energy in the plant passes to the animal. Food chains are short. This is because energy is lost each time it passes from one organism to the next.

Plants change light energy into chemical energy when they make food. Some of this energy is used in plant **respiration**. Some is stored in the plant.

Energy is transferred when herbivores eat plants. Animals absorb nutrients containing energy from digested vegetation. Energy in undigested food is lost in faeces.

Some of the energy animals take in is used in respiration. They use it to move about and to keep warm for example. Animals lose energy in waste materials such as urine.

How energy is lost from a food chain

Carnivores take in energy when they eat their prey. They lose energy in the same ways as herbivores.

By now there is very little of the original light energy left.

When organisms die they are food for **decomposers**. Even faeces are food for something. Decomposer organisms can use the energy in faeces.

Gruesome science

Less than 10% of the energy in plants ends up as stored energy in a herbivore.

Construct a pyramid

- The leaves from a small apple tree fall onto the earth below. In a 10 cm by 10 cm square of apple leaf litter beneath the tree the following animals were found:

  8 small centipedes,
  200 springtails,
  1 harvestman spider.

  Harvestmen spiders eat small centipedes.
  Springtails eat fallen apple leaves.
  Centipedes eat springtails.

  Use the data above to construct a food chain.
  Draw a pyramid of numbers for this food chain.

SUMMARY QUESTIONS

1 ☆ Match each food chain below to its pyramid of numbers:

grass → crane fly (larvae) → swallow
rose bush → aphid → blue tit

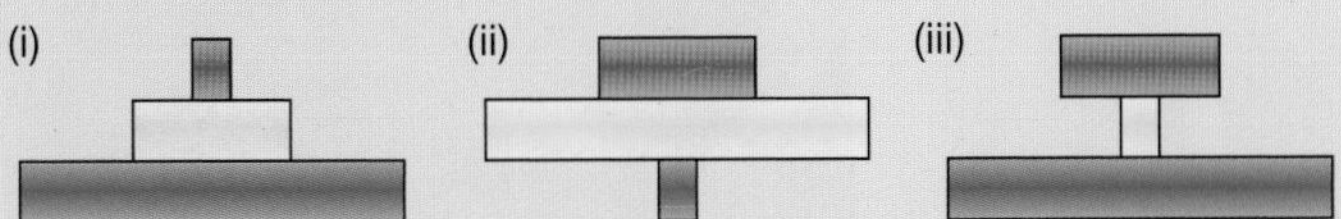

2 ☆ Give *two* ways in which energy is lost from a food chain.

Key words

decomposer
energy
pyramid of numbers
quantitative data
respiration

The case of the disappearing codfish

How many portions of cod are left in the North Sea? We have been fishing for cod for hundreds of years, but it looks as though a fish and chip supper might become a thing of the past.

There are fewer cod in the North Sea because we have been **over-fishing**. We catch more cod than are being replaced by young fish. In the past fish would have reproduced several times before they were caught. Now fish are more likely to be caught before they reproduce, so the numbers are dropping.

We could ban cod fishing. A whaling ban helped to slow down the decline in whale populations. However, banning cod fishing would throw thousands of people out of work. Many coastal communities depend on fishing.

Currently there is a **quota** system. Fishermen can catch a certain number of cod. This has not stopped the decline. Cod swim in shoals mixed with haddock, whiting, herrings and sprats. It is hard not to catch cod while fishing for other fish, but any that are caught have to be dumped.

What can you do to help the situation?

A fishing boat

SCIENTIFIC PEOPLE

Marine ecologists and **fishery scientists** investigate the ecology of the seas. There are many different habitats in the sea. Important habitats include estuaries where rivers run into the sea, shallow water near the shore, and deep water.

It is hard to observe the sea's inhabitants and we still have much to learn. We can monitor fish movement by marking fish, or by using radio-tracking tags on young fish. Sites are regularly sampled to see how the **marine** community changes.

We can investigate some basic fish biology in a laboratory with captive fish – it is rather like a giant aquarium.

One important job is to find out how the populations of different fish species change from year to year. If they stay steady we are happy, but if the numbers go down then scientists have to try and find out why. The decline could be due to:

- adverse physical conditions during the breeding season – this causes a temporary fall in the population
- an epidemic disease
- a change in the population of something else in the marine food web.

A biologist tagging sturgeon. They are an endangered species.

- Plants are affected by the physical conditions in their surroundings.
- Animals and plants compete with each other for the things they need.
- Animals and plants are linked in food chains and food webs.
- Changes in the population of one species in a food web will affect the other species too.
- The number of predators depends on how many prey are available.
- A pyramid of numbers shows how many plants and animals there are in a food chain.
- Energy is lost from each step in a food chain. This is because of respiration, undigested material and wastes.

We found dandelions in 20% of the squares, daisies in 60% and plantain in 30%.
The plants all had flattened leaves in a circle. They would survive here where plants get trampled a lot.
Can I have the binoculars? If the bird has speckles it's a thrush.
You are responsible for the equipment. After you have taken it back, wash your hands carefully.

DANGER! AVOID THESE COMMON ERRORS

Plants do not take food from the soil. Plants make their own food from carbon dioxide in the air and water, using light. They take minerals from the soil to help them make other substances. These minerals are not foods.

When the bottom step of a pyramid of numbers is very narrow, it is because the food chain includes a large plant such as a tree.

Key words

fishery scientist
marine
over-fishing
quota

UNIT REVIEW

REVIEW QUESTIONS

Understanding and applying concepts

1 Copy and complete the following sentences.
   a Food . . . interlink to form a food web of the animals and plants in a community.
   b Decomposers are organisms that use . . . as a food source.
   c Plants compete for resources such as . . ., minerals and water.
   d When predator numbers increase, prey numbers . . .
   e Animals lose energy in food through . . ., and through faeces and wastes.
   f The numbers of individuals in a food chain are represented by a . . . of numbers.

2 Write a sentence using each of these words in a scientific way:

producer consumer decomposer
predator prey sampling

3 Which of these pyramids of numbers pictured below best represents this food chain.

Grass → cow (dung) → dung beetle → badger

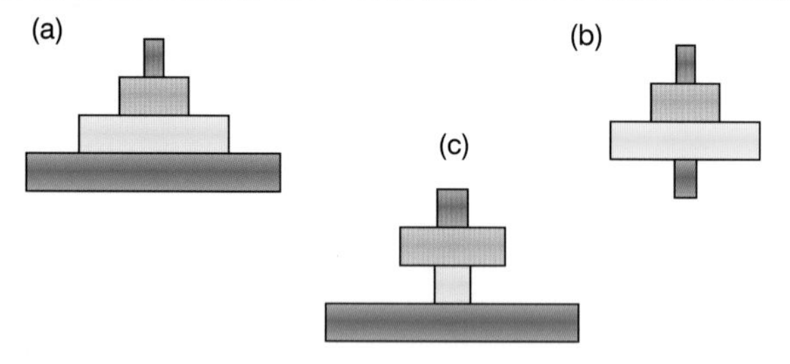

Thinking skills

4 Which is the odd one out in each of these groups?
   a Peacock butterfly, grasshopper, centipede.
   b Arthropod, mollusc, earthworm.

Ways with numbers

5 Draw a pyramid of numbers for the following food chain:

10 cabbages
95 large white butterfly caterpillars
1 robin

SAT-STYLE QUESTIONS

1 The Scientifica crew were investigating how many sorts of plants there were in the school grounds.

They decided to sample using quadrats.

They argued about how many samples to take.

Their teacher showed them a graph drawn by Nina in Year 13 as part of her ecology coursework. It showed the number of plant species she had discovered after taking more and more samples.

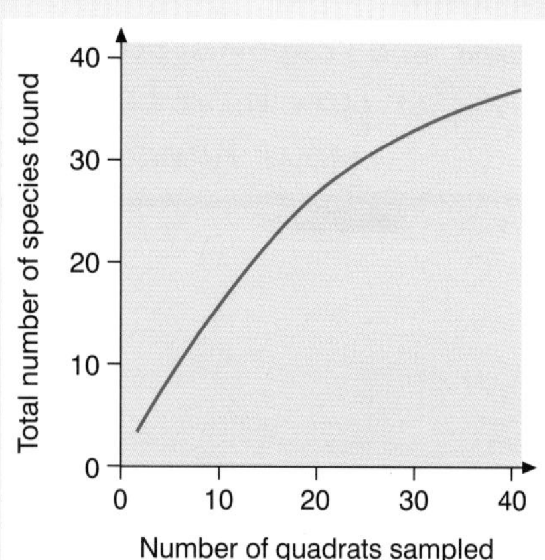

Nina's graph

They decided to use Nina's graph to help them decide on how many samples to take.
   a Describe the pattern shown by the graph. (1)
   b How many samples should they take? Explain why you reached this decision. (2)

2 The food web below shows the feeding relationships between some of the inhabitants of a heath land.

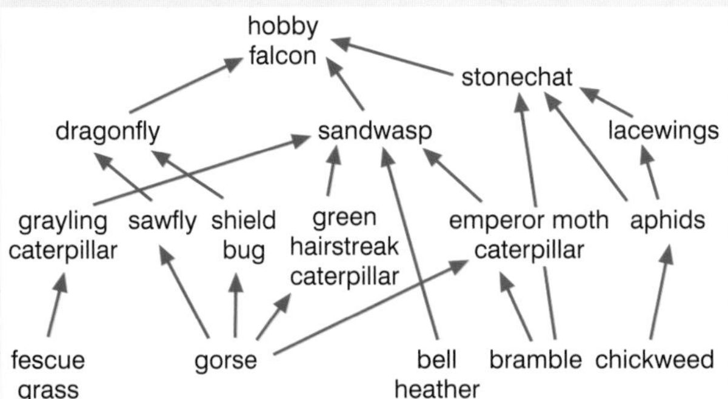

A heath land food web

a Write out one food chain from the food web. (1)

b Choose one producer and one consumer from the food web. (2)

c Choose one predator and its prey from the web. (2)

3 Whiteflies are small insects that feed on plants. They breed very rapidly. They are a serious pest in greenhouses.

Some gardeners do not like to spray insecticides over their plants. They use a predator to control the whitefly. A small wasp called *Encarsia* kills whiteflies. Gardeners can buy the wasps to put in their greenhouses.

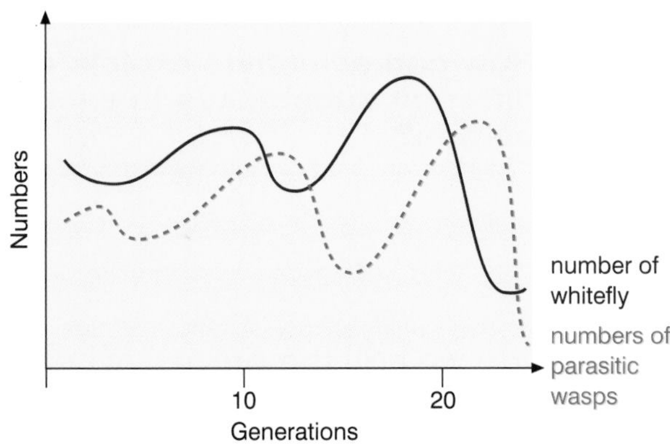

The graph shows what happens when whiteflies and wasps are kept together.

a Why does the population of whiteflies rise between 12 and 18 generations? (1)

b How does the curve for wasps differ from the curve for whiteflies? (1)

c Why do you think the population of wasps falls to such low numbers after 20 generations? (1)

4 Benson and Pete spent one afternoon investigating a field next to their school. The field is used for hay. Some of their results can be seen in the table.

	ox-eye daisy		corn cockle		meadow buttercup		cocks-foot grass		meadow grass	
Quadrat	squares	% cover	squares	% cover	squares	% cover	squares	% cover	squares	% cover
1	3	12	5	20	0	-	0	-	16	64
2	0	-	3	12	0	-	0	-	12	48
3	5	20	1	4	3	12	0	-	3	12
4	2	8	0	-	0	-	14	56	2	8
5	4	16	1	4	3	12	0	-	20	80
6	0	0	3	12	2	8	0	-	16	64
7	12	48	0	-			8	32		

a How do you think they found out the percentage cover of corn cockle? (1)

b Why would it be better for Benson and Pete to measure environmental factors on more than one occasion? (1)

c Benson and Pete could see the white flowers of ox-eye daisies all over the field. They thought that ox-eye daisies must be evenly distributed. Do their results support this first impression? (1)

Key words

Unscramble these:

pooedcrems
etpoor
ming laps
scantter

8E Elements and atoms

COMING SOON

What's it all about?

Just think of all the different substances you can see around you now. How can scientists make sense of all the different materials in the world?

To answer this question we can look more closely at particles. You have met particles before in unit 7G.

Now we will develop our particle model. This will help us to explain more about the way materials behave.

Do I look like a model?
Yes... A very hot particle.

How can scientists explain all the different substances in each person?

What do you remember?

You already know about:

- the differences between solids, liquids and gases.
- changes of state.
- how we can use models to explain our observations.

1 Which state(s) of matter can we compress easily?

solid liquid gas
solid and liquid

2 What do we call the process when a gas turns into a liquid?

melting evaporation
condensation boiling

3 In the particle model, why does a solid expand when we heat it?

the particles get bigger
air inside the particles expands
the particles need heat to grow
the particles vibrate more vigorously

Ideas about elements and atoms

You have to be careful using elements... They get very hot in electric fires and kettles.

Let's see if we can see the atoms in this plant cell.

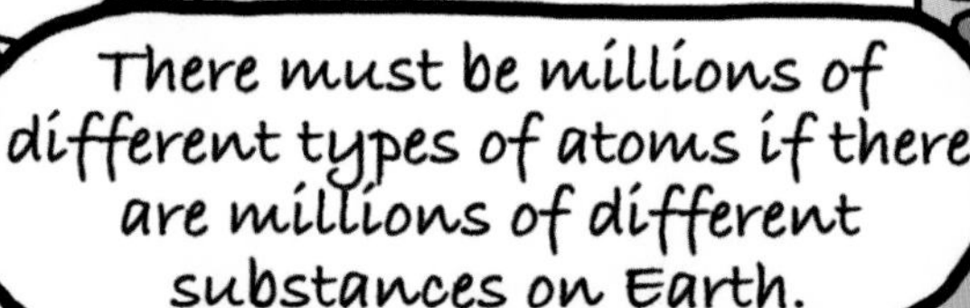

There must be millions of different types of atoms if there are millions of different substances on Earth.

Can we say that gases and liquids are materials... surely all materials are solids?

QUESTIONS

Look at the cartoons above:
Discuss these questions with your partner.

a) The word element has more than one meaning. Find out some different meanings.

b) Do you think Mike can see an atom through a microscope? What small things have you seen using a microscope?

c) How many different types of atom do you think there might be (roughly)? Why did you choose that number?

d) Why is Benson confused about the word 'materials'?

8E1 Different substances

I think you could register this as a new substance, Mike!

Learn about

- the huge variety of materials
- the relatively small number of elements that make up all other substances

Loads of substances

It's difficult for us to imagine all the different **substances** there are on Earth. Nobody knows the exact number.

Scientists try to make sense of all these substances by grouping them in different ways. You looked at solids, liquids and gases in unit 7G.

This is just one way of **classifying** substances.

Classifying substances

Look at the substances on the right:

- Sort the substances in the picture into different groups.

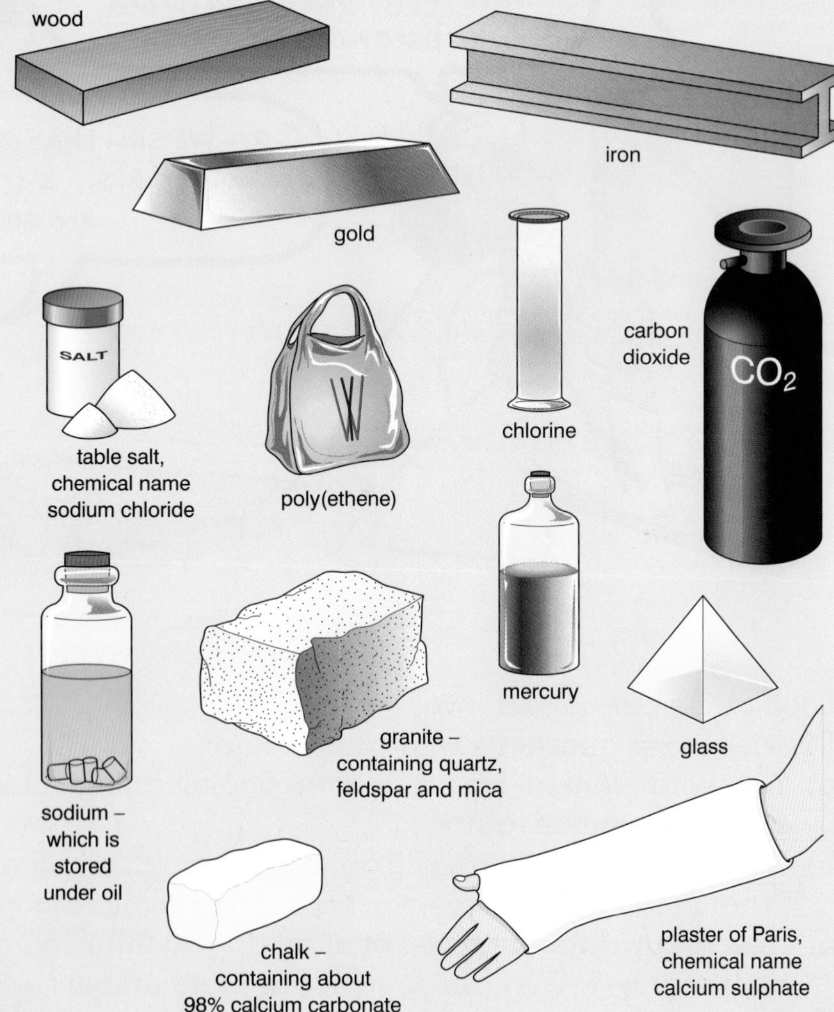

Over 5000 new substances are registered by scientists every day.

Nature's building blocks

Look at the substances on the last page. There are some substances that we call **chemical elements** (or just elements). These are chlorine, iron, sodium, gold and mercury.

Altogether, there are only 92 elements that occur naturally on Earth. All the other substances that exist are made up from just these elements. The chemical elements are like nature's building blocks. They make every substance we know.

We can use models to help us to understand this.

AMAZING SCIENCE!

The human body is made up of just 26 different elements.

Model

Imagine that the chemical elements are the building bricks in a Lego set. The other substances ('non-elements') are all the different things you can make using the Lego bricks.

These bricks represent three substances that are elements

This represents a substance that is one of the millions of 'non-elements'

Q1 Explain the model shown in your own words.

SUMMARY QUESTIONS

1 ☆ Copy and complete the sentences, using words from the list below:

millions **substances** **elements**

There are only about 100 different . . . But these can combine in many different ways to make the . . . of different . . . that exist.

2 ☆☆☆ There are lots more 'non-elements' than elements in the world.

Think up another model that you could use to explain this.

Key words

chemical element
classifying
substance

8E2 Atoms

LEARN ABOUT

- the difference between elements and other substances
- using models to show things we can't see

What are atoms?

You've probably heard of 'atoms' before. The word 'atom' comes from a Greek word. It means something that can't be divided up.

Imagine that you had a magic knife and started chopping up a piece of one of the chemical elements, such as iron. Eventually, the smallest **particle** of iron you would get to would be an **atom**. It would be a single atom of iron.

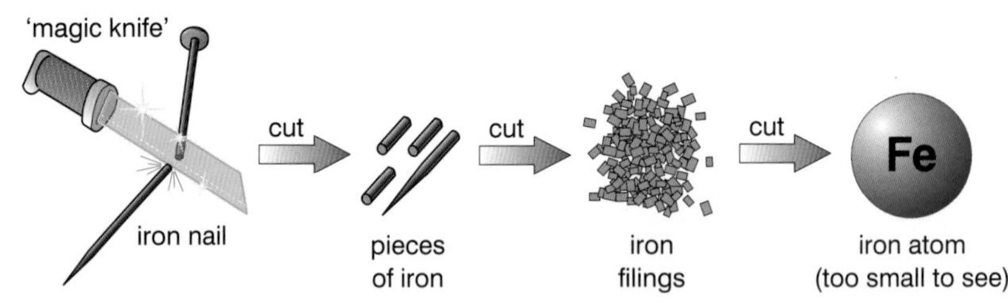

H

An atom of hydrogen

An atom of sulphur

Each atom differs from the others by its size and mass. But we think of them all as spheres.

Chemical symbols

Notice the letter on each atom. This is called the chemical **symbol** of the atom (or of the element). The symbol H means one atom of the element hydrogen. Here are the symbols of some common elements:

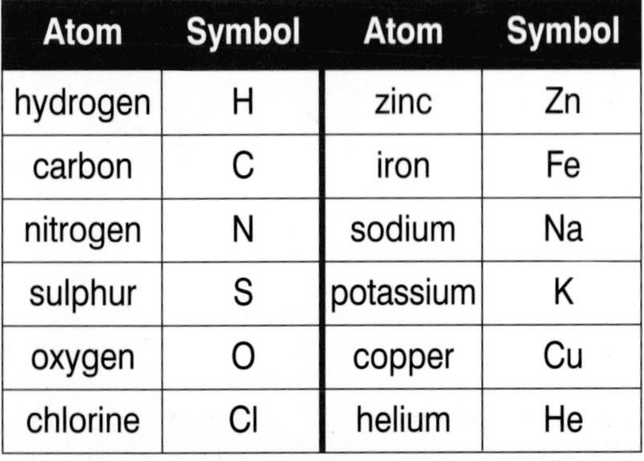

Atom	Symbol	Atom	Symbol
hydrogen	H	zinc	Zn
carbon	C	iron	Fe
nitrogen	N	sodium	Na
sulphur	S	potassium	K
oxygen	O	copper	Cu
chlorine	Cl	helium	He

You can see that the symbol for some atoms is a single *capital* letter. Others have two letters – a capital followed by a lower case letter.

The symbol for some atoms comes from their Latin name. For example, iron's symbol is Fe. This comes from its Latin name, ferrum.

Q1 Imagine that you discovered a new element.
What would you call it?
What symbol would you give it?

Making models

We also have *model kits* to show how atoms join (or bond) to each other.

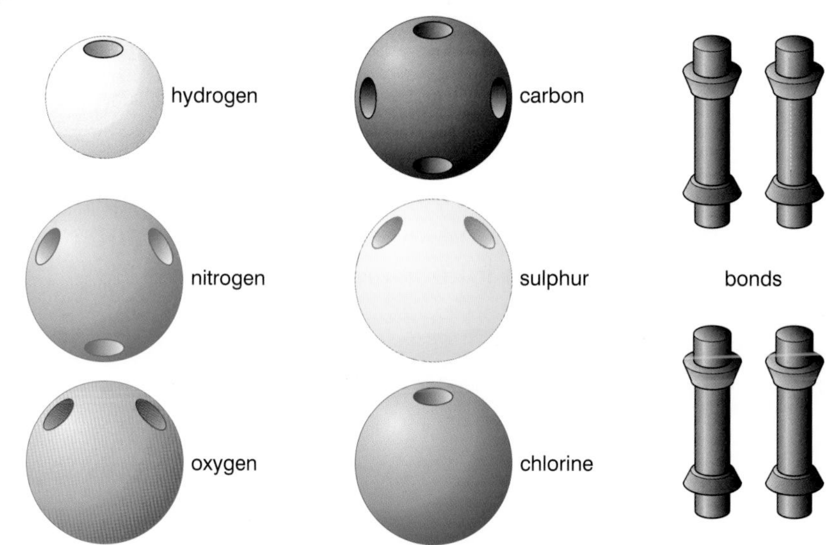

Look at these models below:

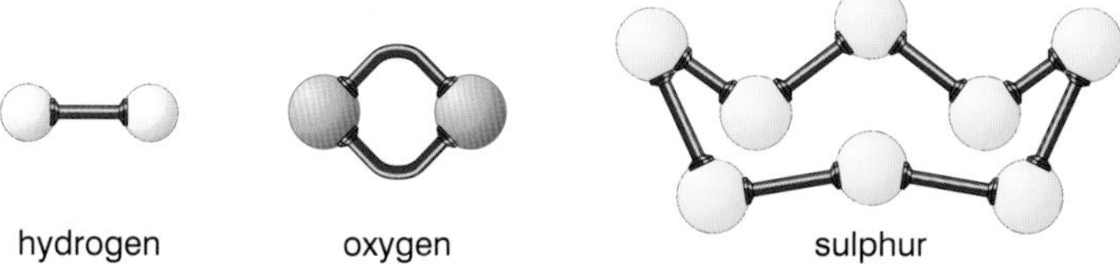

These show how the atoms are joined together in three of the chemical elements.

Notice how each model contains only one type of plastic ball.

***An element** is a substance made of only one type of atom.*

Make your own model

- Use a kit to design your own model.

You can see how a few 'building blocks' can make lots and lots of different substances. Were the models that you made elements or not?

*An **element** is a substance that can't be broken down into simpler substances.*

SUMMARY QUESTIONS

1 ☆ Copy and complete these sentences, using words from the list below.

atom **broken** **simpler** **element**

An . . . is a substance made up of only one type of . . .

They cannot be . . . down into . . . substances.

2 ☆☆ Why don't we use C as the symbol for chlorine? What is the rule about capital and lower case letters in chemical symbols?

Key words

atom
element
particle
symbol

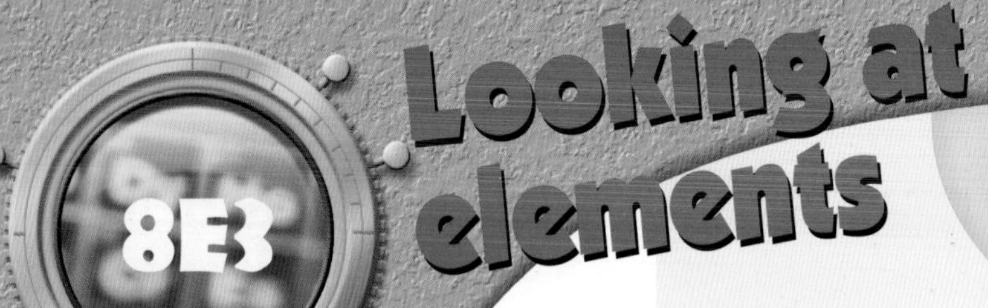

8E3 Looking at elements

LEARN ABOUT

- how elements vary in their appearance and state
- researching some of the elements

The chemical elements

There are around 100 different elements to find out about. Luckily, many of the elements have things in common. So studying them is made a lot easier!

There must be some way to make sense of all these different substances.

Researching elements

Your teacher will give each group about five elements to find out about.

You will need to use books, videos, CD ROMs or the Internet.

- Find out for each of your elements:
  - **a)** its symbol,
  - **b)** its state at 20°C,
  - **c)** whether it is described as a **metal**, a **non-metal** or a **metalloid** (semi-metal),
  - **d)** whether it is magnetic or not,
  - **e)** its appearance, and
  - **f)** any other interesting information about it.

You will be looking for patterns in the information the whole class gathers.

To help us find patterns, record the information on the sides of a cube made from card.

- Record each piece of information on a different side of the cube for each element.
- Write the word *metal* in blue, *non-metal* in red and *metalloid* in green.
- Use a large capital S for solids, an L for liquids and a G for gases.

The element helium was discovered on the Sun before it was found on Earth.

Sorting out the elements

In 1869, a Russian chemist called Dmitri Mendeleev arranged the elements in order of mass. He started with the lightest atoms, getting heavier.

He started new rows so that similar elements lined up in columns. The columns are called **groups**.

He called the arrangement the **Periodic Table**. Periodic means 'repeated at regular intervals'.

Here is a modern version of his table:

The Periodic Table of elements

																	0 (or 8)
			H Hydrogen 1														He Helium
Li Lithium 3	Be Beryllium 4											B Boron 5	C Carbon 6	N Nitrogen 7	O Oxygen 8	F Fluorine 9	Ne Neon 10
Na Sodium 11	Mg Magnesium 12											Al Aluminium 13	Si Silicon 14	P Phosphorus 15	S Sulphur 16	Cl Chlorine 17	Ar Argon 18
K Potassium 19	Ca Calcium 20	Sc Scandium 21	Ti Titanium 22	V Vanadium 23	Cr Chromium 24	Mn Manganese 25	Fe Iron 26	Co Cobalt 27	Ni Nickel 28	Cu Copper 29	Zn Zinc 30	Ga Gallium 31	Ge Germanium 32	As Arsenic 33	Se Selenium 34	Br Bromine 35	Kr Krypton 36
Rb Rubidium 37	Sr Strontium 38	Y Yttrium 39	Zr Zirconium 40	Nb Niobium 41	Mo Molybdenum 42	Tc Technetium 43	Ru Ruthenium 44	Rh Rhodium 45	Pd Palladium 46	Ag Silver 47	Cd Cadmium 48	In Indium 49	Sn Tin 50	Sb Antimony 51	Te Tellurium 52	I Iodine 53	Xe Xenon 54
Cs Caesium 55	Ba Barium 56	La Lanthanum 57	Hf Hafnium 72	Ta Tantalum 73	W Tungsten 74	Re Rhenium 75	Os Osmium 76	Ir Iridium 77	Pt Platinum 78	Au Gold 79	Hg Mercury 80	Tl Thallium 81	Pb Lead 82	Bi Bismuth 83	Po Polonium 84	At Astatine 85	Rn Radon 86

Q1 Why is the table called the Periodic Table?

Q2 How many elements does the Periodic Table above show?

Looking for patterns in the elements

- Now you can use your cubes to search for patterns in the Periodic Table.
- Your teacher will give you a sheet to help.

CHALLENGE

A database for the elements
Set up a database to store your information about the elements in the Periodic Table. Include their melting points and boiling points.

SUMMARY QUESTIONS

1 ☆ Copy and complete the sentences, using words from the list below.

similar   Table   metalloids   groups   metals

The elements can be sorted out into . . ., non-metals and a few . . .

The Periodic . . . shows elements with . . . properties in the same column. The columns are called . . .

2 ☆☆ Why are the chemical symbols for elements useful when scientists from different countries read each other's work?

Key words

groups
metal
metalloid
non-metal
Periodic Table

8E4 Making molecules

Learn about
- new substances made when atoms join together
- molecules and compounds
- chemical formulae

Joining atoms up

You have already seen how we use models to show atoms. You have also tried linking the model atoms together. We call the links between atoms 'bonds'.

When atoms join together, we say that the atoms **bond** to each other.

Q1 Only 92 different types of atom are found naturally on Earth. So how can we have millions of different substances? Use the word 'bond' in your answer.

When atoms bond together, the new particles they make are called **molecules**.

Look at the two molecules below:

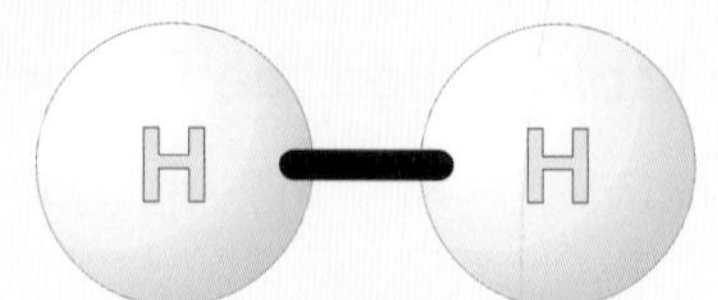

A molecule of hydrogen

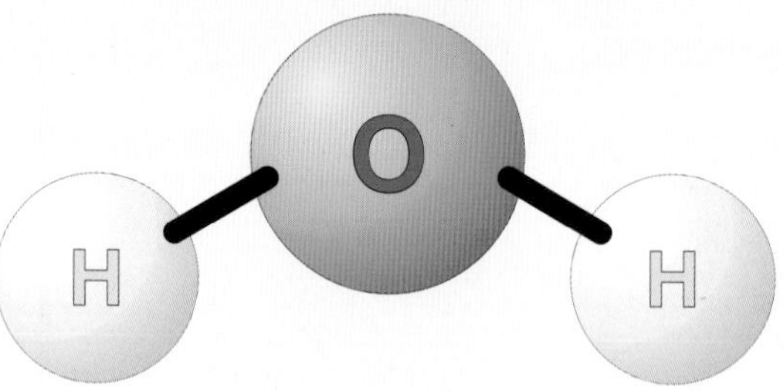

A molecule of water

Two or more atoms bonded together are called ***molecules****.*

Notice that the atoms in a molecule of hydrogen are both the same. We can say that hydrogen is made up of molecules of an element.

But a water molecule contains two types of atom – hydrogen and oxygen. When a substance is made up of two or more different types of atom, we call it a **compound**.

A compound is made up of two or more different types of atom.

It's alright for you... my molecule's not going to be very exciting, is it?

Chemical formula

Scientists use their own short-hand way of showing a molecule. Rather than drawing a molecule, they use its **chemical formula**. It shows us how many of each type of atom there are in a molecule.

The formula does this by using the **symbols** of the atoms, and subscript numbers. An example is CO_2.

Some molecules contain just one atom of a certain element. But we don't bother writing a number 1 in the formula.

Look at more examples below:

Name of molecule	Diagram of molecule	Chemical formula
hydrogen sulphide	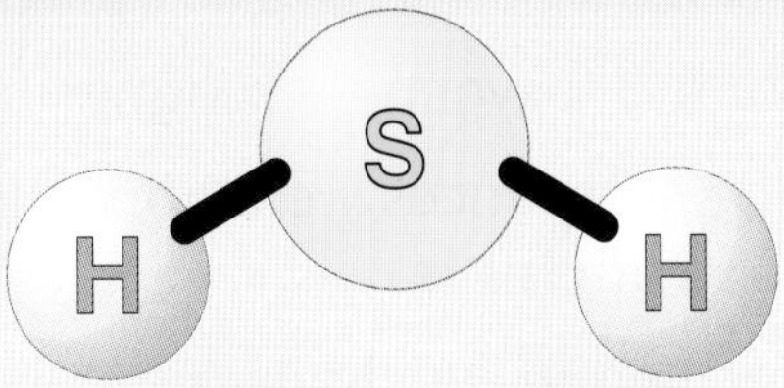 H–S–H	H_2S
chlorine	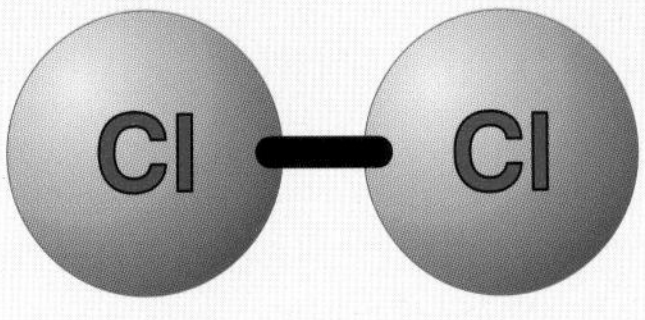 Cl–Cl	Cl_2
methane	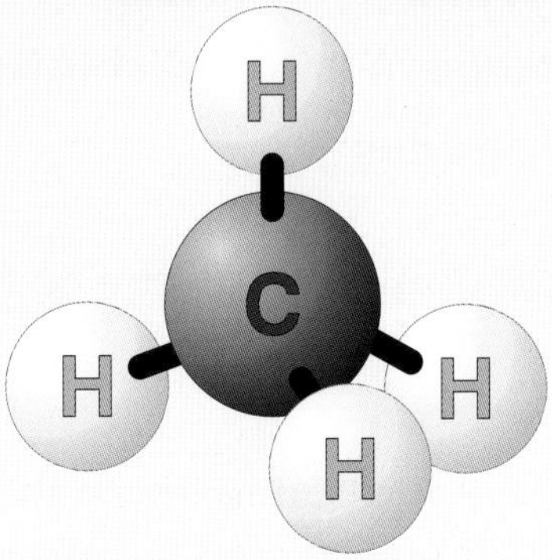 C bonded to four H	CH_4

Q2 You've probably heard of H_2O (H-two-O) before. Which atoms make up an H_2O molecule?

Here's the formula of a larger molecule called insulin. Its formula is:

$C_{254}H_{377}N_{65}O_{75}S_6$!

SUMMARY QUESTIONS

1 ☆ Copy and complete the sentences, using words from the list below.

compound   atom   atoms   molecule

When two or more . . . bond together, we get a . . .

If a substance is made up of two or more different types of . . . it is called a . . .

2 ☆☆ The chemical formula of carbon dioxide is CO_2.
Explain why carbon dioxide is a compound and not an element.

Key words
bond
chemical formula
compound
molecule
symbol

8E5 Reacting elements

LEARN ABOUT

- atoms combining to form compounds
- new substances made in reactions
- using word equations and models to show reactions

From elements to compounds

In Year 7 you saw different elements react with oxygen. The compounds made are called **oxides**.

We represented the reaction by word equations. For example,

magnesium + oxygen → magnesium oxide

Remember that the substances we start with before the reaction are called **reactants**.

The substances formed in reactions are called **products**.

Other non-metals, such as sulphur, chlorine and bromine, also react with other elements to form compounds.

Sulphur makes compounds called **sulphides**.
An example is magnesium sulphide.

Chlorine makes compounds called **chlorides**.

Bromine makes **bromides**.

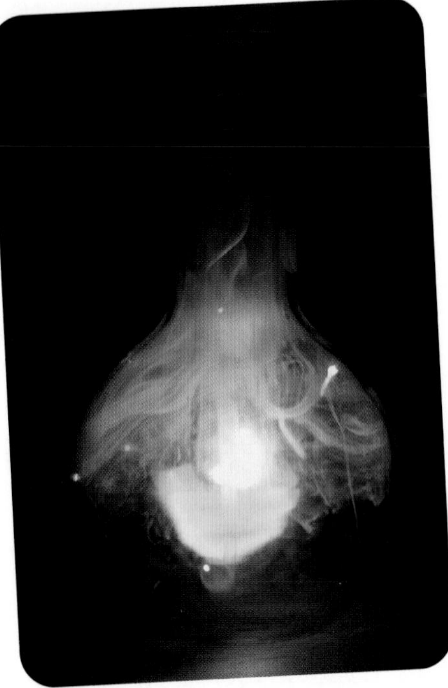

Sodium reacting with chlorine

Q1 What do you think we call the compound made from sodium and bromine?

Q2 Write a word equation to show the reaction between magnesium and sulphur.

Combining two elements

- Watch your teacher demonstrate the following reactions:

hydrogen + oxygen
magnesium + oxygen
sodium + chlorine
copper + sulphur
zinc + sulphur

Your teacher will give you a sheet to help record what happens.

In a chemical reaction, the atoms in the reactants re-arrange to form the products. They 'swap partners'.

Often the new substances formed are nothing like the substances you started with.

We can use models to show a reaction taking place.

Look at the model of hydrogen reacting with oxygen below:

My dance now.
Now that might cause a reaction if she swaps partners!

Modelling reactions

- Use a molecular model kit to show what happens in the reaction between hydrogen and oxygen.
- Draw a diagram to show what happens to the atoms and bonds.
- Now explain your diagram in your own words.

SUMMARY QUESTIONS

1 ☆ Copy and complete the sentences, using words from the list below.

bromine word oxides compounds chlorides iron

Some elements can react together to form . . .

For example, oxygen reacts to form . . . and chlorine forms . . .

We can describe these chemical reactions by . . . equations.

For example, iron + . . . → . . . bromide

2 ☆☆ Hydrogen can react with chlorine.
It forms hydrogen chloride.

Write a word equation to show this reaction.

Key words

bromides
chlorides
oxides
products
reactants
sulphides

IDEAS AND EVIDENCE

A chemical giant – John Dalton

At the start of the 1800s, experiments were playing a bigger part in science. A Cumbrian scientist called John Dalton taught in Manchester. He loved experimenting. He liked to work alone and never trusted the results of other scientists.

His careful experiments suggested to him that all matter was made up of tiny particles. He thought that these particles could not be broken down into anything smaller. He called the particles atoms.

He imagined atoms as hard, indestructible balls. He suggested that each element has atoms of a different mass.

John drew up a list of elements. He couldn't break down the substances in his list. He thought these substances were made of only one type of atom.

Here is Dalton's list of elements:

ELEMENTS

	Wt		Wt
Hydrogen	1	Strontian	46
Azote	5	Barytes	68
Carbon	54	Iron	50
Oxygen	7	Zinc	56
Phosphorus	9	Copper	56
Sulphur	13	Lead	90
Magnesia	20	Silver	190
Lime	24	Gold	190
Soda	28	Platina	190
Potash	42	Mercury	167

An element was defined as something that couldn't be broken down into any simpler substances. However, this led to some compounds getting on John's list of elements. These compounds were very difficult (impossible at the time) to split up so he thought they must be elements.

It's little wonder that scientists at the time had trouble making any sense of the chemical elements. Most had not yet been discovered and others were actually compounds. It was a bit like trying to do a jigsaw puzzle without the picture and with half the pieces missing. Now that's not an easy task!

John Dalton was co-founder of the British Association for the Advancement of Science. Over 40 000 people attended his funeral in Manchester in 1844.

Now I know that the word 'element' can have different meanings. If the element in this kettle is made of iron then it is a chemical element too!

- **Elements** are substances that cannot be broken down into any simpler substances. Elements are made up of only one type of atom.
- The smallest part of an element, that we can still recognise as the element, is an **atom**.
- When atoms bond together they form **molecules**.
- If a molecule contains different types of atoms, then we have a **compound**.
- We can show the number and type of each atom in a molecule by its chemical **formula**. For example, the formula of water is H_2O.

No, we can't see atoms through our microscopes in school... atoms are much too small for that! Even a tiny plant cell contains millions and millions of atoms.
No, the relatively small number of different atoms on Earth can bond to each other in loads of ways. They can make millions of different compounds.
We use the word material, or substance, for anything made up from atoms or molecules.

DANGER! AVOID THESE COMMON ERRORS

People often get confused between the words **A**tom, **M**olecule, **E**lement and **C**ompound. Try building up the ideas in the order **AMEC**.

- **A**toms are the smallest particles.
- They join together to make **M**olecules.
- If the atoms in a molecule are all the same, you have an **E**lement.
- If there are different types of atom in a molecule, you have a **C**ompound.

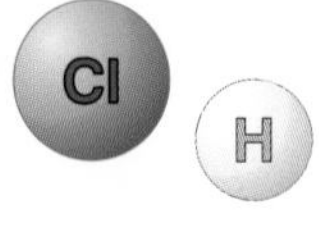

atoms

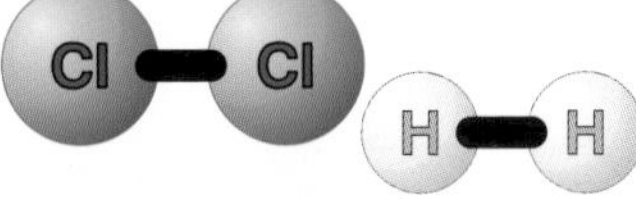

molecules of elements

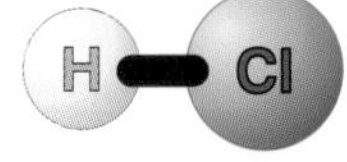

molecule of a compound

Key words

atom
compound
element
formula
molecule

UNIT REVIEW

REVIEW QUESTIONS
Understanding and applying concepts

1 Copy and complete the sentences below. Use the summary on page 89 to help you.

Choose words from this list to fill in the gaps.

atom **bond** **broken** **formula** **water** **molecules** **elements** **number** **compound**

Some substances cannot be . . . down into any simpler substances. We call these substances . . . They are made up of only one type of . . .

When atoms . . . together they form . . .

A . . . contains different types of atoms.

We can show the . . . and type of each atom in a molecule by its chemical . . . For example, . . . is H_2O.

2 a Draw diagrams to represent the following molecules:

i) HBr
ii) Br_2
iii) BF_3
iv) PCl_5

b Which of the molecules in part **a** *(there might be one or more correct answer)*

i) is *not* a compound? Explain your answer.
ii) could be broken down into two elements?
iii) contains one or more bromine atom?

c Copy and complete the table below:

Molecule	Number of atoms in the molecule
HBr	
Br_2	
BF_3	
PCl_5	

3 The chemical symbol of lead is Pb, taken from its Latin name, *plumbum*.

Find five other elements whose atoms have symbols derived from their Latin names. Try to find out their Latin names.

4 Write a word equation to describe the reaction between:

a zinc and oxygen
b sodium and chlorine
c copper and sulphur
d iron and bromine.

5 Look at the molecule below:

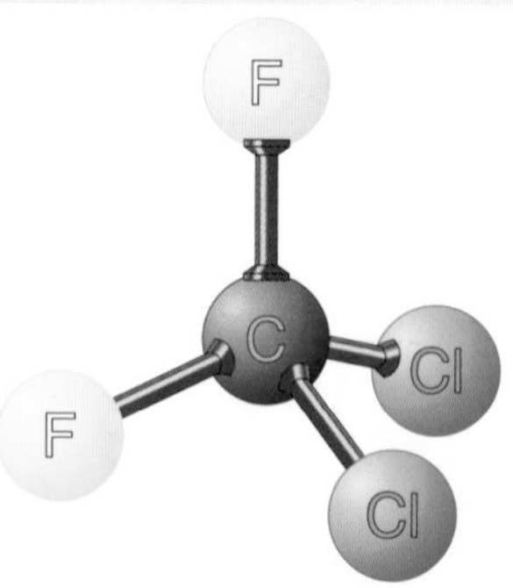

What is the chemical formula of the compound?

6 Draw a concept map like the one below, labelling the arrows. Draw and label any other links you can think of.

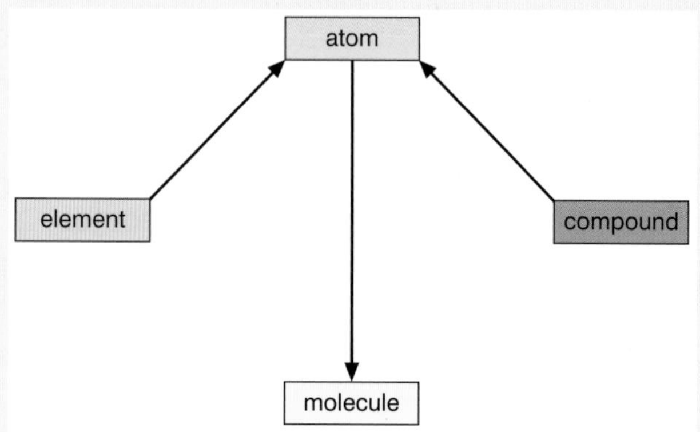

Ways with words

7 Pair each letter with the correct number.

1	Metal	A	A vertical column of elements with similar properties
2	Group	B	Chlorine is an example
3	Periodic Table	C	Sodium is an example
4	Non-metal	D	Shows elements arranged in order

Making more of maths

8 a Draw a bar chart to show this data:

Group 1 element	Melting point (°C)
lithium	180
sodium	98
potassium	63
rubidium	39
caesium	29

b What is the pattern you see as you go down the Group 1 elements?

9 Sort these elements into a Venn diagram like the one shown below:

silver oxygen silicon chlorine lead copper carbon

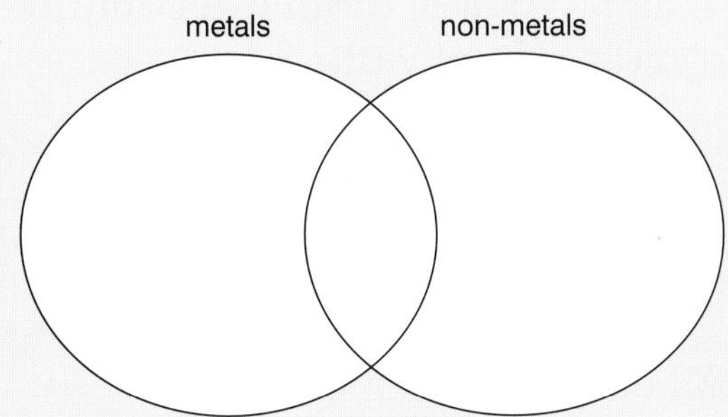

Extension question

10 Carry out some research into the discovery of the Periodic Table.

Find out the names of four scientists who made a contribution.

SAT-STYLE QUESTIONS

1 Read this information:

Sodium, aluminium and zinc are elements that conduct electricity.
Iodine and sulphur are elements that do not conduct electricity.
If zinc and sulphur are heated together, they react vigorously to form a new substance called zinc sulphide.

a Using the information given above:
   i) Name two metals. (2)
   ii) Name two non-metals. (2)
   iii) Give the name of a compound. (1)

b i) Write a word equation for the reaction of zinc with sulphur. (1)
   ii) Why would you carry out the reaction between zinc and sulphur in a fume-cupboard? (2)
   iii) Write the name of the compound formed when magnesium reacts with sulphur. (1)

2 Look at this outline of the areas in the Periodic Table:

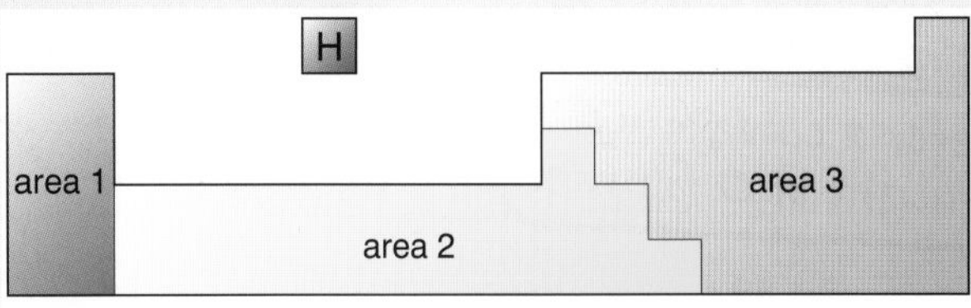

a What does the symbol H stand for? (1)

b In which areas of the Periodic Table would you find:
   i) metallic elements? (2)
   ii) non-metals, such as nitrogen and phosphorus? (1)
   iii) very reactive metals, such as sodium and potassium? (1)
   iv) less reactive metals, such as iron and zinc? (1)

c Why is sodium chloride not found in the Periodic Table? (1)

Key words

Unscramble these:
mota
mylbos
rumafol
omeucell

8F Compounds and mixtures

Coming soon

There's nothing like a good mixture when you're thirsty.
I prefer a compound... Straight H_2O for me.

What's it all about?

In this unit you will build on your work in unit 8E. You already know about compounds. Now we will look at differences between compounds and mixtures.

Most of our chemical industry is all about making useful compounds. But often the raw materials are mixtures, such as air or rocks.

We also make many useful mixtures, such as paints and cosmetics.

Milkshake is a tasty mixture

What do you remember?

You already know about:

- the 100 or so elements each containing only their own atoms.
- compounds being formed when atoms of different elements bond together.
- some chemical reactions.
- making and separating mixtures.

1 Which of the following is an element?

sodium water copper sulphate common salt

2 How would you separate the different dyes from a coloured ink?

filtration evaporation chromatography distillation

3 Which types of atom are contained in a molecule of water?

hydrogen and chlorine
oxygen and helium
helium and hydrogen
hydrogen and oxygen

4 All chemical reactions . . .?

. . . cause explosions.
. . . form new substances.
. . . are easily reversible.
. . . give out light and sound energy.

Ideas about compounds and mixtures

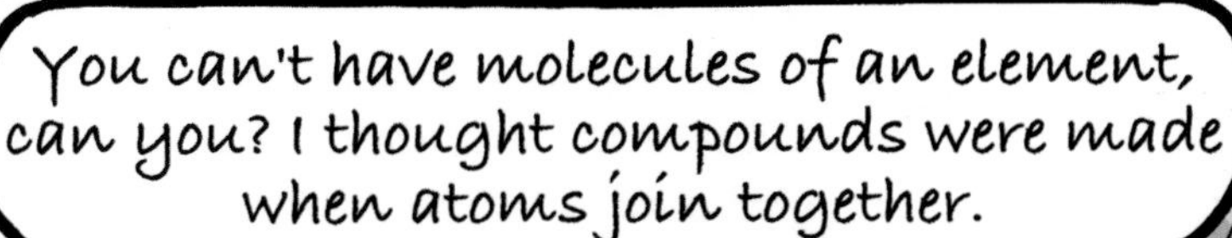

You can't have molecules of an element, can you? I thought compounds were made when atoms join together.

Br2
This is clearly the formula of a compound... It has one atom of B and two atoms of R in its molecules... So it has 2 types of atom.

Why has this been marked wrong? I put 'When magnesium burns in air, we get a mixture of magnesium and oxygen.' What's wrong with that?
Can you ever have pure water? Even if there is nothing dissolved in it, there's still a mixture of hydrogen and oxygen in the H2O, isn't there?

QUESTIONS

Look at the cartoons above:
Discuss these questions with your partner.

a) What is wrong with Pip's ideas about compounds?
b) Do you agree that Br_2 is the formula of a compound? Explain your reasoning to Pete.
c) Add a teacher comment to explain the cross on Molly's book.
d) Do you think water from a tap is pure water? Why?

Making compounds and mixtures

Learn about

- combining elements to make compounds
- the new properties of the compound made
- differences between a mixture and a compound

Elements combining

In unit 8E we looked at elements reacting together to form **compounds**.

Q1 Predict what forms when iron reacts with sulphur.

Sulphur is found as an element underground in Texas. Super-heated water is pumped down pipes to melt the sulphur. The liquid sulphur is then forced to the surface.

Reacting iron and sulphur

Now you can look at a **mixture** of elements before they react together. Then compare the mixture with the compound formed in the reaction.

Your teacher will give you a sheet to help.

Symbol equation

The formula of iron sulphide is FeS. We can write an equation, using symbols and the formula. It shows how we make iron sulphide:

$$\mathbf{Fe + S \rightarrow FeS}$$

We call this a **symbol equation**. Notice that we have the same number of Fe and S atoms on either side of the equation. We can then say that this is a '**balanced** symbol equation'.

Q2 The formula of zinc sulphide is ZnS.
Write a symbol equation for the reaction between zinc and sulphur.

Comparing a mixture and a compound

SAFETY

- Look at a sample of the compound iron sulphide. Then compare it with a mixture of iron and sulphur.

  a) What differences do you notice?

- Wrap a magnet in plastic film. Then use it to test the compound and the mixture.
- Add iron sulphide to some water in a beaker and stir it. Repeat this with the mixture of iron and sulphur.

  b) What happens in each test?

- Watch your teacher add some dilute hydrochloric acid to the compound and to the mixture. This should be done in a fume-cupboard.

  c) What differences do you notice between the reactions?

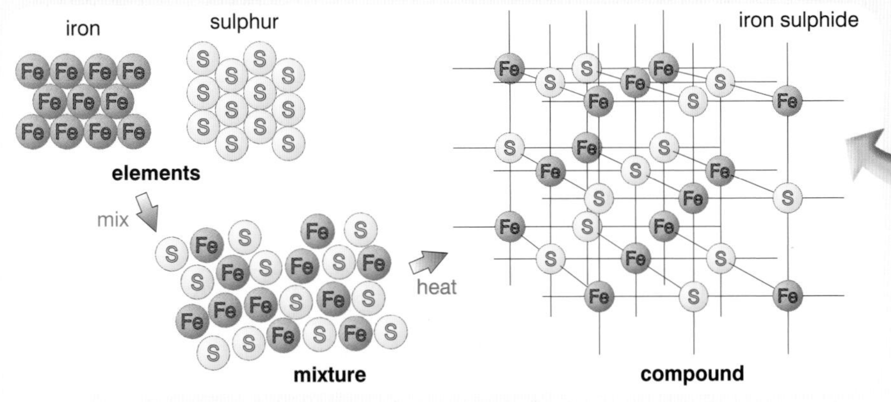

Any compound always has **fixed proportions** *of its elements. This is shown by its chemical formula.*

The amounts of substances in a mixture can vary.

SUMMARY QUESTIONS

1 ☆☆ Copy and complete the sentences, using words from the list below.

formula mixture vary fixed elements

The properties of a compound differ from those of the . . . it is made from.

A compound always has . . . proportions of each element (shown by its chemical . . .). However, in a . . . the proportions can . . .

2 ☆☆☆ List *two* differences between water and the elements that make it.

Key words

balanced
compound
fixed proportions
mixture
symbol equation

Reacting compounds

LEARN ABOUT

- making observations and drawing conclusions
- compounds undergoing chemical changes
- differences between mixtures and compounds

Physical and chemical changes

So far you have looked at elements reacting to make compounds.

You have seen that in chemical reactions new substances are formed.

Q1 How can you tell that a reaction takes place when magnesium burns in air?

We also refer to reactions as 'chemical changes'. These are the opposite of 'physical changes'. Here is a table showing the differences between physical and chemical changes:

Chemical changes	Physical changes
New substances are formed	No new substances are formed
Often cannot be reversed	Usually easy to reverse

Examples of chemical changes that you have come across are neutralisation and combustion (burning).

On the other hand, changes of state are not chemical changes. No new substances are formed and the changes are easily reversed. Melting and boiling are examples of physical changes.

Q2 Give two more examples of physical changes.

Sorry! I think my beaker has just undergone a physical change.

Can compounds react too?

In the next experiment we will use compounds as reactants in chemical changes.

- Mix the following compounds together.
  1. **sodium carbonate solution** and **iron(II) chloride solution**
  2. **dilute hydrochloric acid** and **solid magnesium carbonate**
  3. **ammonia solution** and **copper sulphate solution**
  4. **lead nitrate solution** and **sodium iodide solution.**

  Your teacher will give you a sheet to help.

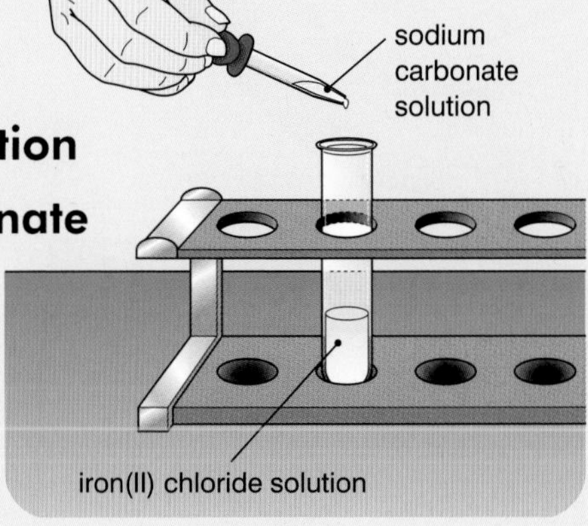

Compounds and mixtures

You have seen that there are differences between mixtures and compounds.

Here is a table that shows these differences:

Compounds	Mixtures
Have a fixed **composition**. There will always be the same **proportion** of elements in any particular compound	Have no fixed **composition**. Their **proportions** vary depending on the amount of each substance mixed together
Need chemical reactions to separate the elements in them	The substances can be separated again more easily. You can use the differences in properties of each substance in the mixture to separate them.
Are single substances	Contain two or more substances
Have properties different to those of the elements combined in the compound	Have properties similar to those of the substances in the mixture

SUMMARY QUESTION

1 ☆☆ Copy and complete the sentences, using words from the list below.

separate reaction mixtures composition

Compounds have a fixed ... but ... can have any proportions of substances in them.

We can ... the substances from a mixture quite easily. However a chemical ... is needed to break down a compound into its elements.

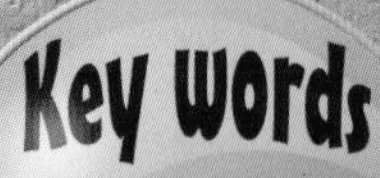

composition
compound
proportion
mixture

8F3 More about mixtures

Learn about

- some useful mixtures
- the mixture of gases in air
- separating these gases and some of their uses

Useful mixtures

We use lots of mixtures in everyday life. We can make all sorts of useful mixtures by mixing substances that don't dissolve well in each other.

Sometimes we get one of the substances finely spread throughout the other substance. Then we call the mixture a colloid.

Aerosol sprays are examples of colloids. You have fine droplets of liquid mixed with the gas that spurts out of the can. You can see some other useful colloids below:

Foams are a mixture containing a gas trapped in a liquid.

Emulsions are a mixture containing two liquids, such as oil and water.

Shaving foam

Many cosmetics are emulsions

There are other types of mixture, such as a sol. In a sol fine particles of an insoluble solid are spread through a liquid.

You can also get solid foams. In these a gas is spread throughout a solid, like in a sponge.

Q1 Think of an example of a solid foam that you can eat.

Raw materials

Here are some useful mixtures that we use as **raw materials.** These are the materials used in industry to make new products:

air sea water crude oil
rocks (some are called ores)

Air is not a single substance, but a mixture of different gases.

ICT CHALLENGE

Make an information booklet for the government on 'The importance of air as a raw material for industry'.
Work as part of a group.
You can use ICT
- to find the information you need, and
- to present your findings in a professional way.

Separating the gases from liquid air

We can separate and collect liquids with different boiling points from liquid air. The process is called **fractional distillation**.

In industry we get air cold enough for it to condense into a liquid. The air has to be cooled to a temperature of almost −200°C.

Look at the table on the right. It shows the boiling points of the main substances left in the liquid mixture:

Substance	Boiling point (°C)
nitrogen	−196
argon	−186
oxygen	−183

Q2 Which of the gases in the table has the lowest boiling point?

Then the liquid is allowed to warm up, and at −196°C, nitrogen boils off first. It is collected from the top of a tall column.

The remaining mixture contains mainly oxygen.

SUMMARY QUESTION

1 ☆ Copy and complete the sentences, using words from the list below.

foam liquid mixing cream fractional dissolve mixture

We can make many useful materials by . . . substances that do not . . . well in each other.

Examples include face . . . and shaving . . .

Air is a . . . of gases. We can separate the gases from . . . air using . . . distillation.

Key words

argon
fractional distillation
nitrogen
oxygen
raw material

Pure or impure?

Learn about
- melting points and boiling points
- pure and impure substances

Pure water?

Look at this label from a bottle of mineral water:

Q1 Would you call mineral water 'pure' water?

Q2 How could you get a sample of pure water from mineral water?

Aquavic water is specially produced to be fresh and light. We use our own formula to blend a unique balance of ingredients to create maximum refreshment.

AQUAVIC

Composition in mg/litre:

Calcium	78	Bicarbonates	357
Magnesium	24	Sulphates	10
Sodium	5	Chlorides	4.5
Potassium	1	Nitrates	3.8
Silica	13.5		

Q3 What would be the best way to describe mineral water:

an element a compound
a mixture a mineral

Melting points and boiling points

We can show the **melting point** and **boiling point** of a substance on a temperature line.

For example, the data for bromine has been put on this line:

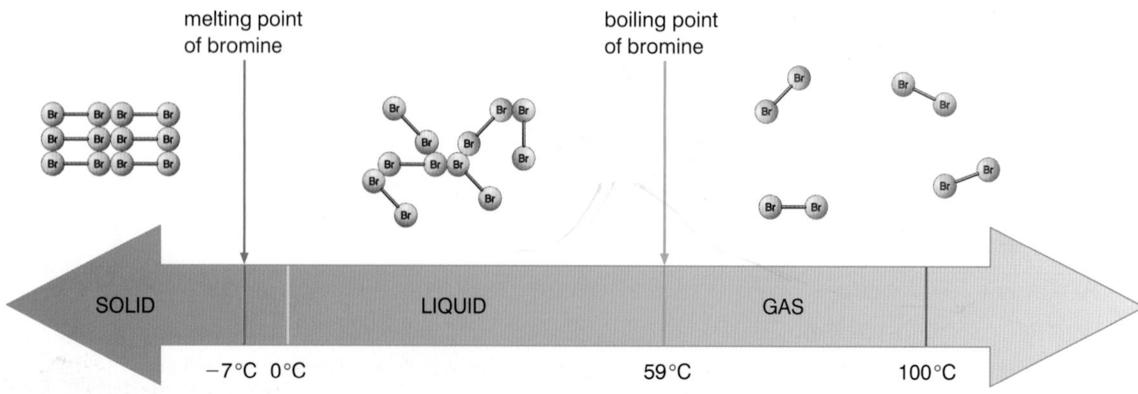

This shows that the element bromine is a solid below −7°C.

It melts at −7°C, turning into liquid bromine. The liquid boils at 59°C, turning into a gas.

So at room temperature (taken as 20°C) bromine is a liquid.

Pure substances and mixtures

We can use boiling points and melting points to identify pure substances. The melting point and boiling point of an element or a compound are called its **fixed points**.

Pure substances can be compounds or elements, but they contain only one substance. An **impure** substance is a mixture of two or more different substances.

We can use melting points or boiling points to identify substances. That's because pure substances have characteristic temperatures at which they melt and boil.

The melting point and boiling point of a mixture will vary. They depend on the composition of the mixture.

A mixture does not have a sharp melting point or boiling point. It changes state over a range of temperatures.

Which is pure?

Your teacher will give you two liquids and a help sheet.

- Your task is to find out which liquid is pure water and which is salt solution.

SUMMARY QUESTIONS

1 ☆ Copy and complete the sentences, using words from the list below.

range **compound** **state** **fixed** **mixture**

A pure element or . . . can be identified from its . . . points.

However, a . . . will change . . . over a . . . of temperatures.

2 ☆☆ Bromine is one of only two elements that exist as a liquid at 20°C.

a) Name the other liquid element.

b) Give one use of this liquid element.

Key words

boiling point
fixed points
impure
melting point
pure

IDEAS AND EVIDENCE

Chocoholics – can you resist the mixture we know as chocolate?

Why is chocolate so lovely? Why do some of us crave it so much? But why do we feel guilty after munching loads of that yummiest of all mixtures? Chemical research has revealed some, but not all, of the answers.

It turns out that chocolate is a mixture of around 300 different substances. Some of these are chemicals that can act like drugs and affect the way your brain works. These are only present in tiny quantities. But they might explain our liking for chocolate.

Chocolate is mainly a mixture of cocoa butter, sugar and dried milk. Like all mixtures, its composition can vary. It is obvious that plain, dark chocolate must contain a different mix to milk chocolate and white chocolate.

Chocolate bars are made so that they are solid at normal room temperature and can be snapped into pieces. The trick is to vary the components of the mixture. You don't want chocolate that will melt in your hands but you do want it to melt at the slightly warmer temperature inside your mouth.

Chocolate gets its taste from chemicals extracted from cocoa beans. One of these chemicals is called theobromine. Its chemical formula is $C_7H_8N_4O_2$.

Look at the model of a molecule of theobromine below:

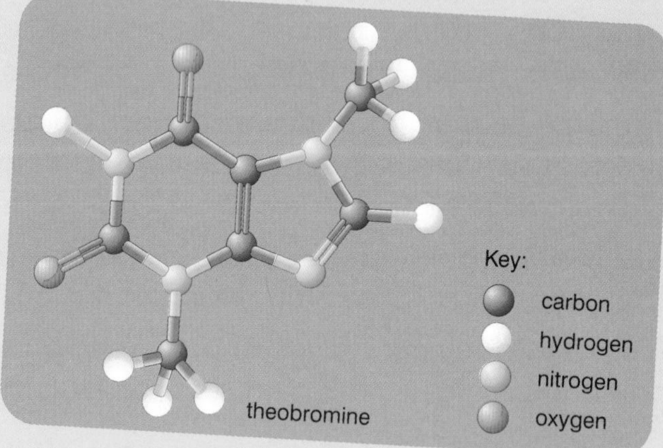

This compound is only a weak stimulant, although this might be why chocolate makes you feel good.

There is no doubt that for some people it works. However, warnings of the fat and high sugar content leave many of us feeling guilty for giving in to the pleasures of chocolate!

Other choco-facts

- The chemicals in red wine that protect against heart disease are also found in chocolate. There is the same amount in one square of milk chocolate as there is in a whole glass of red wine.
- The average person in the UK eats about 9 kg of chocolate each year. Only Swiss chocoholics can beat that, with 10 kg per year.

Gruesome science

Chocolate can act as a poison to some animals, such as dogs. The animal can experience vomiting and diarrhoea.

- **Compounds** contain more than one type of atom bonded together.
- The **ratio** (or **proportion**) of each element is fixed for any particular compound.
- The elements in a compound can only be separated by some kind of chemical reaction.
- On the other hand, **mixtures** do not have any fixed **composition**. The amount of each substance in a mixture can vary.
- No new substances have been formed in a mixture. So it is usually possible to separate out the different substances from a mixture. (We can use methods such as filtration, evaporation, distillation and chromatography.)

You can have molecules of elements... If all the atoms bonded together are the same type, just like we have in the model.
No, this is the formula of an element... There's a capital B and a little r meaning there are 2 atoms of Br in Br_2... So only one type of atom here!
Br_2
There is a chemical reaction when magnesium burns in air to make magnesium oxide. There are bonds between magnesium and oxygen in the new compound made... You can't call it a mixture.
Now I see that you can have pure water if the only substance in the beaker is H_2O. If there is anything dissolved in it, you get a mixture.

DANGER! AVOID THESE COMMON ERRORS

Some people confuse 'compounds' and 'mixtures'.

Compounds contain atoms of different elements bonded together. The properties of the new compound made are not related at all to those of its elements.

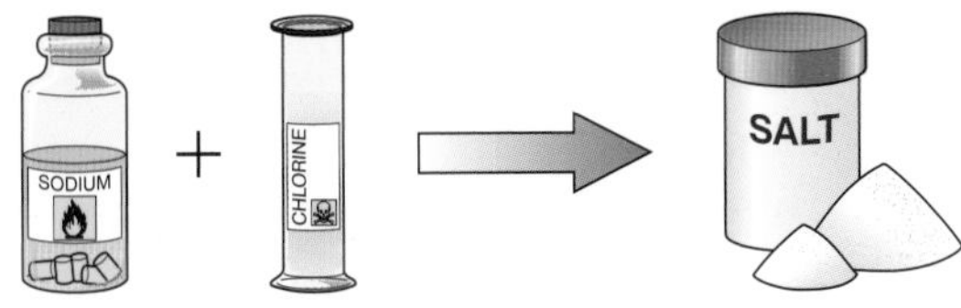

Fortunately, salt is nothing like sodium or chlorine!

Key words

composition
compound
mixture
proportion
ratio

UNIT REVIEW

REVIEW QUESTIONS
Understanding and applying concepts

1 Copy and complete the sentences below. Use the summary on page 103 to help you.

If a substance is made up of more than one type of . . . bonded together, we call it a . . .

We can only separate the . . . in a compound by using a chemical . . .

The amount of each substance in a . . . can vary.

We can usually . . . out the different substances from a mixture. We can use methods such as:

f. . .

e. . .

d. . . and

c. . .

2 Explain the difference between a mixture of elements and a compound.

Use diagrams to help with your explanation.

3 Look at the boxes below:

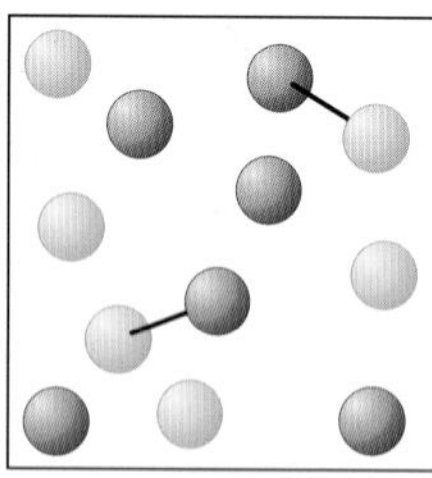
Box A

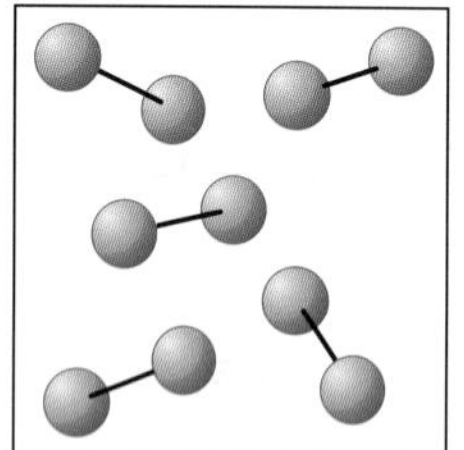
Box B

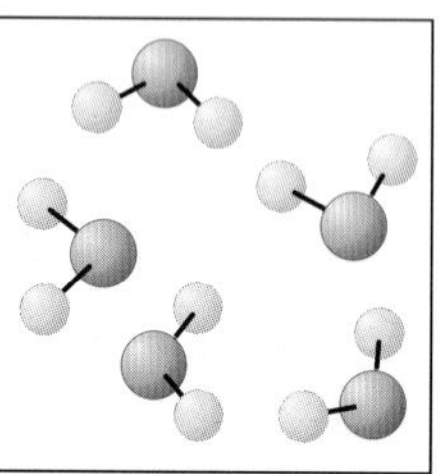
Box C

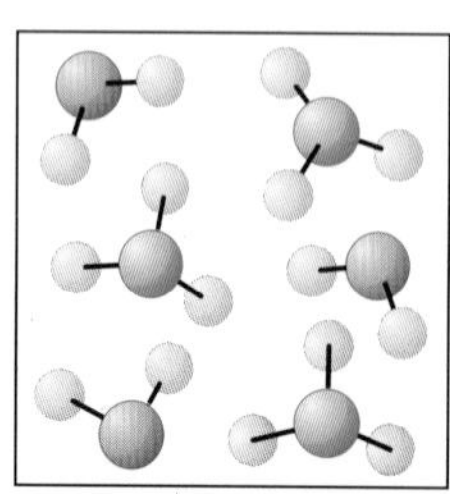
Box D

a Which boxes contain mixtures?
b Which boxes contain a pure substance?
c Which box contains a pure element?
d Which box contains a mixture of compounds?
e Which box shows a chemical reaction taking place?
f Which box contains ammonia, NH_3?

4 Look back to page 102 and answer **a** and **b** below.

a Which elements make up theobromine?
b How many atoms are there in each theobromine molecule?
c Why does theobromine have a sharp melting point while chocolate melts over a range of temperatures?

5 Explain these statements:

a Rock salt is put on roads when there is a forecast of freezing conditions.
b Boiled potatoes cook slightly more quickly if you add salt to the water in the pan.

6 The gases in air can be separated by fractional distillation of liquid air.

The boiling points of the substances in the liquid mixture are given in the table:

Substance	Boiling point (°C)
nitrogen	−196
argon	−186
oxygen	−183

a Which gas boils off after nitrogen?
b Why is it difficult to obtain 100% pure oxygen?
c Which statement is true?
  A Nitrogen, argon and oxygen are elements.
  B Nitrogen, argon and oxygen are compounds.
d Explain why there is no such thing as the 'chemical formula of air'.

7 Look at this table showing the gases in air:

Gases in the air	Formula of gas	Approximate proportions (%)
nitrogen	N_2	78
oxygen	O_2	21
carbon dioxide (about 0.04%) water vapour (varies) argon (about 0.9%) and other noble gases various pollutants	CO_2 H_2O Ar He, Ne, Kr, Xe, Ra e.g. SO_2 or NO_2 or CH_4	1

Give the formula of any gas in the air that can be described as:

a atoms of elements
b molecules of elements
c molecules of compounds.

Ways with words

8 a Does the word 'pure' mean the same in the food and drink industry as it does to a scientist? What is the difference in meaning?
b What do advertisers mean by the word 'pure' when describing a product?
c Try to think of some products that are advertised as 'pure'.

Making more of maths

9 The chemical formula of insulin is $C_{254}H_{377}N_{65}O_{75}S_6$.
a Name the elements that make up insulin.
b How many atoms are there in an insulin molecule?

Extension question

10 Look at these natural mixtures that we use as raw materials in the chemical industry:

sea water crude oil
rocks (some are called ores)

Choose one of the mixtures above and find out some of the products we can make from that raw material. Present your information as a spider diagram.

SAT-STYLE QUESTIONS

1 The diagrams below show the different arrangement of atoms in six substances.

Each atom is represented by a circle labelled with its chemical symbol.

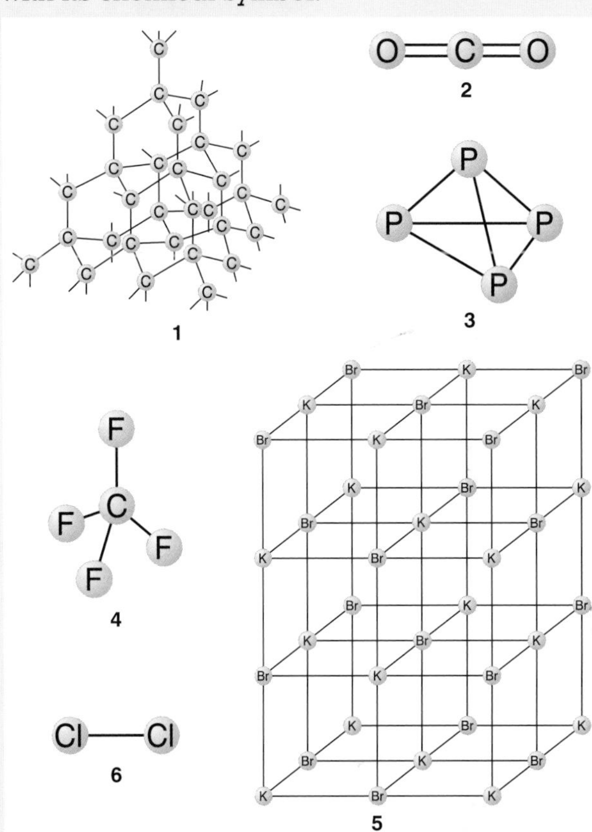

a i) Which of the diagrams represent the structures of chemical elements? Write down the correct numbers. (1)
ii) Explain how you decided which are elements. (1)
b Give the formula of two of the compounds shown in the diagrams. (2)
c Give the name of the substance labelled 5. (1)
d Give the names of the chemical elements whose atoms can be represented by:
i) C
ii) Cl
iii) Cu (3)

Unscramble these:
uprime
meetlen
pocmound
otari

8G

Rocks and weathering

Coming soon

What's it all about?

We are never very far away from rocks. Beneath the concrete of our cities, we will find it. The soil contains fragments of rock. Sometimes we can see bare rock piercing the surface.

This muscle is as hard as rock.
I've heard some rocks are actually very soft.

How on earth did these form?

But how do the rocks make all those interesting shapes? How do they get into the soil? How are they broken down in nature?

In this unit we will start looking for the answers to these questions.

What do you remember?

You already know about:

- soils coming from rocks, and rocks being under the surface of the Earth.
- some examples and uses of rocks.
- the particles in solids, liquids and gases.
- the pH scale.
- what happens when solutions evaporate.

1 Which of these rocks can you see in the face of a white cliff?

granite slate sandstone chalk

2 Which of the following is the best use of slate?

bricks roof tiles gutters fence posts

3 In which of these states of matter do particles slip and slide over each other?

solids liquids gases none of these

Ideas about rocks and weathering

This can't be proper rock, can it? Look, it's all crumbly.

Surely water couldn't have caused that huge cavern we just visited.

This rock must have been put here by the park rangers... It's nothing like any of the other rocks around.

Can scientists really look at rocks and work out what happened millions of years ago... How can anybody tell what happened that long ago?

QUESTIONS

Look at the cartoon above:
Discuss these questions with your partner.

a) What do you think rocks are like? Can you generalise and say 'All rocks are . . .'?

b) How do you think that underground caverns could form in limestone regions?

c) Do you think Pete is right? How can large rocks be moved in nature?

d) Think of some things that you know happened millions of years ago. What evidence convinces you to believe them?

8G1 Looking at rocks

LEARN ABOUT
- the mixtures of mineral grains in rocks
- the textures of rocks
- using evidence and models to explain different textures

Diamond is a mineral that is an element. It is one form of the element carbon (C).

Halite is a mineral that is a compound. Its chemical name is sodium chloride (NaCl).

What are rocks?

There are many different rocks. They are usually made up of different *mixtures of minerals*. A **mineral** is a solid compound or element found naturally in the ground.

For example, diamond is a mineral that is an element. It is an element made up of carbon atoms.

On the other hand, halite is a mineral that is a compound. It is made up of sodium chloride. Most minerals are compounds.

Q1 Which elements make up halite?

Q2 Why do minerals have a chemical formula but rocks do not?

Look at the photo of granite rock:

Granite **is a rock made from a mixture of minerals. This type is called blue pearl granite.**

Q3 How many different minerals can you see in this granite?

Texture

The **texture** of a rock describes the way its grains fit together.

There are two main types of texture in rocks:

- **Crystalline texture**. The mineral grains are crystals in the rock. The grains all interlock. There are no gaps between the crystals.
- **Fragmental texture**. The minerals form randomly shaped fragments or grains. The grains do not fit together neatly.

The grains in *sandstone* are non-interlocking

The textures of granite and sandstone

- Use a hand lens to look at the structure of granite and sandstone.
  Your teacher will give you a sheet to help.

Porosity

The **porosity** of a rock tells us how well it soaks up water.

Rocks that have spaces between their grains can soak up water better than rocks with interlocking crystals. The water fills the gaps between grains in rocks like sandstone.

We say that sandstone is a porous rock.

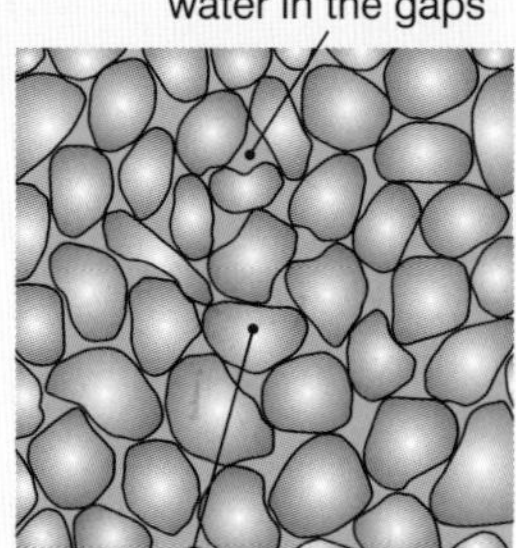

Porous rocks have grains that do not interlock

Modelling rock

Imagine that the people in your class are the minerals in a rock.

Try to think up a model you could use to help explain the porosity of rocks to a child in Year 6. It should show the interlocking and non-interlocking grains.

SUMMARY QUESTION

1 ☆ Copy and complete the sentences, using words from the list below.

porous **textures** **fragmental** **compounds**
mixtures **solid** **interlock** **soak**

Minerals are . . . elements or . . . found naturally. Most rocks are . . . of minerals.

The two main types of rock . . . are crystalline and . . .

When the grains in a rock do not . . . the rock is . . ., meaning it can . . . up water.

Key words

crystalline
fragmental
granite
mineral
porosity
sandstone
texture

Chemical weathering

LEARN ABOUT

- the breakdown of rocks in chemical changes
- how to record results over a period of time
- explaining changes that happen to rocks over time

I knew weathering could be slow, but this is ridiculous!

Breaking down rocks

Some rocks, such as granite, are very hard indeed. But even the surface of granite is broken down by the reactions with rain water. We say that the granite gets **weathered** by the rain water.

Weathering *breaks down rocks.*

Rain water is slightly acidic. That's partly because of carbon dioxide gas in the air.

Q1 Why does the amount of carbon dioxide in air vary in different places?

Carbon dioxide gas dissolves slightly in water. It forms a *weakly acidic* solution. Over time, this acid can attack some of the minerals in rocks.

Acid on carbonate rocks

Let's see what happens when we add acid to three types of rock containing carbonates.

We can test limestone, chalk and marble.

Your teacher will give you a sheet to help.

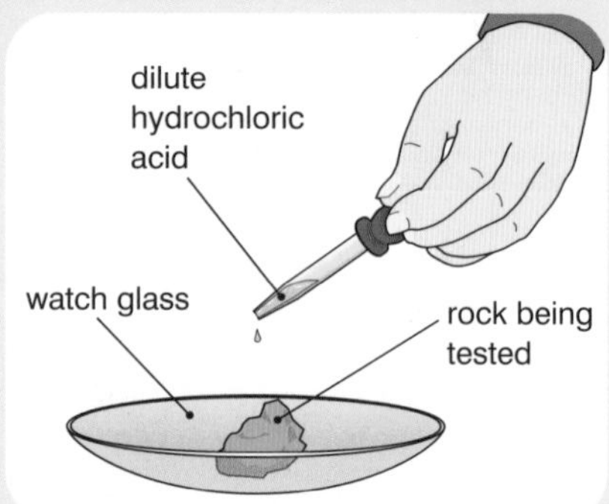

Q2 Do stalactites grow downwards or upwards?

Limestones (which include chalk) and marble contain the mineral **calcite**. Its chemical name is calcium carbonate ($CaCO_3$).

Acids react with carbonates. They form a salt, plus carbon dioxide and water. The salt formed is often soluble in water.

So any carbonate in the rock breaks down in acid. It forms a solution. That's how carbonate rock gets weathered by acids in soil or in rain water.

Limestone can be weathered over time to form caverns

Chemical weathering of granite

We can also model the effect of rain water on granite rock.

The effect of acid on granite

This reaction happens very slowly. You will have to observe the changes to the granite over several weeks.

Your teacher will give you a sheet to help you.

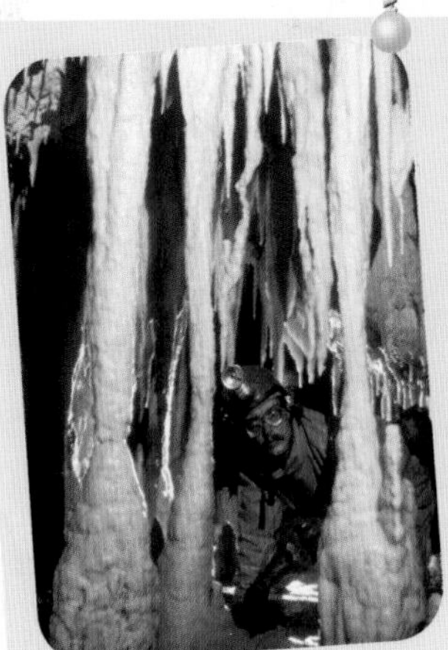
Stalactites and stalagmites form from solutions of weathered limestone. The water evaporates. It leaves behind tiny crystals of calcite.

Granite is a mixture of three types of mineral – quartz, feldspar and mica.

The acid in rain water attacks the feldspar and mica minerals. Eventually the granite is weathered into small particles of clay.

These are carried away by the water, along with any compounds formed in solution.

***The breakdown of rock by reactions is called* chemical weathering**.

SUMMARY QUESTIONS

1 ☆ Copy and complete the sentences, using words from the list below.

chemical weathered broken acids

When rocks are ... down in nature, we say that the rocks have been ...

This can happen as a result of ... reactions with ... in rain water or in soil.

2 ☆☆ Carry out a survey of school building materials that have been weathered.

Key words

calcite
chemical weathering
granite
limestones
weathered

8G3 Physical weathering

LEARN ABOUT
- freeze/thaw weathering
- weathering caused by temperature changes

Forces that break down rock

Rocks can be broken down by natural forces.

We call this **physical weathering**.

Freeze/thaw

Most liquids contract slightly when they solidify.

Q1 Why do most liquids contract slightly when they change to a solid?

However, water expands as it freezes to form ice. Sometimes water collects in rocky places. If it freezes and thaws again and again, pieces of rock can be broken away.

Look at the diagrams below:

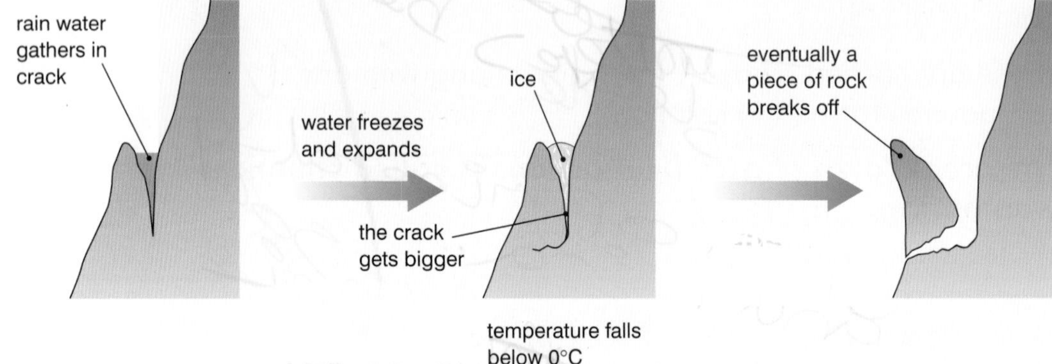

temperature falls below 0°C

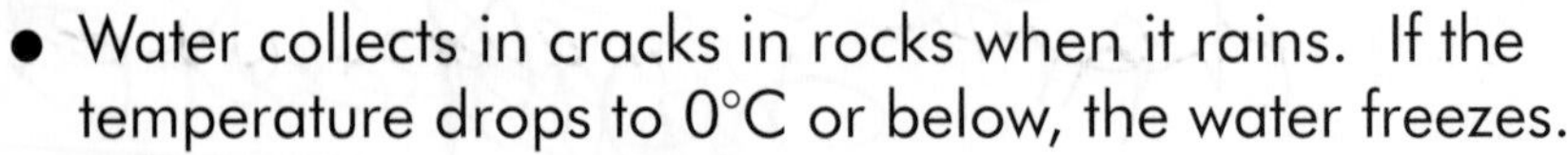

- Water collects in cracks in rocks when it rains. If the temperature drops to 0°C or below, the water freezes.
- As the water turns to ice, it expands and opens the crack a little wider.
- This happens many times.
- Finally the crack gets big enough to break off a rock fragment.

The fragments of broken rock can collect at the bottom of the rock face. This is called a **scree slope**.

A scree slope in the Lake District

Changing temperatures

As you know, when solid materials get hot they expand. When they cool down they contract.

Q2 Why do solids expand and contract with changes in temperature?

Rocks in a desert will get very hot in the baking sun. At night the temperature quickly drops. This repeated heating and cooling of rocks is another cause of physical weathering.

Rocks are mixtures of minerals. During heating and cooling, each of the minerals expands and contracts by different amounts. This sets up stress forces within the rock. Eventually these forces cause the surface to crack and break away.

On individual pieces of rock we can get an effect called 'onion-skinning'. The rock splits into layers that fall away. It's like peeling off the layers of an onion.

On large masses of rock this flaking off is called **exfoliation**.

Rocks in the desert get very hot in the day and very cold at night

Rocks can also be broken down by plant and tree roots. Even burrowing animals can scrape away at the surface of rocks, breaking bits off. Some people call this biological weathering.

SUMMARY QUESTIONS

1 ☆ Copy and complete the sentences, using words from the list below.

fragment **broken** **freeze** **crack** **temperature**

Water that collects in a . . . in a rock can . . . and expand.

This splits the rock further until a . . . breaks off. Rocks can also be . . . by stress forces produced within rocks by changes of . . .

2 ☆☆ Give a difference between physical weathering and chemical weathering.

Key words

exfoliation
freeze/thaw
physical weathering
scree slope

LEARN ABOUT
- how rock fragments become sediment grains
- how rock fragments and sediments are moved and deposited

Transporting fragments

We know that weathering breaks down rock. But what happens to the bits that come away from the rock?

The **fragments** or minerals in solution get moved to another place. They are **transported** by:

- gravity,
- wind,
- ice (in glaciers – rivers of ice), or
- water (in streams, rivers and seas).

Q1 How will minerals in solution be carried away?

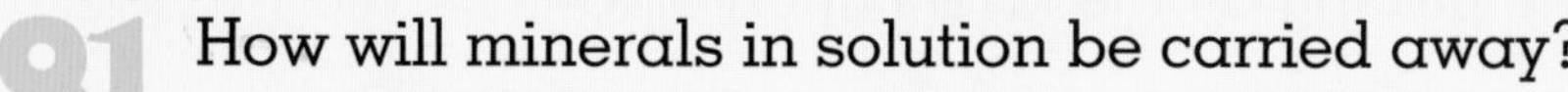

Modelling transport by water

- Use a length of square guttering to channel water into a deep trough.
  Your teacher will give you a sheet to help.

Depositing sediments

Weathered rock is often carried away in streams and in rivers. At first, high in the mountains, fast-flowing water races down steep slopes.

Here the water has enough energy to carry quite big pieces of rock. They bounce along the bottom of the river.

The river starts to slow down as the land levels off. Then the larger bits of rock get deposited on the riverbed first.

Deposited pieces of rock are called **sediments.**

The smaller pieces of rock get carried along further before they are also deposited.

It has been estimated that the Mississippi River in the USA deposits almost 2 million tonnes of material each day at its delta.

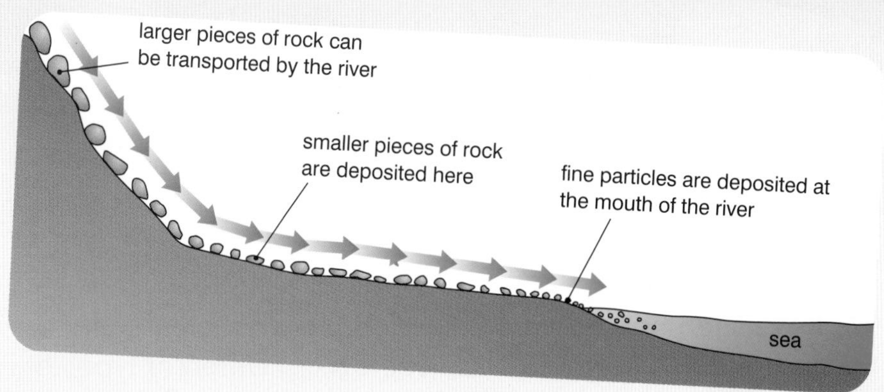

Sediments tend to be sorted by size as the river deposits them

The fine bits of rock, such as clay, can be carried all the way to the river mouth (estuary). If the fine bits of sediment build up there, they form a **delta**.

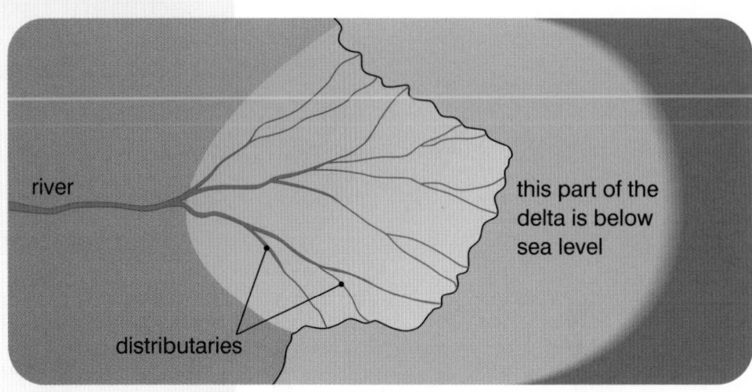

The fine sediments deposited at the mouth of a river can form a delta

Erosion

Erosion is the wearing away of rock as surfaces rub against each other. Weathered fragments will erode the rock that they pass over.

For example, rocks in riverbeds will be worn away (eroded) as fragments bounce along the river.

The weathered fragments themselves also get worn down. They lose their sharp edges. They will get smaller and smaller, as they get carried along by the river.

Q2 Is erosion a physical change or a chemical change? Why?

SUMMARY QUESTIONS

1 ☆ Copy and complete the sentences, using words from the list below.

smaller **water** **transported** **eroded** **wind**

Weathered rock can be . . . by gravity, . . . , ice and . . .

The weathered pieces of rock become . . ., smoother and rounder as they get . . .

2 ☆☆ What is a river delta? How does it form?

Key words

delta
erosion
fragments
sediments
transport

Forming layers

LEARN ABOUT
- forming sedimentary layers
- explaining observations

Layers of sediment

We have seen how sediments get deposited. Eventually these sediments turn into rock (see 8H1). Different types of sediment form layers of different rocks.

Look at these two rocks taken from different layers in a cliff face:

Sandstone rock

Conglomerate rock

Q1 What can you say about the sediments that were deposited to form the two rocks in the photos?

Look at the photo below. It shows layers of rock formed from sediments deposited millions of years ago:

Layers of sediment formed these beds of rock

Q2 Why can we see the layers now?

The layers of rock are called **beds**. The boundaries between different layers are called **bedding planes**.

The layer of rock at the bottom of the layers is usually the oldest. Its sediment was probably laid down before the others.

However, we can't be certain. That's because sometimes layers are put under great stress by powerful movements in the Earth's crust. They can be snapped, folded and even turned upside down.

AMAZING SCIENCE!

A 3 metre depth of sea water must evaporate to leave a layer of minerals 5 centimetres thick.

Layers of minerals

We can also get layers of minerals that were once dissolved in water forming layers of rock. These were mainly formed when ancient seas evaporated. They left behind the salts that were dissolved in them.

This is thought to have happened when seas became cut off and surrounded by land. Eventually the water evaporated, leaving the layers of minerals behind.

The sea can return and evaporate many times. This builds up thick layers of the rock.

We call rocks formed like this **evaporites**.

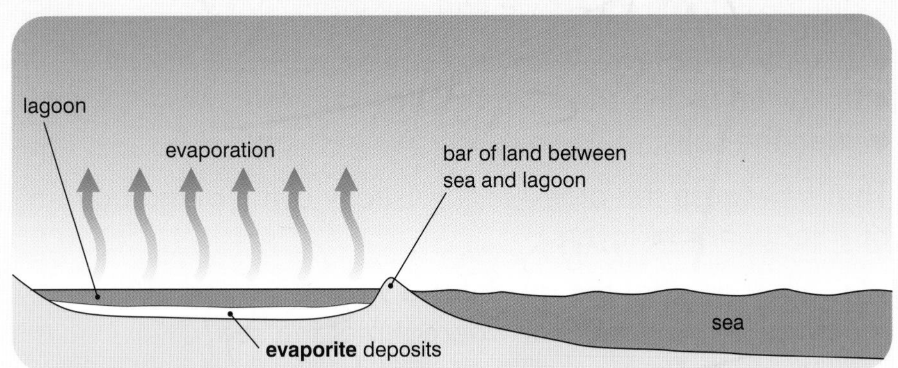

SUMMARY QUESTIONS

1 ☆ Copy and complete the sentences, using words from the list below.

water sediment below beds evaporite

Older layers (or . . .) of rock are usually found . . . layers made from . . . laid down more recently.

Other layers of rock can be formed when . . . evaporates from sea water. Rock formed like this is called an . . .

2 ☆☆ Explain how a layer of rock salt can be formed.

Key words

bedding plane
beds
conglomerate
evaporite
sandstone

Evidence from layers

Learn about

- sediments from once living things
- using evidence from rocks to sequence events
- using evidence from fossils

Evidence in the rock

We can make deductions from the layers of rock we see.

For example, look at the layers below:

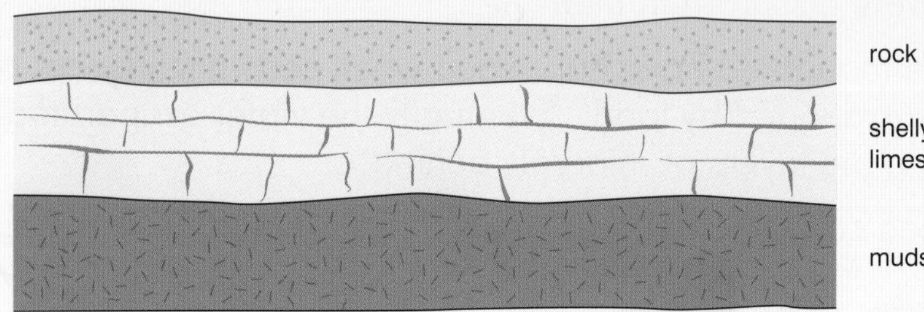

From these three layers we can say that:

- a sediment of mud was laid down first,
- followed by the shelly limestone,
- then the salt.

That's because the oldest rocks usually come at the bottom of a sequence of layers.

We can guess that the **mudstone** was deposited at the mouth of an ancient river where it met the sea.

Sometime later this part of the shore became covered by the sea. A layer of sea creatures was deposited as sediment to form the layer of limestone.

This part of the sea must then have been cut off from the rest of the ocean. The new in-land sea was surrounded by land. The water evaporated from the sea. This left behind a layer of rock salt.

It's a bit like being a detective really. You can try to work out what happened from the clues left in the rocks.

Q1 Why do sediments vary in size?

Chalk was made millions of years ago from tiny sea plants. The plants were called coccoliths. Each coccolith measured only a few thousandths of a millimetre across. Yet layers of chalk 1000 metres thick have been formed – now that's a lot of coccolith!

Layers from living things

Sometimes the layers of sediment found in rock can be formed from the remains of plants or animals. These often lived in the sea.

Chalk was made from the 'hard bits' of a tiny sea plant called **coccolith**. The sediments from living things build up in layers.

Coal is another rock made from sediments. It was formed millions of years ago from layers of plant material.

The chalk, which was laid down in thick layers, is clearly visible in these cliffs in Kent

Evidence from fossils

We can find fossils in some rocks which were formed from sediments. A **fossil** can show an imprint made by a living thing. They can also form from the skeletons of the once living things.

This is a fossil of a fern found in coal

Fossils help us to compare rocks found in different parts of the world. Rocks containing fossils of the same species must have been formed at about the same time.

They can also give us **evidence** about the conditions on Earth at the time. For example, we find tropical fern-like fossils in the coal seams under Britain.

This suggests that our climate was very different millions of years ago.

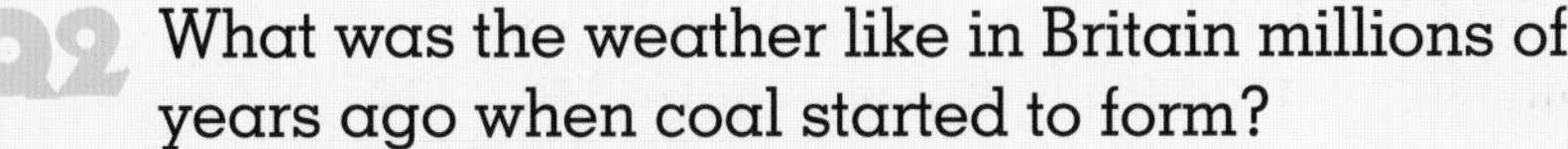

Q2 What was the weather like in Britain millions of years ago when coal started to form?

SUMMARY QUESTIONS

1 ☆ Copy and complete the sentences, using words from the list below.

millions **chalk** **fossils** **coal**

Rocks and . . . give us clues to events that happened . . . of years ago.

Rocks, such as limestone, . . . and . . . were formed from once living things.

2 ☆☆ What type of fossils are you likely to find in **a)** coal **b)** chalk? Explain your answers.

Key words

coccolith
evidence
fossil
mudstone

Mary Anning – famous fossil hunter (1799–1847)

Mary's great find

Discovering the fossil of a large prehistoric creature in one piece is very rare. But a girl called Mary Anning did just that when she was only 11 years old.

She discovered the fossil of a complete Ichthyosaurus. Her brother first spotted the position of the fossil. She returned to the spot later. Mary carefully brushed the earth away, and there it was – the remains of a reptile 30 metres long!

It is thought that Mary Anning gave rise to the tongue-twister 'She sells sea shells on the sea shore'

The fossil is now kept in the Natural History Museum in London.

Mary went on to be described as the greatest fossil collector ever. She was one of the first ever palaeontologists. These are people who study fossils and evidence from prehistoric times.

Mary's place in science

Mary did not really gain the credit that her discoveries and great knowledge about fossils deserved.

At the start of the 19th century, men dominated British society. Women were treated as second-class citizens. Poor people were also looked down upon by the rich. Schooling was not provided for all children. The rich and the clergy did receive a good education. But even rich women couldn't go to university.

The world of science reflected these attitudes. Many scientists were wealthy men who enjoyed science as a hobby. Little wonder that Mary struggled to get respect from fellow scientists. She was poor, had received little formal education and was a woman!

However, she did eventually win over the scientists of her time. She discovered the first ever fossil of a Plesiosaur.

Mary was able to discuss scientific theories on equal terms with famous geologists. She was even made a member of the Geological Society of London before she died. She was finally accepted into the scientific community.

- Rocks are broken down by weathering. **Chemical weathering** happens when weakly acidic rain water attacks rocks.
- Rocks are also broken down by **physical weathering**. Changes in temperature and freeze/thaw break off pieces of rock.
- The weathered rock is then **transported** to another place, often by moving water. On its journey the rock fragment will get smaller, smoother and rounder. It will also wear away rock that it passes over. This is called **erosion**.
- Eventually, the rock fragment is **deposited** as a **sediment**. These sediments build up in layers. The sediment can be made from bits of rock or from the remains of animals and plants.
- Other layers are formed as water evaporates from rivers, lakes or seas. We call these **evaporites**.

Not all rocks are hard, you know. Did you know that talc is a soft rock?
We can't see the chemical weathering as it happens... It's too slow... But it has had millions of years to break down the rock!
Glaciers are rivers of ice. They can carry large boulders along and dump them where they melt.
There are all kinds of clues in rocks if you know what to look for. Look at this fossil and the sediments that make up the rock.

DANGER! AVOID THESE COMMON ERRORS

Many people think that the words 'weathering' and 'erosion' mean the same thing. But they don't!

- **Weathering** takes place at the site of the original rock. The rock is *broken down* in weathering.
- When bits of rock are moved along they collide with other rock. The rocks get *worn away* and we call this **erosion**.

Some people don't think coal is a rock because it is also a fuel. Geologists refer to sand, peat and clay as rocks too!

Key words

deposit
erosion
evaporites
sediment
transport
weathering

UNIT REVIEW

REVIEW QUESTIONS

Understanding and applying concepts

1 Copy and complete the sentences, using words from the list below. Use the summary on page 121 to help you.

thaw erosion chemical wear evaporites layers acidic deposited physical smoother temperature sediment transported evaporated

When weakly . . . rain water attacks rocks, we call it . . . weathering.

Changes in . . . and freeze/. . . break off pieces of rock. We call this . . . weathering.

As the weathered rock is . . . to another place, it gets smaller, . . . and rounder the further it is carried along. It will also . . . away rock that it passes over. We call this . . .

When the rock fragment gets . . . we call it a . . . These build up in . . .

Sometimes ancient seas . . . and we got layers of rock called . . . laid down.

2 You go on holiday in winter and forget to leave some kind of heating on at home.

- **a** Why might you need a plumber when you get back? Why does this happen?
- **b** How does a similar process result in the physical weathering of rocks?

3
- **a** Bits of weathered rock can be transported. Name four ways that rocks can be moved from place to place in nature.
- **b** Think up a situation that could involve rocks transported in two different ways.

4
- **a** Where do rocks go through regular large and rapid changes of temperature?
- **b** Explain what happens to a rock during exfoliation.

5 Here is a scree slope:

- **a** The number of rock fragments at the bottom of the scree slope is increasing. Do you think that the temperature:

  A stays below 0°C all the time?
  B falls below 0°C, then rises above 0°C often?
  C stays above 0°C all the time?

  Explain your answer.
- **b** How are the rock fragments on a scree slope transported to the slope?

6
- **a** Why are the sediments at the mouth of a river usually small in size?
- **b** Sediments are usually bits of weathered and eroded rock. Name *two* rocks made from this type of sediment.
- **c** Sediments eventually form layers of rock. What is another word for one of these layers?
- **d** What do we call the boundary between two layers of rock?
- **e** How does a delta form at the mouth of a river?
- **f** Name *two* rocks that were formed from sediments of things that were once alive.
- **g** Look at this bend in a river: Would you expect more sediment to be deposited at A or B? Explain why.

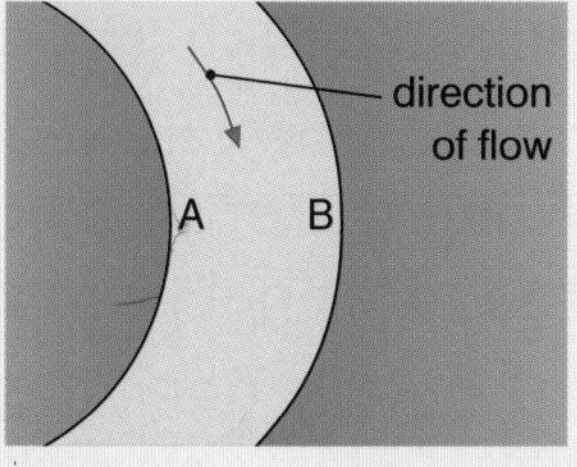

7 Look at the sequence of layers found at the face of a cliff:

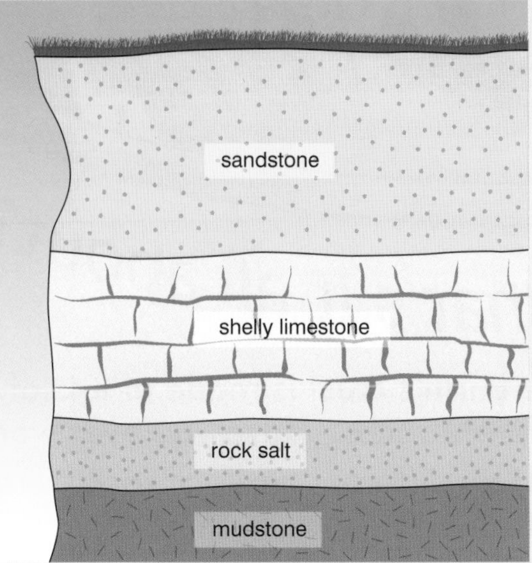

Describe a possible sequence of events that led to the layers being formed.

Ways with words

8 Write definitions for the following:

chemical weathering
physical weathering
transport
erosion
deposition
sediment
evaporite
coal

9 Imagine you are a piece of rock. Write a poem about the processes of weathering, transport, erosion and deposition.

Making more of maths

10 It has been estimated that it would take about 30 years for a 1 millimetre layer of chalk to build up from the skeletons of coccoliths. Calculate how long it took to build up a layer of chalk that is 1 metre thick.

Extension question

11 Carry out research into the formation of fossils.

Write a booklet for Year 6 children.

Explain how fossils can form in different ways.

SAT-STYLE QUESTIONS

1 Weathering breaks down rocks. This can happen when:

i) Water collects in cracks in rocks.
ii) The water turns to ice at its freezing point and expands.
iii) Pieces of rock get split off.

What other things must happen during this type of weathering? Choose *two* of these options:

A The temperature does not change.
B The temperature rises above 0°C.
C The temperature remains below 0°C.
D Expansion forces all the water out of the cracks.
E Expansion causes the cracks to widen.
F Expansion forces the cracks to close up.

(2)

2 Aisha and Tom carry out an investigation into the porosity of rock.

They have a piece of sandstone and a piece of basalt rock.

They weigh each piece of each rock when dry. Then they soak both in water and weigh them again.

Here are their results:

Rock	Mass when dry (g)	Mass after soaking (g)	Increase in mass (g)	Percentage increase in mass (%)
sandstone	200	230		
basalt	50	51		

a Copy and complete the table. (2)

b Which rock is more porous? How do the results show this? (1)

c How could Aisha and Tom improve the reliability of their results? (1)

Key words

Unscramble these:
sotepid
roonies
poisartvee
rotprants

8H

The rock cycle

Coming soon

I don't think that's the rock cycle we'll be studying!

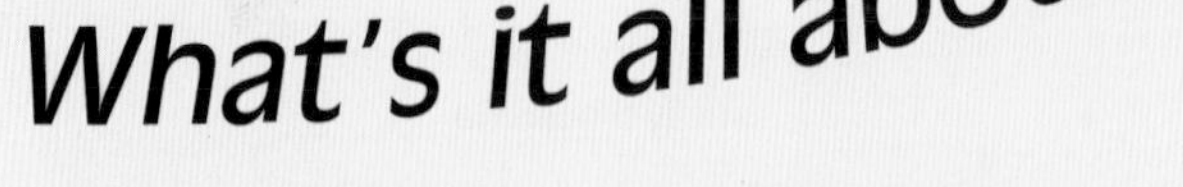

What's it all about?

The Earth's crust is made of lots of different rocks. Have you ever wondered:

- How different types of rock were formed?
- Why some rocks are really hard, but others crumble in your hands?
- Why they are different colours and densities?
- Why some are made of crystals and others of grains?

This unit will help you to answer these questions and others about rocks.

What do you remember?

You already know about:

- rocks under the surface of the Earth and that soils come from rocks.
- the names of some rocks and their textures.
- weathering processes and how sediments are formed.
- the differences between the way particles are arranged in solids and liquids.

1 Weathered rock fragments wear away rocks they come into contact with. What do we call this wearing away of rock?

deposition **erosion** **weathering** **sedimentation**

2 Which of the following describes the texture of sandstone?

intermingling **non-intermingling** **interlocking** **non-interlocking**

3 Which of these processes is described as chemical weathering?

freeze/thaw **changes in temperature** **attack by acid** **breakdown by tree roots**

4 The particles are very close together, touching, and vibrating. Which state of matter does this describe?

solids **liquids** **gases** **none of these**

Ideas about rocks

Every rock on Earth must be millions and millions of years old.

They say 'Diamonds are forever'... But I suppose rocks are too.

This rock can't be made of sediments... It's really hard.

Do you know the chemical formula of granite?

Can you find fossils in any kind of rock? Let's look closely at granite.

That can't be limestone... it looks nothing like the limestone we used at school.

QUESTIONS

Look at the cartoon above:
Discuss these questions with your partner.

a) The Earth is about 4600 million years old. Are all rocks that old too?
b) Do rocks last forever? What might change them?
c) How do you think you can get hard rocks made from sediments?
d) Why would it be impossible to find the formula of granite?
e) Which type of rocks do you know that fossils are found in? How might fossils be destroyed as a new rock forms?
f) Why do you think that different kinds of limestone can look so different?

Sedimentary rocks

LEARN ABOUT

- how sedimentary rock can form
- the characteristics of sedimentary rocks

How do sediments turn to rock?

We have seen in unit 8G how weathered rock eventually settles as a sediment.

Over time, layers of sediment build up. The separate bits of rock become a layer or bed of rock. But how does this happen?

Sand and sandstone

- Squeeze a handful of wet sand.
  a) What do you see happen?
- Now compare your damp sand with a piece of sandstone. You can use a hand lens or microscope to help your observations.
  b) How do you think the grains in sandstone are held together? Use your observations.

You can imagine the pressure building up as layer upon layer of sediment is deposited. This squeezes water out from the gaps between the grains of sediment. Under this pressure, the edges of the grains can join together. This is called **compaction**.

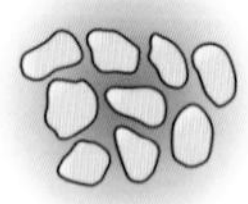

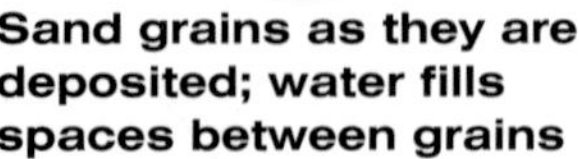

Sand grains as they are deposited; water fills spaces between grains

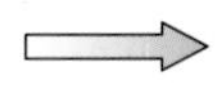

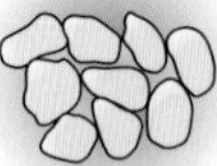

As more sediments build up, the pressure increases and pushes grains of sand closer together, squeezing out the water

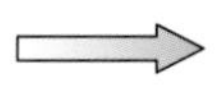

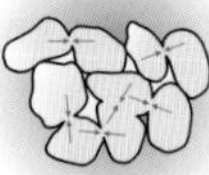

The edges of the grains can fuse together under this pressure, forming solid rock

Another process also helps the sediments to form rock. Water that passes between the gaps in the grains can evaporate. This leaves behind any solids that were in solution. The solid that comes out of solution acts like cement. It sticks the grains of sediment together. This is called **cementation**.

Rocks that form like this are called **sedimentary rocks**.

Sedimentary rocks are formed by compaction and cementation.

The individual pieces of sediment are compressed and 'stuck' together to form rock.

There are many different sedimentary rocks. We can classify them by their **texture**.

Look at the examples:

Sandstone is made of sand with particles between 0.5 mm and 2 mm in diameter. This is medium grained sedimentary rock.

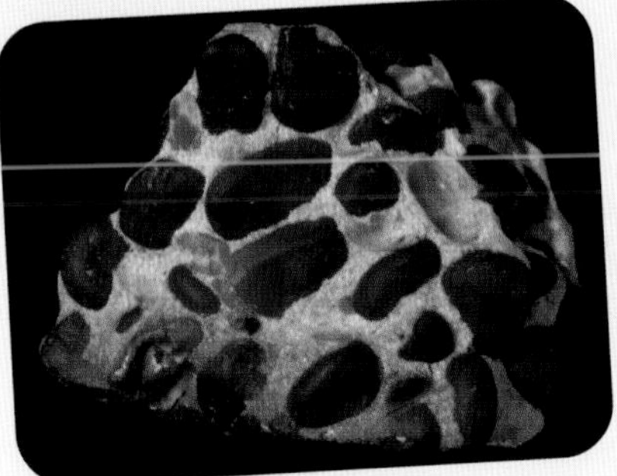

Conglomerate is a sedimentary rock made from a sediment containing pebbles. This is called coarse grained sedimentary rock.

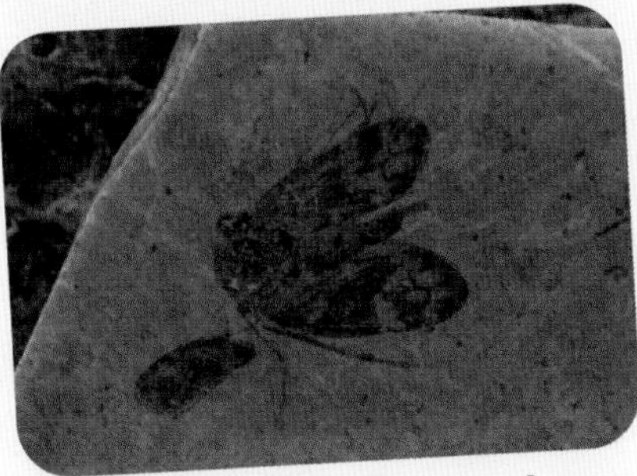

Mudstone is classed as fine grained sedimentary rock. The particles of clay sediment are less than 0.5 mm in diameter.

From this lesson and your work in unit 8G we can say that sedimentary rocks:

- are **porous** (absorb water)
- usually have grains that don't interlock
- can contain fossils.

Observing texture

- Use a hand lens or microscope to examine some samples of sedimentary rock. Your teacher will give you a sheet to help.

Q1 Which of the rocks shown is made of the largest bits of sediment?

Q2 Which of the rocks shown is made of the smallest bits of sediment?

SUMMARY QUESTION

1 ☆ Copy and complete the sentences, using words from the list below.

grains pressure together Solids cement compaction layers cementation

Sedimentary rock is formed by the processes of . . . and . . .

The . . . increases as . . . of sediment and rock build up above.

This causes the edges of . . . to fuse . . ., and water is squeezed out.

. . . left behind act as a . . . between the grains, forming rock.

Key words

cementation
compaction
porous
sedimentary
texture

8H2 Looking at limestones

LEARN ABOUT

- trialling your ideas to solve a practical problem
- describing and evaluating your method and conclusions
- how different limestones were formed

Limestone is a popular building material

What is limestone?

Limestone paving and tiles have become very popular. These are a light beige colour. But there are lots of different rocks called limestone.

Limestones are sedimentary rocks. The main mineral in all limestones is calcite (**calcium carbonate, $CaCO_3$**).

Often the calcium carbonate is in the 'hard bits' of sea creatures and plants. They use it to make their shells and skeletons.

When they die, these build up on the seabed. Over long periods of time, they form sedimentary rock.

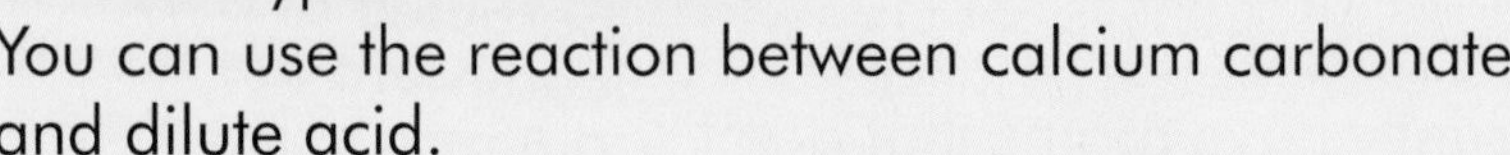

How much calcium carbonate in limestones?

SAFETY

- Find out how much calcium carbonate is in different types of limestone.
  You can use the reaction between calcium carbonate and dilute acid.
  Your teacher will give you a sheet to help you plan your enquiry.

Forming limestones

Different types of limestone were formed under different conditions.

Shelly limestones

These formed from sediments of shells deposited on ancient seabeds.

In clear waters, these shells will be the main sediment collecting on the seabed. Then we find lots of calcium carbonate in the limestone.

Sometimes there are other sediments mixed with the shelly bits. Then we find less calcium carbonate.

Brown limestone contains minerals of iron

Chalks

We have already seen how **chalk** formed slowly over millions of years. It formed from the remains of **coccoliths** (tiny sea plants).

Chalk is almost pure calcium carbonate (about 98%). This means that there were few other sediments settling on the seabed at the same time.

Q1 Which part of Britain is famous for its 'white cliffs'?

Other types of limestone

Coral reefs are made up of the shells of sea creatures. They fasten themselves to the bottom of the sea in warm conditions. These reefs build up over time. They form a very hard rock called **reef limestone**.

Corals form very hard deposits of calcium carbonate in their shells

Q2 Do you think that selling coral to tourists should be banned? Why?

Sometimes calcium carbonate comes out of solution when some sea water evaporates off. The sediment is often mixed with mud. So the rock formed is dark grey with very fine grains. It is called **lime 'mudstone'**.

A fine white mud of calcium carbonate can also coat other bits of sediment that roll across it. The sediment gets coated with an outer layer of calcium carbonate. These can go on to form another type of limestone (**oolitic** limestone).

Oolitic limestone

SUMMARY QUESTIONS

1 ☆ Copy and complete the sentences, using words from the list below.

formed **calcium** **sedimentary**

All limestones are . . . rocks.

Their main mineral is . . . carbonate.

Their characteristics depend on how they were . . .

2 ☆☆ Read the information above and draw a 'spider diagram' with the word 'limestone' in the middle. Your diagram should explain how each type of limestone mentioned is formed.

Key words

chalk
coccoliths
calcium carbonate
coral
limestones
oolitic

8H3 Metamorphic rocks

Learn about

- how metamorphic rocks are formed
- some examples of metamorphic rocks

Slate – a metamorphic rock

Slate is a metamorphic rock

Slate can be split into very thin sheets along one direction. Look at the photo:

Slate was made from mudstone or shale, both examples of sedimentary rock. In mudstone the clay minerals are mainly jumbled up.

Sometimes sedimentary rocks are subjected to very high temperatures and/or pressures. When this happens, chemical reactions take place in the solid rock. New minerals will form crystals.

No new elements can be added within the rock. Those already in the minerals are re-arranged to make the new minerals. The new rock formed is called a **metamorphic rock**.

Slate is formed under high pressure. This is caused by movements in the Earth's crust or being buried under many layers of rock. The new minerals in slate are all lined up in one direction:

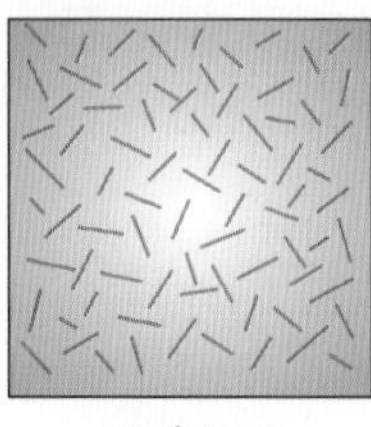

mudstone

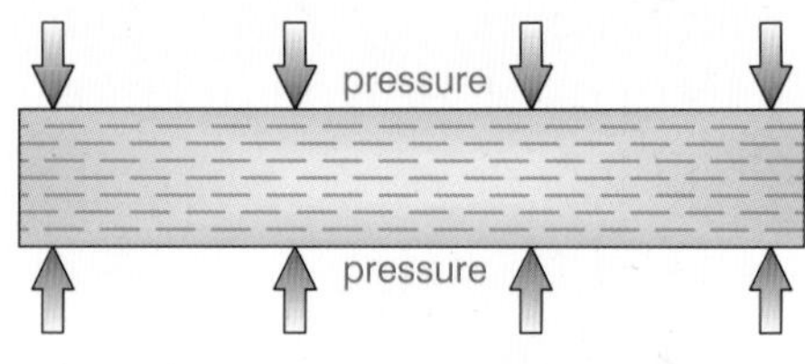

slate

Q1 The new minerals in slate are made of the same atoms that were in the clay minerals. Can you explain this?

Gneiss is a metamorphic rock. It was made when mountains were formed.

Sometimes mudstone and shale are subjected to higher pressures and temperatures. Then we get a rock called **schist**. You can see bands of minerals running through this metamorphic rock.

Then under even more extreme conditions, **gneiss** (pronounced 'nice') is made. Its bands of minerals stand out clearly.

Baking rocks

Beneath the Earth's surface, rocks can get very hot. They are subjected to extreme heat near molten rock called **magma**.

The magma rises towards the surface in areas where we find volcanoes. The Earth movements that build mountains also generate great heat.

During **metamorphism**, the rocks may get very hot but they do not melt.

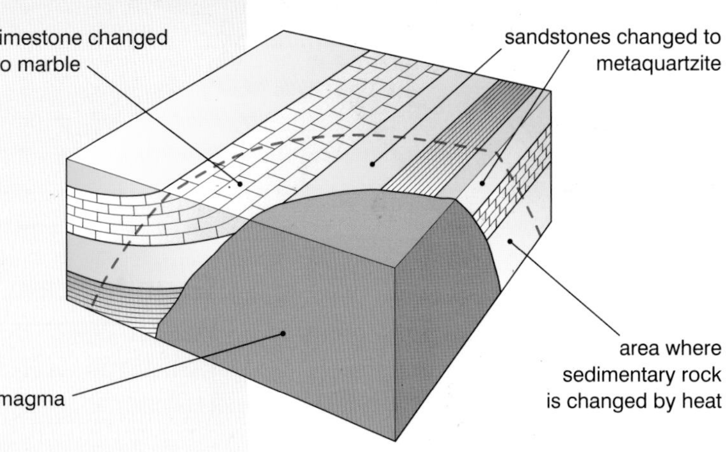

Marble can be formed by the action of heat on limestone or chalk.

In general, the characteristics of metamorphic rocks are:

- they are made of crystals that are often too small to see with the naked eye
- their crystals are usually interlocking. (This makes the rocks non-porous.)
- they often have bands of minerals running through the rock
- they usually contain no fossils.

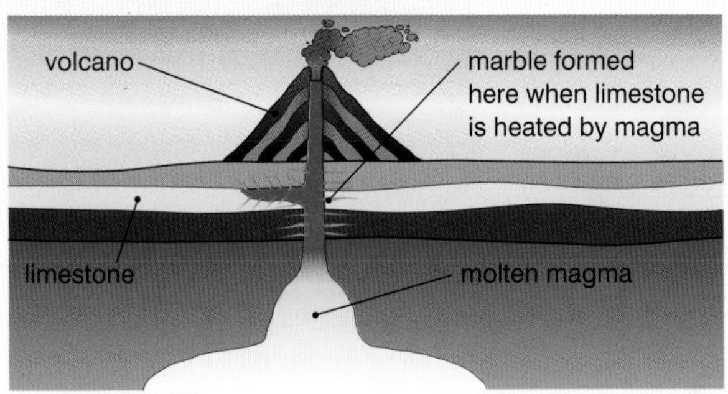

The outer part of the Earth is divided into huge slabs of rock called tectonic plates. These plates are still moving at a rate of a few centimetres each year. That's about the rate at which your fingernails grow.

SUMMARY QUESTIONS

1 ☆ Copy and complete the sentences, using words from the list below.

bands **pressure** **melting** **metamorphic**

New rocks that have been formed by the action of . . .and/or heat (without . . . the rock) are called . . . rocks.

You can often see . . . of minerals running through the rock.

2 ☆☆ Which metamorphic rock is formed from limestone? How does it form?

Key words

gneiss
magma
metamorphic
metamorphism
schist
slate

8H4 Igneous rocks

LEARN ABOUT
- how igneous rocks form
- the differences between igneous rocks

Forming crystals

Granite is the hard, shiny rock you see on some kitchen worktops. It is also used sometimes for pillars and steps in buildings. Granite is an example of an **igneous** rock.

Why is granite used for kitchen worktops?

You have seen how molten rock, called magma, can rise towards the Earth's surface. Sometimes it actually escapes from the surface, as in a volcano.

The molten mixture of materials that breaks through the surface is called **lava**.

When molten rock (magma or lava) solidifies we get igneous rock formed.

As magma or lava cools down, it forms interlocking crystals. These crystals make the igneous rock.

This lava contains a mixture of minerals and gas

Gruesome science

A volcano on the island of Martinique in 1902 killed about 30 000 people in a nearby town.

Crystal sizes

It is difficult to melt rock in a science lab. So here we will use a solid that melts quite easily. This will model what happens when molten rock **crystallises**. The solid is called salol.

Your teacher will give you a sheet to help.

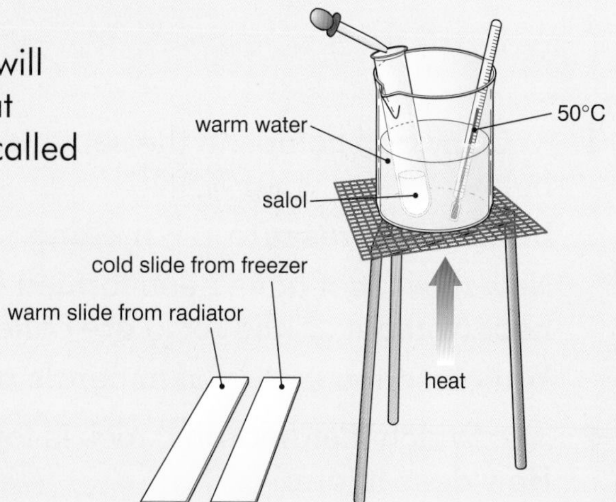

Look at the two examples of igneous rock below:

Granite's large crystals formed as molten rock cooled slowly under the ground.
It is called an intrusive igneous rock.

Basalt's small crystals were formed as molten rock cooled quickly at or near the surface. The crystals are so small that you need a microscope to see them. It is called an extrusive igneous rock.

The slower the rate of cooling, the larger the crystals formed.

Q1 Why is granite called an 'intrusive' igneous rock and basalt 'extrusive'?

Q2 Think of a factor that might affect how viscous (thick) and slow-moving lava is.

Modelling crystallisation

Imagine that you and your classmates are the particles in molten rock.

- In a large space, model the movement of the particles.
- When your teacher gives you a signal, cool down and start forming crystals. You will have to link together.
- Stop the crystallisation on another signal.
- Repeat the process a second time but now you will have longer to crystallise.

What do you notice about:

a) the number of crystals formed, and

b) the size of the crystals?

c) Explain the difference in crystal size between granite and basalt. Think about the particles in their minerals.

SUMMARY QUESTION

1 ☆ Copy and complete the sentences, using words from the list below.

slowly intrusive magma Basalt molten large Granite igneous solidifies quickly extrusive

When molten rock (. . . or lava) cools down, it usually . . . into crystals of . . . rock.

If the . . . rock cools down . . . , deep underground, then we get . . . crystals. . . . is an example of such an . . . igneous rock.

If it cools down . . . at or near the surface, small crystals form. . . . is an example of one of these . . . igneous rocks.

Key words

basalt
crystallise
extrusive
granite
igneous
intrusive
lava

LEARN ABOUT
- the minerals in igneous rocks
- the rock cycle

The minerals in igneous rocks

In intrusive igneous rocks, with larger crystals, it is easy to see the different **minerals**.

Compare the granite and gabbro in the photographs:

Q1 What differences can you see?

Q2 Why will the minerals in different igneous rocks vary?

Granite

Gabbro

In order to work out the density of a rock we will need to use this equation:

$$\text{density} = \frac{\text{mass}}{\text{volume}}$$

Your teacher will give you a sheet to help.

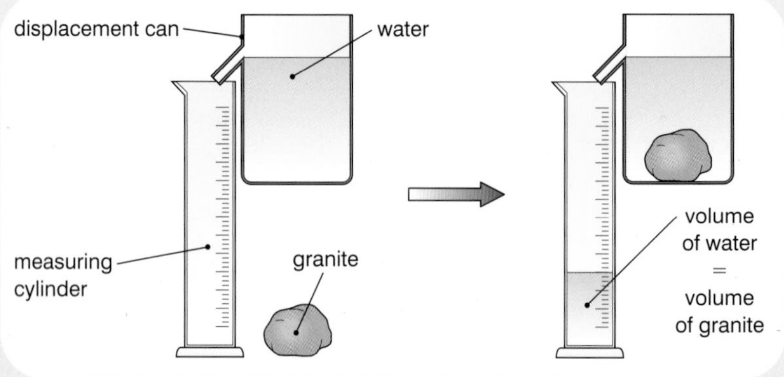

ICT CHALLENGE

Test some other examples of igneous rock to see if they are more like granite or gabbro. Set up a spreadsheet to do your calculations in this experiment.

When Krakatau (a volcano near to Java) erupted in 1883 the sound of the blast could be heard over 4000 kilometres away.

Iron content of igneous rock

Granite is a light coloured igneous rock. It is rich in the elements silicon and oxygen. It contains the mineral, **quartz**.

On the other hand, **gabbro** is much darker in colour. It is rich in minerals that contain iron.

The minerals containing iron are more dense, so gabbro has a higher density than granite.

In general the characteristics of igneous rocks are:

- they are made of interlocking crystals
- they are hard and non-porous.

The rock cycle

The three main types of rock – sedimentary, metamorphic and igneous – are involved in a long cycle of change. Some changes take place rapidly. Others can take thousands or millions of years to happen.

The changes can be shown in the **rock cycle** (see below):

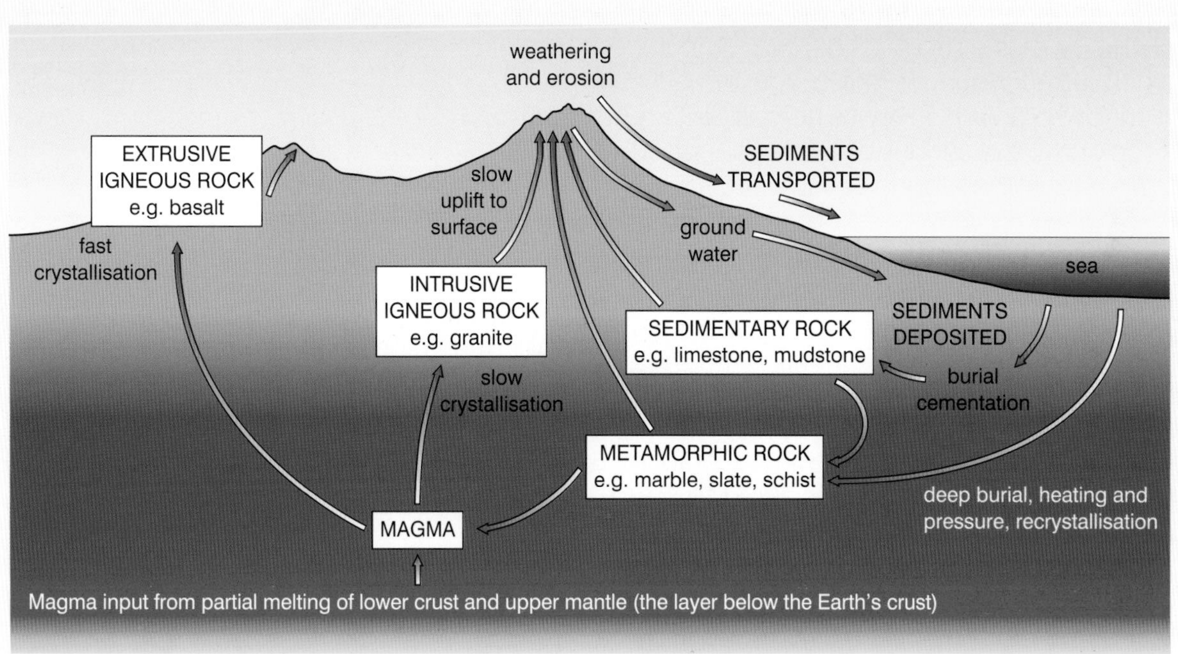

The rock cycle

SUMMARY QUESTIONS

1 ☆ Copy and complete the sentences, using words from the list below.

high cycle sedimentary density iron quartz

Granite is a low . . . igneous rock that contains . . . , whereas gabbro is a . . . density igneous rock rich in . . . bearing minerals.

The rock . . . shows how the processes that form igneous, . . . and metamorphic rocks are linked together.

2 ☆☆ Get a blank copy of the rock cycle. Fill in as much as you can using information from this unit and unit 8G.

Key words

gabbro
granite
minerals
quartz
rock cycle

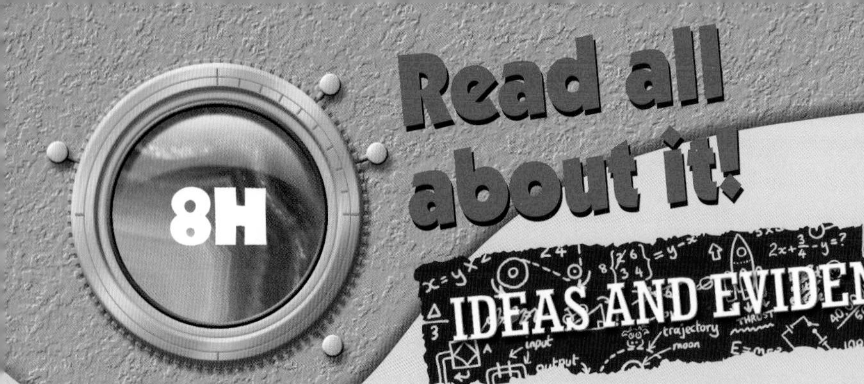

Drifting continents – the story of Alfred Wegener

The idea that continents are moving around on the surface of the Earth is difficult to believe. And it was in 1915 when Alfred Wegener first suggested his theory of continental drift. Few of his fellow-scientists took his ideas seriously. It took about 50 years for them to come around to his way of thinking.

Alfred was born in Berlin in 1880. As a boy, he read everything he could about Greenland. He dreamed that one day he would get to explore there.

At first Alfred was interested in astronomy. Then he started to study meteorology. Studying the weather in a scientific way was quite a new branch of science. In 1906 and 1912 he was asked to be the meteorologist on expeditions to Greenland.

Alfred was interested in many different areas of science. One day he was studying a scientific paper on fossils. He noticed how alike fossils found in Africa and South America were. This made him curious. Looking at an atlas of the world, people had already spotted that the coastlines of Africa and South America looked like two pieces in a jigsaw puzzle. But Alfred went further and suggested that at one time, millions of years ago, they had been joined together. He thought they had slowly drifted apart.

Alfred could offer scientific evidence to support his idea. As well as the matching fossil evidence, he also used fossils of tropical plants found in the Arctic. They must have grown on land much nearer the equator millions of years ago. He argued that the land had drifted thousands of miles.

Alfred Wegener (1880–1930) on one of his expeditions to Greenland

Evidence that Africa and South America were once joined together

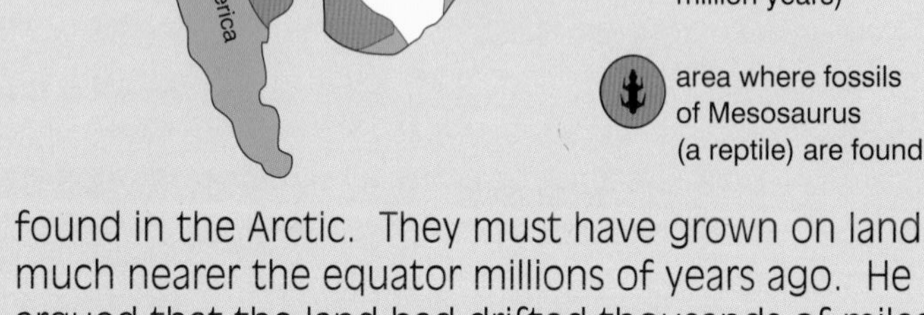

He also noticed matches between the types of rock found in Africa and South America. There were also matching rocks across other continents, for example, between Scotland and North America. This led him to think that millions of years ago all the continents had been joined together. He called this 'super-continent' Pangaea.

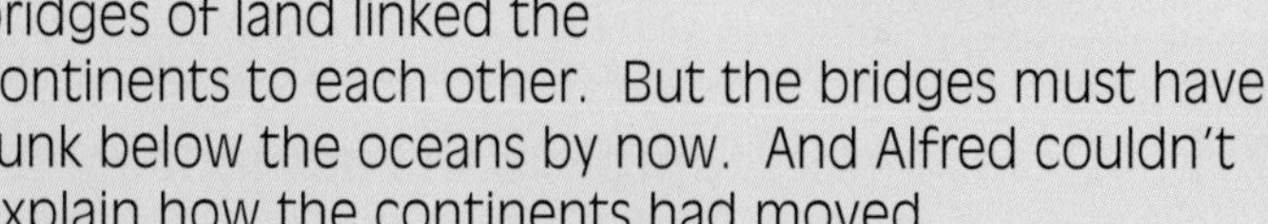

Pangaea

Scientists already had a theory that could explain the similar fossils on different continents. They believed that in the past bridges of land linked the continents to each other. But the bridges must have sunk below the oceans by now. And Alfred couldn't explain how the continents had moved.

Alfred's ideas were never accepted in his lifetime. In 1930 he led his last expedition to Greenland and was never to return. He was lost in a snowstorm and died there.

Over 20 years later, scientists discovered direct evidence of Alfred's drifting continents. Exploring the ocean floor, they found new rock forming on either side of massive cracks that ran between continents. Then the old 'land bridge' theory was dropped. A new theory, called plate tectonics, which could explain Alfred's ideas, became accepted by the scientific community.

This new rock from the volcano formed an island off Iceland. The processes of weathering and erosion will now start on the rock.
Sedimentary rocks form when layers of sediment are buried under more recent deposits. Under the pressure (compaction), and with the help of mineral 'cements' (left behind when water evaporates from between the particles of sediment – cementation), rocks are formed.
Metamorphic rocks form when existing rock experiences high pressure and/or temperature (without melting). The original rock has its structure and possibly its minerals changed. Bands of minerals are often visible if the metamorphic rock is formed under high pressure.
Igneous rocks form when molten rock solidifies. Slow cooling, inside the Earth's crust, produces rock with large crystals. Granite is an example. Faster cooling, at or near the Earth's surface, produces rock with small crystals. Basalt is an example.
We can show how rocks form in the rock cycle (see page 135).
But sometimes sedimentary rocks have really hard minerals joining their grains together, you know.
Hold on, remember most rocks are mixtures... So they don't have a chemical formula like a compound.
There are lots of different looking limestones... Depending on their sediments and how they were formed.

DANGER! AVOID THESE COMMON ERRORS

Some sedimentary rocks crumble easily but others are surprisingly hard. That's because their mineral cement, such as quartz, is strong.

Not all metamorphic rocks have visible bands. High pressure causes the banding. So you will not see any bands if the rock was changed by only high temperatures. The crystals in metamorphic rocks are often so small you need a microscope to see them.

The crystals in extrusive igneous rock, such as basalt, are also very small. In fact some igneous rocks, such as obsidian, form so quickly that crystals don't have time to form! However, most types of igneous rocks are made up of crystals.

Key words

cementation
compaction
igneous
metamorphic
rock cycle
sedimentary

UNIT REVIEW

REVIEW QUESTIONS

Understanding and applying concepts

1 Copy and complete the sentences, using words from the list below. Use the summary on page 137 to help you.

Metamorphic **large** **small** **temperature** **pressure** **minerals** **basalt** **water** **melting** **sediment** **cementation** **Igneous**

Sedimentary rocks are formed when layers of ... get buried under more layers.

Under the ... (**compaction**) from layers above, rocks are formed. The sediment is also stuck together by mineral 'cements', left behind when ... evaporates from between the particles of sediment. We call this ...

... rocks form when rock experiences high pressure and/or ... (without ...). Bands of ... are often visible if the metamorphic rock is formed under pressure.

... rocks are formed when molten rock solidifies. Slow cooling makes rock with ... crystals, such as granite. Faster cooling, at or near the Earth's surface, produces rock with ... crystals, such as ...

2 Identify the rocks below as igneous, metamorphic or sedimentary.

Rock X: It is made from plate-like crystals all lined up in the same direction. The rock fragment has parallel flat sides where it has been cleaved.

Rock Y: There are particles of sand visible held together by an orangey-brown mineral. Bits of sand crumble off the surface of the rock quite easily.

Rock Z: There are three different types of interlocking crystal arranged randomly in this hard rock.

3 a i) Name *two* igneous rocks made up of large crystals.
ii) What do we call this type of igneous rock?
iii) How is this type of rock formed?

b i) Name an igneous rock with very small crystals.
ii) What do we call this type of igneous rock?
iii) How is this type of rock formed?

c Crystals in igneous rocks can be different sizes. Explain this using the particle theory.

Ways with words

4 Write a story imagining you are a particle in a lump of granite. Describe your many adventures before arriving at your 'not-so final' resting place in the granite!

You might like to present your story as a comic strip.

Making more of maths

5 Look at the two graphs below. They show the minerals in granite and gabbro:

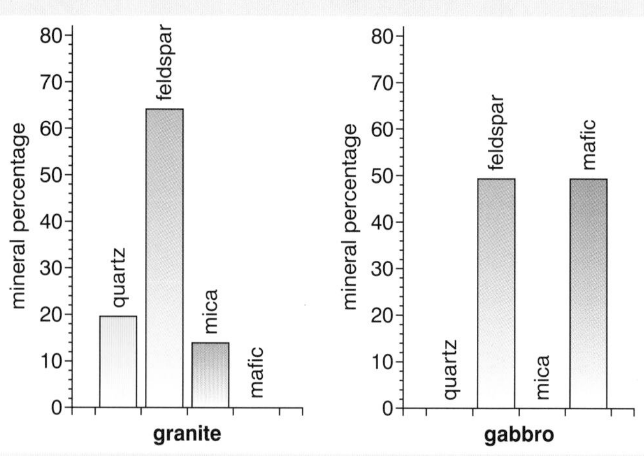

a Gabbro is more dense than granite. Which do you think is the dense mineral in gabbro.

b A piece of the mineral quartz has a volume of 50 cm^3 and mass of 130 g. What is the density of quartz? (Remember: density = mass/volume.)

Thinking skills

6 Look at the rocks below:

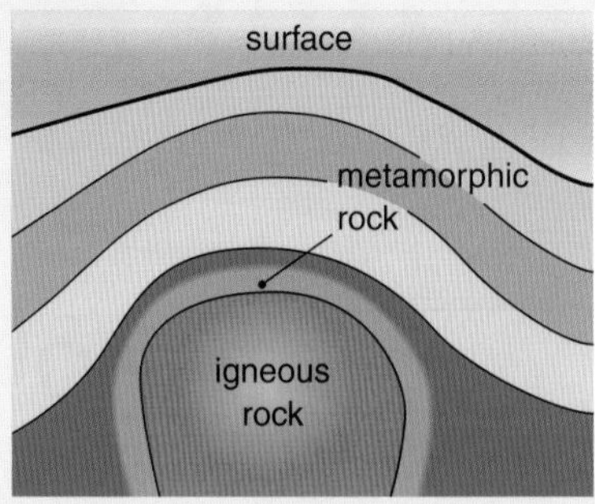

Suggest the order in which the events to form the rock structure happened. Use your knowledge of rock formation where possible.

Extension question

7 Decide on a question to investigate on some aspect of volcanoes that interests you.

Use a variety of sources to gather information. Present your findings as a poster.

SAT-STYLE QUESTIONS

1 Molly and Pete were investigating how rocks can be worn down.

They made six cubes from plaster of Paris. They weighed the cubes then put them in a tin can with a lid. They shook them for 30 seconds then weighed the six largest blocks again, making sure no bits were lost from the can. They replaced the blocks in the can and repeated this several times.

Here is a graph of their results:

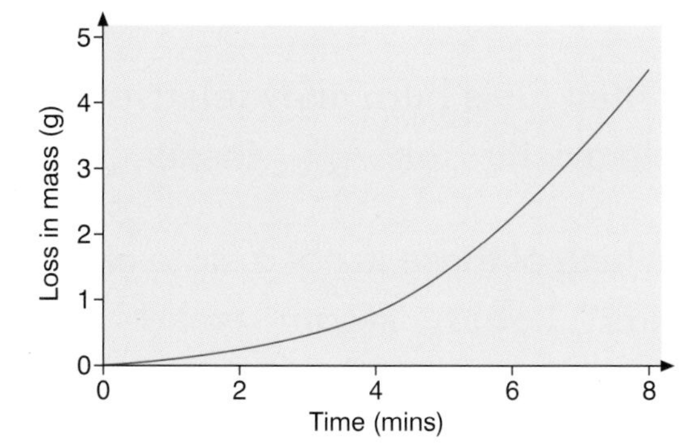

- **a** Name the process Molly and Pete were modelling. (1)
- **b** Why did the blocks lose mass? (1)
- **c** What happens to the edges of the cubes in their experiment? (1)
- **d** If they weighed the tin can plus its contents before and after the experiment, what should they find?
  - **A** The mass had decreased after the experiment.
  - **B** The mass had increased after the experiment.
  - **C** The mass remained the same. (1)
- **e** **i)** What do we call the rock formed from fragments of rock that settle in layers? (1)
  - **ii)** If these rocks are put under high pressure and baked at high temperatures, what type of rock forms? (1)

2 The list below describes some processes that occur in the rock cycle.

- **A** Layers of new minerals form as the mudstone is squeezed.
- **B** Deep in the Earth's crust rocks can be subjected to high temperatures and pressures. New crystals can then be formed in bands running through the rock.
- **C** Grains collect on the sea bed.
- **D** As molten magma cools deep underground, large crystals form.
- **E** Grains of sediment get cemented together as they are buried under more and more sediment.

- **a** Give the letters of *two* processes that describe the formation of metamorphic rock. (2)
- **b** Give the letter of a process that describes the formation of igneous rock. (1)
- **c** Which *two* letters could lead to the formation of sandstone? (2)
- **d** Which letter describes the process of deposition? (1)

Key words

Unscramble these:

egtrain
sougine
teardesinmy
cocomatpin

81 Heating, cooling

Coming soon

I'm the good conductor...
...And I'm the bad conductor!

What's it all about?

In unit 7I on energy resources, you learned about fossil fuels. If you hold a lump of coal, you are holding a store of energy that is hundreds of millions of years old. When you burn coal, heat energy is released.

Heat energy is tricky – it tries to escape. You may want to warm your home, or have a barbecue. The heat energy from the burning fuel spreads out. Perhaps you make a hot drink. The drink cools down as energy escapes from it. It will soon be cold.

In this unit, you will learn about how heat energy moves about, and why.

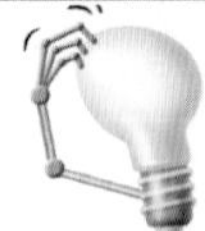

What do you remember?

You already know about:

- keeping things warm.
- how materials change state.
- what happens when fuels burn.
- the particle model of solids, liquids and gases.

1 A material which helps to keep things warm is a good . . .
conductor indicator insulator radiator

2 When fuels burn, they release:
electricity energy fossils oxygen

3 Which of these is *not* a state of matter?
gas liquid steam solid

4 A liquid can change to a gas by (choose *two*):
boiling condensing evaporating melting

Getting warm?

It gets cold at night because the Sun doesn't shine.

Close the door. You're letting all the cold in from outside.

I've caught a cold. My temperature must be below 0°C.

So why do you feel so hot?

That warm scarf will melt the snowman.

SCIENTIFICA HIGH

QUESTIONS

It's winter at Scientifica High. Do you agree with what the different characters have to say?

a) If you leave the door open on a cold day, what comes in? What goes out?

b) Do warm clothes make you warm, or stop you from getting cold?

c) What happens to your temperature when you catch a cold?

d) Why is it colder at night than during the day?

8I1 Taking temperatures

LEARN ABOUT

- the Celsius temperature scale
- thermometers

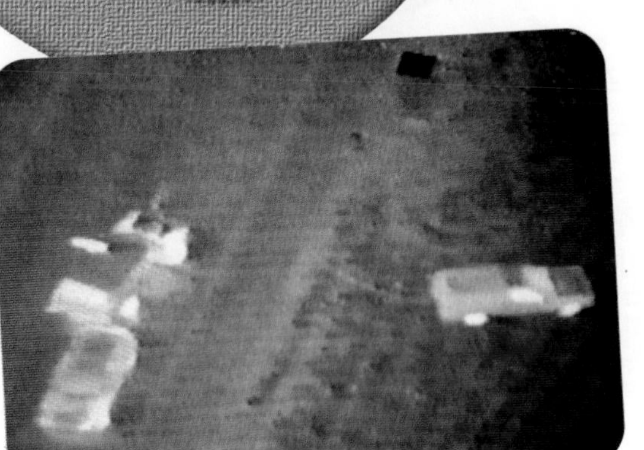

The police sometimes use heat-sensitive cameras to watch suspected criminals (and their cars) at night. People and cars show up because they are warmer than their surroundings. The car on the right has just turned off the road – you can even make out its tracks, because its tyres make the road warmer.

Q1 Look at the photo. Warm objects appear white. What colour are cold objects?

No hiding place

If you go outside on a snowy day, you need to be dressed in warm clothes. Otherwise, you will soon start to feel cold.

Ice and snow are cold. Human beings are warm. (That's because we are warm-blooded, like other mammals.) Our bodies have a **temperature** close to 37°C.

The police can make use of this. They can use a heat-sensitive camera to spot people and cars at night.

Feeling warm

When you go outside in the morning, you soon know if it's a freezing cold or boiling hot day. That's because your body is covered in nerve-endings which detect temperature. They help us to judge how hot things are.

If you are unwell, the doctor or nurse may touch your forehead. They want to know if your temperature is 'above normal'. Because our nerves are **sensitive**, we can detect quite a small rise in temperature.

Getting in hot water

Take two bowls of cold water. Add a little hot water to one. Try this:

- Put your right hand in one, then in the other. Can you tell the difference?
- Now use a thermometer to check that your answer is correct. Put the thermometer in one bowl of water. When its reading is steady, write it down. Then use the thermometer to find the temperature of the water in the other bowl.
  Take care! Glass thermometers are easily broken.

  a) Why do you have to wait until the reading on the thermometer is steady?

  b) Why is a thermometer a better way of finding out which bowl of water is warmer?

Getting scientific

In science, we use **thermometers** to measure temperatures. They show the temperature in **°C**. (We say '**degrees C**' or 'degrees Celsius'.)

The photos show some different types of thermometer.

Liquid-in-glass thermometer: the alcohol or mercury rises up the tube as it gets warmer

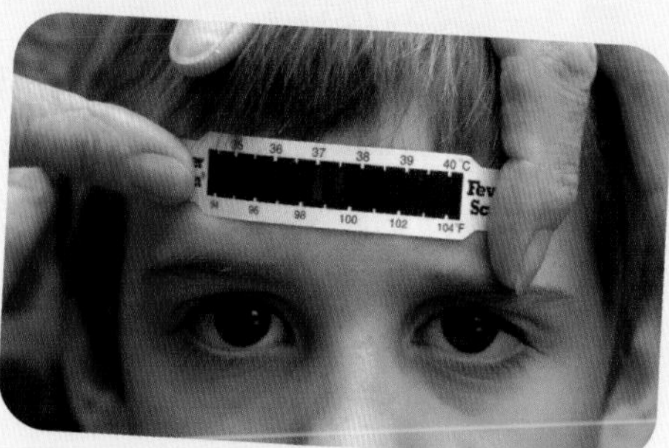

Liquid-crystal thermometer: different colours show up as the temperature changes

Electronic thermometer: the sensor detects how hot something is, and the display shows the temperature

Boiling point of pure water
100°C
Too hot to touch!
60°C
Normal body temperature (humans)
37°C
Heated swimming pool water
30°C
A comfortable, mild day
20°C
Inside the fridge
5°C
Freezing point of pure water
0°C
Inside a freezer
−20°C
alcohol

Q2 Which type of thermometer do doctors and nurses use? (You may know of more than one type.)

AMAZING SCIENCE!

Bacteria have been discovered that can live in super-hot water at over 100 °C!

SUMMARY QUESTIONS

1 ☆ What instrument do we use to measure temperature?

2 ☆☆ Look at the diagram on this page.
a) At what temperature does pure water boil?
b) At what temperature does pure water freeze?
c) What is normal body temperature?

3 ☆☆ Do you have a thermometer at home? What type of thermometer is it?

Key words

degrees C (°C)
sensitive
temperature
thermometer

812 Getting hotter, getting colder

LEARN ABOUT
- why things cool down or warm up
- how heat energy flows

Cooling off

Have you noticed a pattern like this in your eating habits?

- In the winter, when it is cold, you eat big meals. You may eat more snacks between meals.
- In the summer, when it is warmer, you eat less food. In very hot weather, you may not feel like eating at all.

Your body tries to stay warm. On a cold day, energy escapes quickly from your body. Your food is your energy supply, so you need more in the winter, to make up for the energy which escapes.

Energy escapes quickly in the winter, because Reese is much warmer than her surroundings

Heat energy

It isn't just people that cool down when it's cold. Any object that is warmer than its surroundings loses energy like this.

Think about what happens when you make a cup of tea. It starts off hot, but it soon cools down. Eventually it reaches the same temperature as the room.

Energy moves from a warmer object to a colder one. Energy moving like this is called **heat energy**.

In summer, there is only a small difference in temperature, so energy escapes more slowly

Q1 Have you ever been in a sauna? In a sauna, your surroundings are hotter than you! So heat energy will move:

out of your body   into your body
nowhere   everywhere

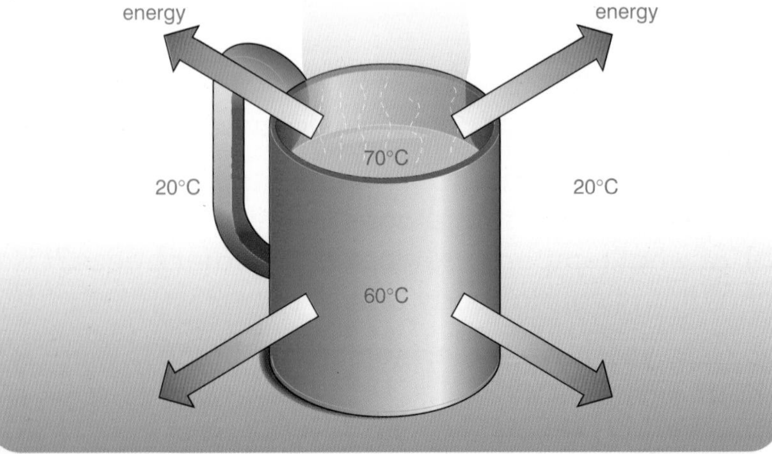

The giant freezers where manufacturers store frozen food for a long time are at –60°C.

Warming up

Hot drinks cool down and cold drinks warm up. We say that heat energy escapes from hot objects. So does 'cold energy' escape from cold objects?

That's not the scientific way of explaining things. There's only heat energy. A cold object warms up because heat energy spreads into it from its surroundings.

That's why a snowman eventually melts.

- While the weather stays cold, no heat energy spreads into the snowman, so it remains frozen.
- When the weather warms up, the air is warmer than the snowman, and heat energy spreads from the air into the snowman.

Q2 You take a cold can of drink from the fridge and put it on the table. Draw a diagram to show how heat energy flows. What happens to the temperature of the can?

The flow of heat

- You will be given a drawing of a room. Try to decide which things are hot, and which are cold.
  - **a)** Use colours to show the different temperatures. (The photo of the fridge may give you some ideas.)
  - **b)** Add arrows to show how heat energy is flowing in the room.

In this special photo, the colours tell you how cold things are. Purple and blue show the lowest temperatures; red is the warmest.

SUMMARY QUESTIONS

1 ☆ Copy and complete this sentence by choosing the correct bold word.
Heat energy flows from a **hot/cold** object to a **hot/cold** one.

2 ☆☆ Look at the photo of the fridge. Which shelf is coldest? Which containers are warmest?

3 ☆☆☆ You make a hot drink, and leave it on the table.
a) Choose the graph that shows how the drink's temperature will change.
b) Think up an experiment you could do to check your answer. List the equipment you would need.

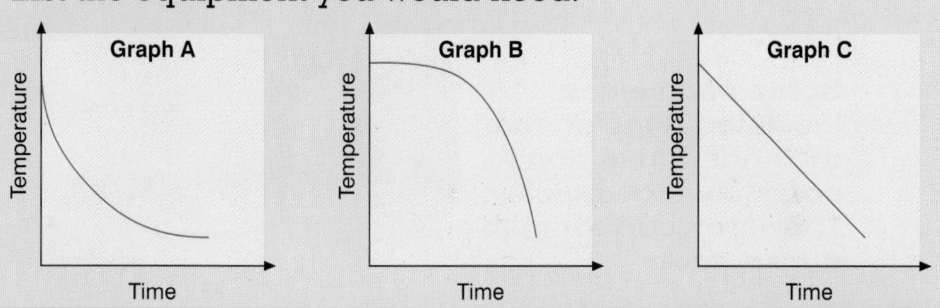

Key words

heat energy

Conduction, insulation

Learn about
- thermal conductors
- thermal insulators

Slowing the flow

Heat energy is always escaping from our bodies. In cold weather, we try to slow down this flow by wearing suitable clothes – coats, hats, scarves, etc.

Insulating clothing keeps your body heat in on a cold day. A hat can save up to 50% of the heat loss.

'Warm clothes' are made of materials like wool. Wool is a good insulating material – a **thermal insulator**.

Wool is a good insulator because, mostly, it isn't wool! Most of the volume of a woolly jumper is air. And air is a good insulator.

Q1 If you were a farmer, in which season would you shear your sheep?

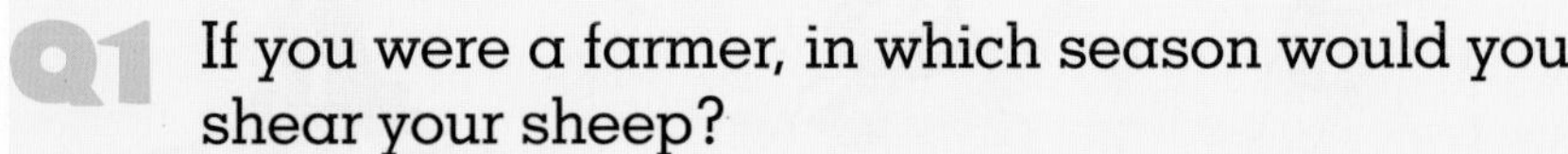

Keeping warm

An insulated cup can help to keep a drink hot.

Your task is to test some different insulating materials. How good are they at keeping a cup of hot water hot?

- Collect the equipment you think you will need.
- Discuss with your teacher how you will carry out your investigation.

Safety: Take care with hot water.

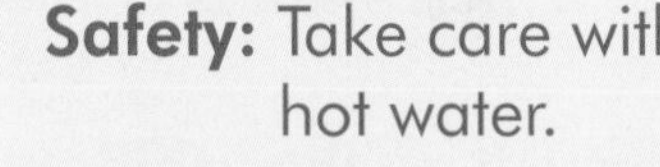

Some people use insulated cups so that their hot drinks don't cool down too quickly. They are good for cold drinks, too.

Gruesome science

Never touch the inside of a freezer with damp hands, because you may become stuck. Ice can stick harder than superglue!

Faster flow

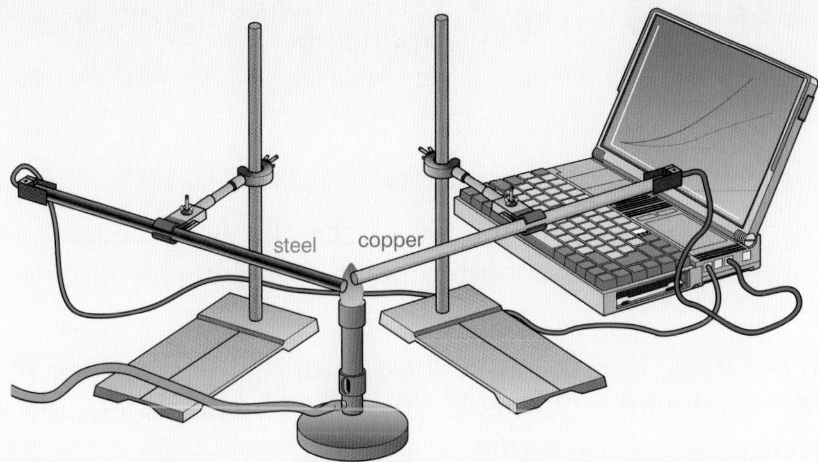

This experiment can show which metal is the best thermal conductor. The temperature sensor detects the increasing temperature at the cold end of the rod.

Metals are good **thermal conductors**. Heat energy can flow easily through them. That's why radiators are made of steel – energy can spread out from the hot water inside into the room. Some metals are better at conducting heat than others. Copper is twice as good as aluminium, and steel is a poorer conductor than both.

Other materials such as plastic and glass are good insulators.

Seeing where the heat goes

Thermocolour film is a sheet of special plastic. It starts off black. If you press on it with your hand, it turns blue. Heat energy from your hand warms up the plastic, and it gets warm and changes colour.

The photo shows an experiment. The student wore a glove on one hand, and then pressed on the sheet with both hands. Can you explain what he observed?

- Try out some other experiments using thermocolour film.

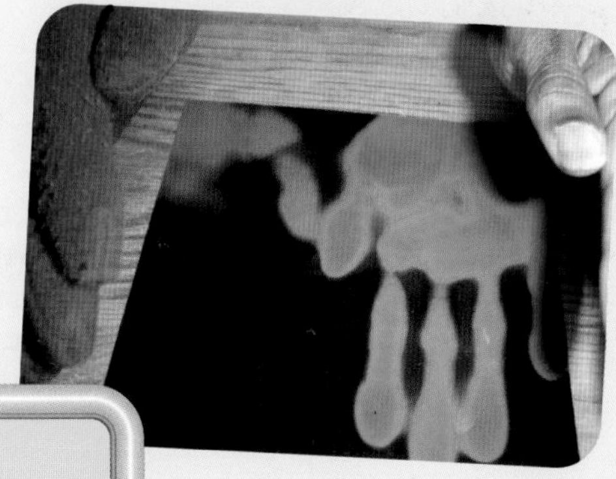

SUMMARY QUESTIONS

1 ☆ Copy and complete the sentences:
   a) A material which allows heat to flow through it easily is called a thermal . . .
   b) Heat cannot flow easily through a material which is a . . . . . .

2 ☆ Put the following words in the correct boxes:
plastic **water** **air** **copper**

good insulator					good conductor of heat

3 ☆☆ Think about the clothes you have at home. Make two lists, headed 'winter clothes' and 'summer clothes'. How do winter clothes differ from summer clothes?

Key words

thermal conductor
thermal insulator

Expanding and explaining

LEARN ABOUT

- solids, liquids and gases expanding

The oldest thermometer

Over 2000 years ago, the Greek scientist Archimedes ('Eureka!') invented a thermometer. You can see it in the picture.

coloured water

air

On hot days, the air in the flask expanded and pushed the water up the tube. On cold days, the air contracted and the water moved down again.

Archimedes had noticed that air expands when it is heated. It only expands a little. That's why he designed his thermometer with a big flask containing a lot of air, and a thin tube so that the water would move further when the air expanded.

Q1 How is a liquid-in-glass thermometer similar to Archimedes' thermometer?

Expanding solids

Railway lines are designed to survive temperatures as high as 40°C, but recent hot summers have caused some to expand and buckle

Experimenting with expansion

Watch some demonstrations of solids expanding.

Most materials **expand** when they get hotter, and **contract** when they get colder. Solids, liquids and gases all behave like this.

Sometimes, expansion can be a problem. On very hot days, railway lines may expand so much that they buckle. Then the trains have to stop running.

Particles explain expansion

You have studied the **particle model** of matter. Remember that everything is made of particles, which are too small to see.

In a solid, the particles are packed closely together. They vibrate about their fixed positions.

- When a solid is cold, its particles vibrate a little.
- When the solid gets hotter, its particles have more energy, so they vibrate more. Each particle pushes on its neighbours, and takes up more space, and so the solid gets bigger – it expands.

Take care! The particles don't get bigger, they just take up more space.

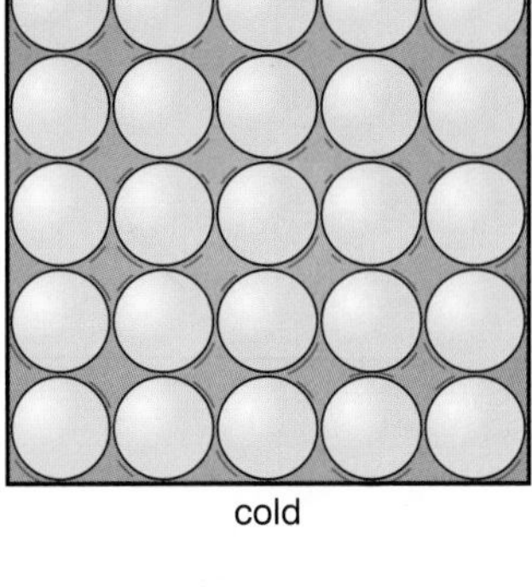
cold

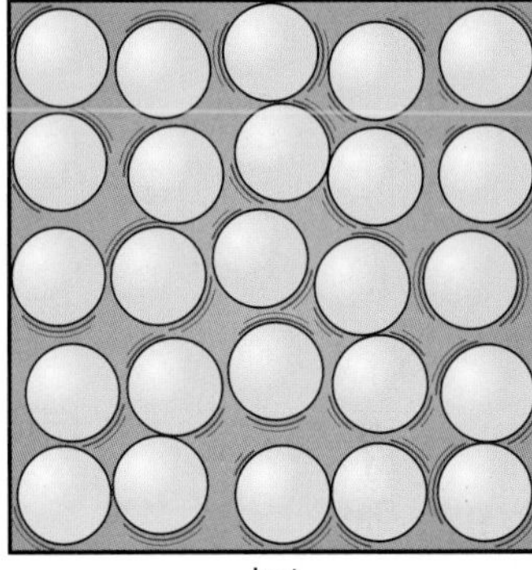

hot

The 'particle people' play

You could act out a little drama to show why solid materials expand when they get hot.

Each member of the class plays the part of a particle.

- How would you arrange the class to show the particles of a cold solid?
- How will they change as the solid gets hotter?
- How will you show that the solid expands as it gets hotter?

Discuss your ideas with the rest of the class.

SUMMARY QUESTIONS

1 ☆ Copy these sentences, replacing the words in italics with the correct scientific words.

When a steel bar is heated, it *gets bigger*. When it cools down, it *shrinks*.

2 ☆☆ The picture shows the wires that carry electricity across the countryside.

a) Make a copy of the picture.

b) On your picture, show what will happen to the wires on a hot, sunny day.

c) Write a sentence to explain why this might be dangerous.

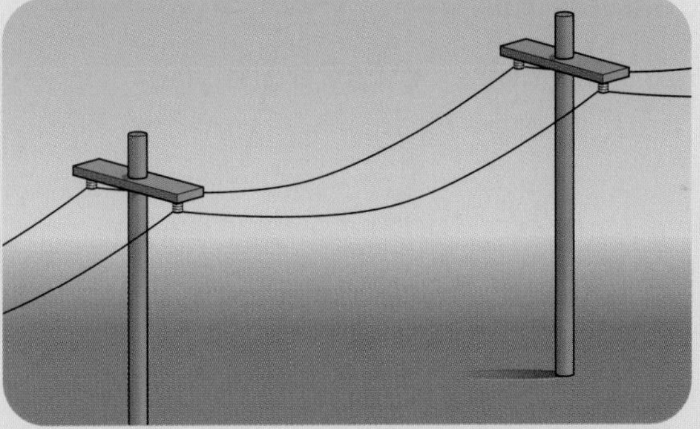

Key words

contract
expand
particle model

8I5 Radiation and convection

LEARN ABOUT
- radiation of heat energy
- convection of heat energy

Heat energy radiates out from the Sun all the time

Heat energy spreading out

The Sun is very hot, so it loses energy all of the time.

- Rays of light reach us from the Sun. That's one kind of energy.
- We also get heat energy from the Sun – we can feel it on our skin.

When heat energy spreads out like this, we call it **radiation**. Radiation can pass through the air.

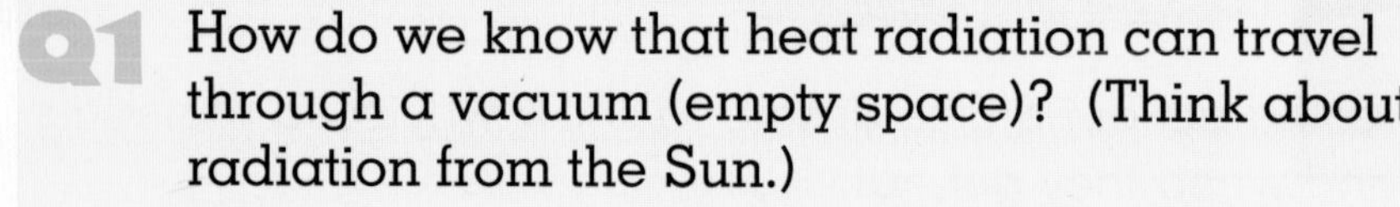

Q1 How do we know that heat radiation can travel through a vacuum (empty space)? (Think about radiation from the Sun.)

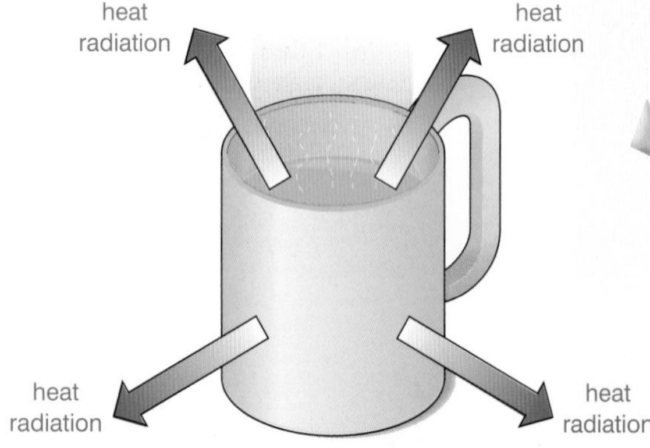

Rays spreading out

Heat energy spreads out from any object that is warmer than its surroundings. It travels in straight lines, like rays of light.

Q2 Think of some other words that start 'radi-'. Can you think how they might be connected to the word 'radiation'?

Hot lips

- Hold a test tube under the hot tap, or stand it in a beaker of hot water, until it is hot.
- Then hold it a couple of millimetres away from your top lip. Can you feel the heat energy radiating from the hot test tube?
  (Your lip is very sensitive to heat. That's so that it can detect if your food is too hot.)

Heat moving upwards

The vultures in the photograph can't take off first thing in the morning. They are waiting for the wind to blow. What makes the wind blow? No, it's not the trees waving their leaves. (You knew that.)

Hot air rises. (Everyone knows that.) This gives us a clue to the wind. Heat and light energy from the Sun warms the air. Warm air rises, and colder air flows in to replace it. This is called a **convection current**.

Ready for lift-off – these vultures make use of rising air

Seeing and using convection currents

You can have convection currents in liquids as well as gases. The picture shows one way to see how water moves when it is heated.

- Try out this experiment, and some ways of using convection currents in the air.

Safety: Use forceps to handle the coloured crystals.

The colouring in the water shows how the convection current flows

When you studied the water cycle, you learned how rising air carries water vapour upwards.

SUMMARY QUESTIONS

1 ☆ What processes are being described here? Choose from:

conduction **convection** **radiation**

a) Heat energy travelling along a metal rod.
b) Heat energy spreading out from a hot object, travelling through a vacuum.
c) Heat energy being carried by a current of water or air.

2 ☆☆ Which radiates most energy: a hot object or a cold object?

3 ☆☆ Why are convection currents important to people who enjoy hang-gliding or hot-air ballooning?

Key words

convection
convection current
radiation

816 Conserving energy

Learn about
- insulating houses
- saving energy

Weather worries

People who live in cold countries need houses designed to keep energy in

Some people think they have noticed changes in our weather. We're getting hotter summers, and the winters are wetter and stormier.

Some scientists predict that our climate will become colder, and we will have to adjust the way we live. We will have to redesign our houses so that we can survive colder winters. We will need to use more **insulation**.

Switching off

You can tell from this photo where energy is escaping from the houses. Yellow and orange are hot; purple and blue are the coldest.

If you turned off the heating in your house, it would gradually cool down. That's because it is warmer than its surroundings. In the winter, you would feel very chilly.

Heat leaves a house in all of the ways you have been learning about:

- Heat escapes by **conduction** through the floor into the ground below. It conducts through the walls, windows and ceilings.
- Heat escapes by **convection**. Warm air rises above the house, and cold air replaces it.
- Some energy also escapes by **radiation**, from the outer walls.

Q1 Draughts are an example of heat escaping by:

conduction
convection
radiation

Keeping it in

All of the energy that escapes is energy that has been paid for. Fuel and electricity cost money. It makes sense to **conserve** energy, because that saves money.

There is another reason, as you saw when you studied energy. Our use of energy damages the environment.

The picture shows that there are lots of ways of making sure a house loses less energy.

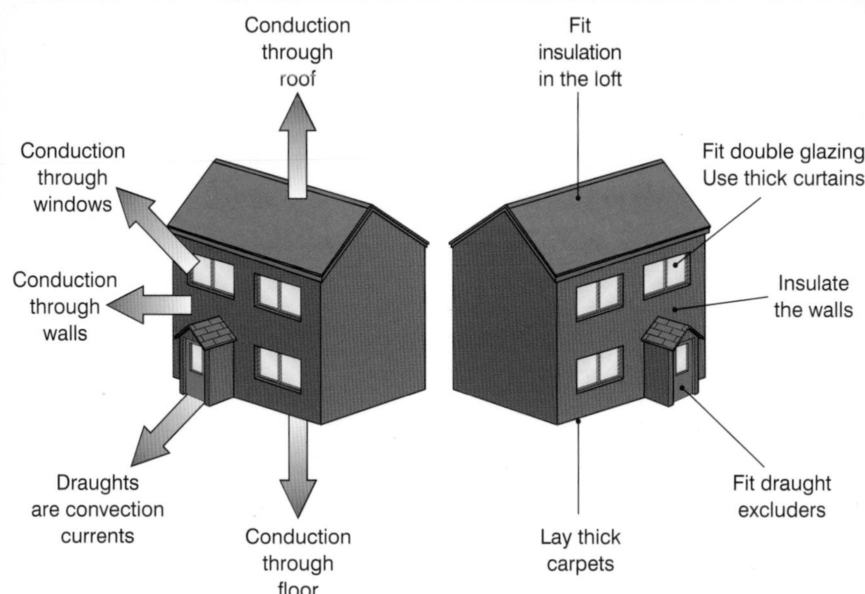

You can save more energy by turning down the thermostat on your central heating so that the house is a little cooler. You might need to wear warmer clothes.

Q2 Look at the 'thermogram' of the houses on the opposite page. How can you tell that they are losing heat quickly through their windows? Do you think that any of the houses has an insulated loft?

Ideal homes

- Use a model house with a small light bulb inside, to heat it. Switch off the heating and investigate the pattern of the temperature inside the house as it gets colder. Investigate how you can use insulation so that energy escapes more slowly from it. Your teacher must check your plan before you start.

SUMMARY QUESTIONS

1 ☆ Copy and complete the sentences.

It is a good idea to reduce the amount of energy we use to heat our houses.

This saves m. . ., and causes less damage to the e. . .

2 ☆ Fitting thick carpets can help stop heat escaping through the floor. Less energy escapes by:

conduction **convection** **radiation**

3 ☆☆ Find out about double-glazed windows. In what ways are they different from ordinary windows?

Key words

conduction
conserve
convection
insulation
radiation

Changing state

Learn about

- changes of state
- finding melting and boiling points

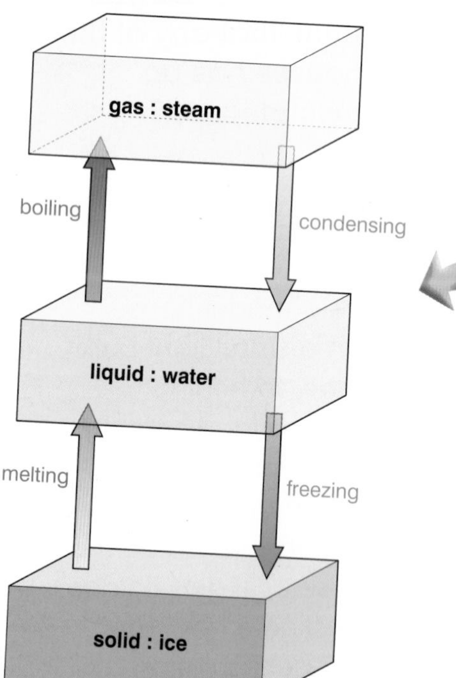

Hard, runny, invisible

Ice is very hard. If it's thick enough, you can skate on it.

Ice is just frozen water. However, if you came from a hot planet and weren't familiar with ice, you might be very surprised to find that a runny liquid can turn into a hard solid. And it can become completely invisible when it boils to become steam.

Melting and freezing, boiling and condensing – you already know about these **changes of state**.

Particle explanations

We can use the particle model to explain what happens when a substance changes state.

In a solid, the particles are closely packed together

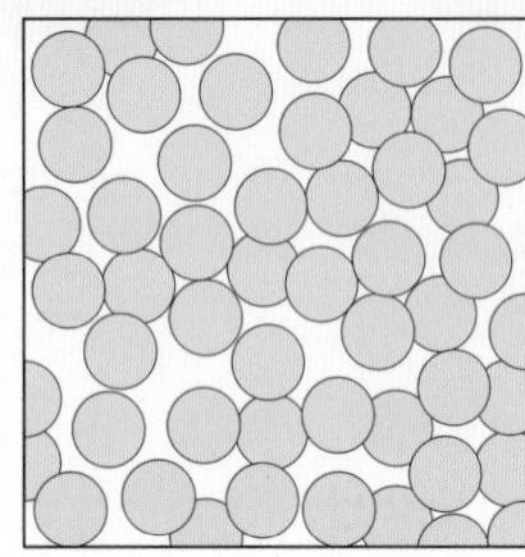

In a liquid, the particles are less tightly packed. They can slip past each other.

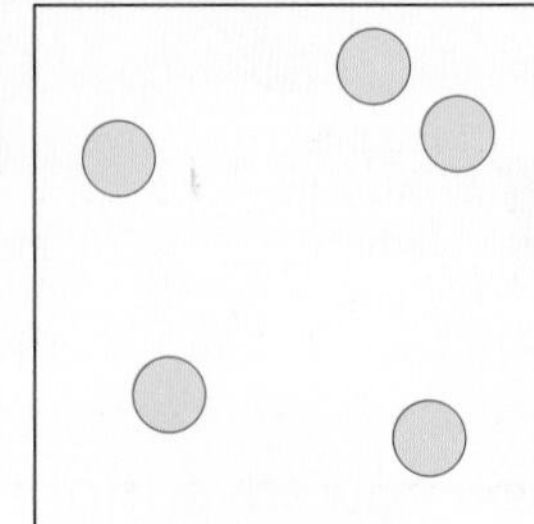

In a gas, the particles are far apart, so they can move around easily

Imagine heating a solid. Its particles vibrate more and more. Eventually the vibrations are so strong that the particles become free to move about – the solid has become a liquid.

Now imagine heating the liquid. As its particles gain more energy, they move more quickly. Eventually, the particles fly apart – the liquid has become a gas.

We thought ice skating was cool.
Now we're freezing!

Q1 Discuss how the class could pretend to be particles in a solid as it turns into a liquid and then into a gas. How would you act out this drama?

Meanwhile, back in the kitchen . . .

If you put a pan of water on the stove, it will soon come to the boil. Leave it there for a while, and the water boils away. Here's what the graph shows:

- The temperature of the water rises to 100°C. That's when the water boils.
- While the water is boiling, its temperature stays at 100°C – that's its **boiling point**.

When you heat water on the stove, its temperature rises until the water boils. Then it remains steady – that's how you can find the boiling point of water.

If you want to make ice cubes, you put water in the freezer. It takes a while for the ice to form. While the water is freezing, its temperature stays at 0°C – that's its **freezing point**.

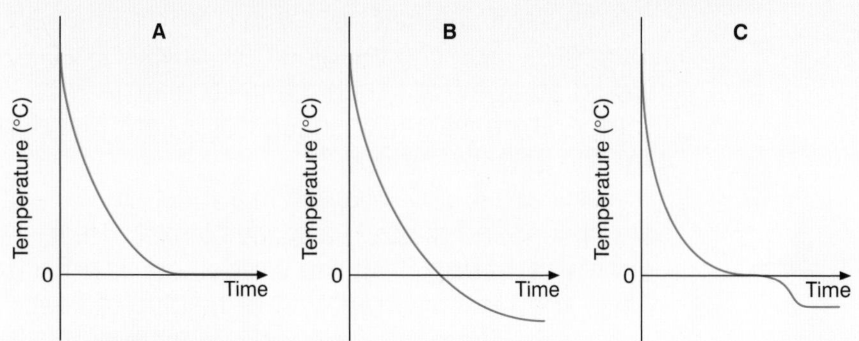

Q2 Which graph shows how the temperature of water changes when you put it in the freezer?

Freezing hot

Salol is a kind of wax. If you warm it up in a beaker of warm water, it melts. When it cools down, it freezes again. It's still very hot when it freezes.

- Carry out an experiment to find the freezing point of salol. Start with some liquid salol, and measure its temperature as it cools.

Safety: Wear eye protection.

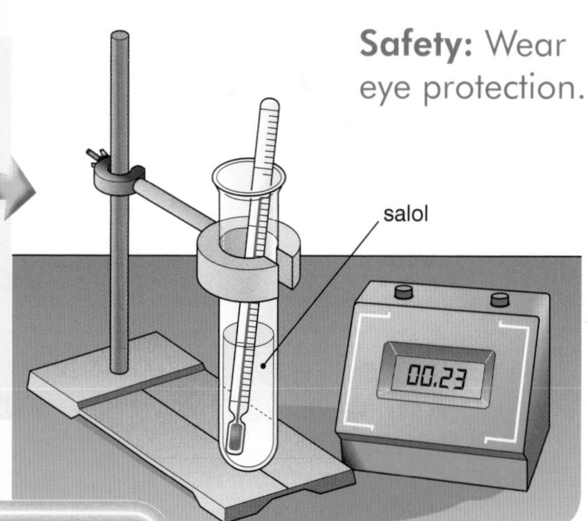

SUMMARY QUESTIONS

1 ☆ Which change of state is the opposite of boiling?

2 ☆☆ What do we call the temperature at which something melts? Give two names for it.

3 ☆☆ If you heat some water to 200°C, it will be:

ice **water** **steam**

4 ☆☆ When water boils, its temperature:

falls **is low** **rises** **is steady**

Key words

boiling point
change of state
freezing point

Using science today

Have you ever eaten Baked Alaska? It's a surprise pudding. When you take it out of the oven, it has hot meringue on the outside, and frozen ice-cream on the inside. How can that be?

The cook puts a block of ice-cream on a cold dish, and then heaps the meringue mixture on top.

When the meringue goes in the oven, it cooks quickly. It's mostly air. Air is a good insulator, so heat can't get through to the ice-cream.

A scientist recently invented another surprise pudding, ice-cream with hot jam inside. You put runny jam inside the ice-cream, and cook it in a microwave oven. The jam **absorbs** the **microwaves** and melts but the ice-cream doesn't absorb any of the energy of the microwaves.

Keeping baby warm

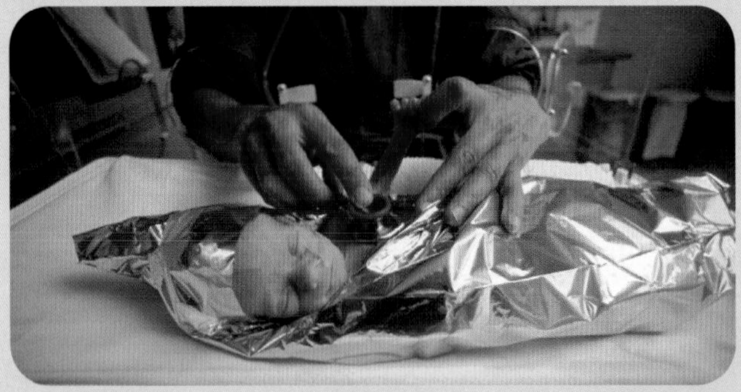

This baby was born prematurely. She doesn't have much body fat to keep her warm, and she would die quickly if she had not been transferred to an incubator. You can imagine how quickly heat would escape from such a thin little arm. The temperature inside the incubator is kept just right for the baby to survive.

This baby is also wrapped in a sheet of aluminium and plastic – a space blanket. Heat energy **radiating** from the baby's body is reflected back, another important way of helping to keep her warm. The doctor is checking her heart.

Even very tiny babies like this one have a good chance of survival provided they are kept warm, fed, and protected from infection.

Cooking chips

Computer chips like this need constant cooling to ensure they do not over-heat

Why does your computer hum? Doesn't it know the words? No, that constant hum is the fan, which blows cool air over the chips that do all the work in a PC.

Chips get hot because electric currents flow through them as they operate. The chips must be cooled or they would over-heat.

Blowing away hot air is known as '**forced convection**'. It's what you do when you blow on a hot drink to cool it down.

It gets cold at night because heat energy radiates away into space!
I've caught a cold. My temperature is two degrees above normal.
I can feel heat energy flowing from your body to my cooler hand.
That warm scarf will help prevent heat energy from flowing in and melting the snowman.
I'm closing the door to prevent a convection current from bringing cold air in from outside.

- Thermometers measure temperatures in °C.
- Heat energy is energy moving from hotter places to colder places. It travels by conduction, convection and radiation.
- When a solid is heated, it may melt to become a liquid, and then boil to become a gas. These are changes of state.

DANGER! AVOID THESE COMMON ERRORS

Don't get confused between heat energy and temperature.

Temperature tells you how hot something is. If you put a thermometer into a hot object or place, it will tell you that the temperature is high.

Heat energy is energy moving from one place to another. It moves from a hotter place to a colder one.

Key words

absorbs
forced convection
microwaves
radiating

UNIT REVIEW

REVIEW QUESTIONS

Understanding and applying concepts

1 Look at the 'thermogram' photo of someone making a pot of tea. Say as much as you can about what the photo tells you.

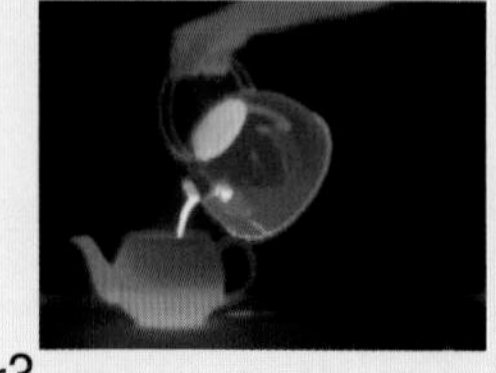

What colour is the hot water?
What colour are cold objects?
What do you notice about the person's arm?
How full is the teapot?

2 A saucepan is usually made of metal, but its handle is made of plastic. Explain why these are good choices of materials. Why would a plastic pan with a metal handle be a bad idea?

Ways with words

3 You have learned about thermal conductors and insulators. Who might wear 'thermal clothing'? How is it different from ordinary clothing?

4 We talk about the Celsius **scale** of temperature. A mountaineer might **scale** a mountain. A pianist might play a musical **scale**. Explain what these different scales have in common with each other.

Making more of maths

5 The table shows the melting points of four different substances, A, B, C and D. The diagram shows the same information.

Substance	Melting point (°C)
A	0
B	120
C	80
D	44

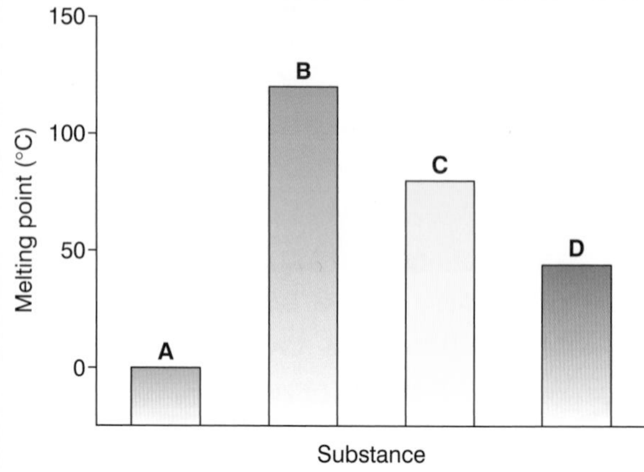

a Which substance has the highest melting point?

b Can you guess the name of substance A?

c When the temperature is 50°C, is substance C a solid or a liquid?

d If you cooled all of the substances down, starting at 200°C, which would be the last to become solid?

Extension question

6 Doctors use disposable thermometers to measure their patients' temperatures. Find out what these thermometers look like, and how they are used. Why is it a good idea to use thermometers that can be thrown away after they have been in a patient's mouth?

SAT-STYLE QUESTIONS

1 Tess was investigating how a beaker of hot water cooled down. The drawing shows her apparatus.

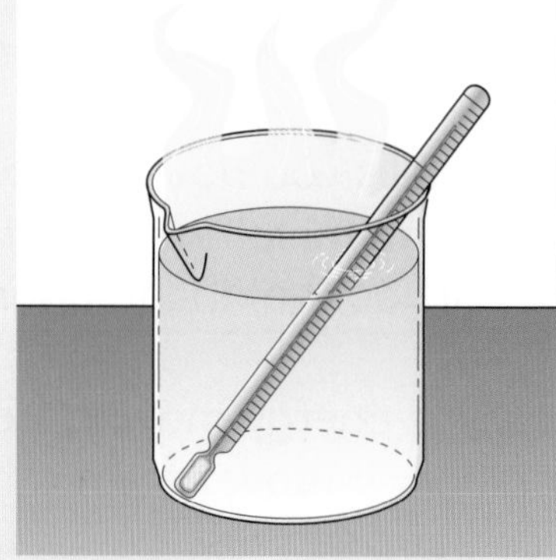

a Name the instrument she used to measure the temperature of the water. (1)

b Heat energy escaped from the beaker of water in several different ways. The table shows some of the ways heat energy escaped from the water. Complete the table by filling in the last column. Choose from:

conduction **convection**
insulation **radiation**

How the heat energy escaped	Name for this
Heat energy passed through the glass of the beaker and spread into the top of the table.	
Heat energy was carried away by warm air rising above the beaker.	

(2)

c After a while, Tess measured three temperatures:
temperature of water in beaker = 20°C
temperature of air near beaker = 20°C
temperature of table under beaker = 20°C
Predict whether the water would continue to get colder. Give a reason to support your answer. (2)

2 Benson was investigating the freezing of sea water. He put a plastic beaker of sea water into a freezer, together with a temperature sensor connected to a computer to record the temperature of the water.

The graph shows how the temperature of the water changed:

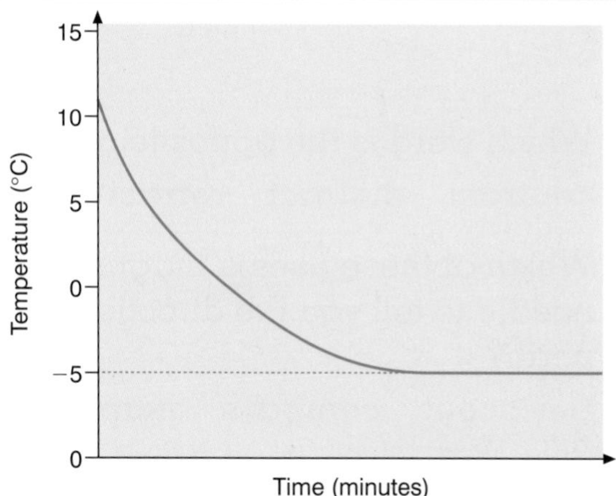

Use the graph to help you answer these questions:

a What was the temperature of the water when Benson put it in the freezer? (1)

b At what temperature did the water freeze? (1)

The sea water froze at a different temperature to pure water.

c At what temperature does pure water freeze? (1)

d Benson repeated the experiment with pure water instead of sea water. On a copy of the graph, show how you think his results would appear. (1)

3 In Pete's room, there is an electric heater. Heat energy is carried around the room by convection currents.

Air close to the heater is heated.

a How does the temperature of the air change? (1)

b How does the density of the air change? (1)

c Copy the diagram, and add an arrow to show how the air close to the heater moves. (1)

d Add another arrow to show how the cold air in the room moves to form a convection current. (1)

Key words

Unscramble these:
remothertem
venscore
prematurete
daniatior
inourlast

8J Magnets and electromagnets

COMING SOON

My big brother THINKS he's got a magnetic personality!
That explains why he repels everyone!

What's it all about?

Magnets are fun to play with. They seem slightly magical, because they can make a force act on something without actually touching it. They can attract and repel another magnet.

In this unit, you are going to learn more about magnets and magnetic materials. You may have learned about Michael Faraday, the scientist who did most to explain how electricity and magnetism are linked. Now you can learn about how electricity can make a magnet.

Later in your studies of science, you will find out about the other half of Faraday's idea, how magnetism can make electricity.

What do you remember?

You already know about:

- how magnets are used.
- magnetic and non-magnetic materials.
- how to represent forces using arrows.

1 Magnets can be made from . . .
copper plastic steel wood

2 Which *two* of these can be picked up by a magnet?
copper iron plastic steel

3 Which word is the opposite of *attract*?
contract distract retract repel

4 Which of these uses a magnetic needle to tell you the direction of north?
boy scout compass map Pole Star

Ideas about experimenting with magnets

QUESTIONS

You already know quite a lot about magnets and magnetic materials.

a) What can you say about the magnets which Pip and Molly are trying to pull apart?

b) Can you help Pete with his problem? Has Reese got the answer?

c) Can magnets do strange things to your hair, like Mike and Benson think?

8J1 What magnets do

LEARN ABOUT
- magnets
- magnetic materials

I spy magnets

Magnets keep the fridge door shut. Magnets are a handy way of pinning up notices. There are magnets in electric motors and in headphones. They're all around us.

Q1 List some places where magnets are used. Try to think of some unusual examples.

Magnetic materials

A magnet can attract a piece of steel – a paper clip, for example. This tells us that steel is a **magnetic material**.

- Iron and steel are magnetic materials. That means that they are attracted by a magnet.
- Iron oxide is another magnetic material. It's used to make fridge magnets.
- Aluminium, copper, gold and many other metals are *not* attracted by a magnet. They are **non-magnetic materials**.
- Most other materials are also non-magnetic – paper, wood, water, plastic, air, etc.

Most magnets are made of steel or iron oxide

Q2 Have a guess: Is silver magnetic or non-magnetic? Give a reason to support your idea. How could you check it?

Magnetic all over?

- Examine some magnets. Test each one with a paper clip. Does every part of the magnet attract the clip?
- Stick lots of paper clips to your magnet. Where do they stick?
- Draw a diagram of a bar magnet. Think of a way of showing where the magnet's attraction is strongest, and where it is weakest.

Pairs of poles

A bar magnet has two ends. It is strongest at the ends, and we call these its north and south **poles**. Usually, a magnet is marked so that you can tell which is its north pole.

Two magnets can **attract** each other, or they can **repel** each other. The picture shows how we can represent these forces, using arrows.

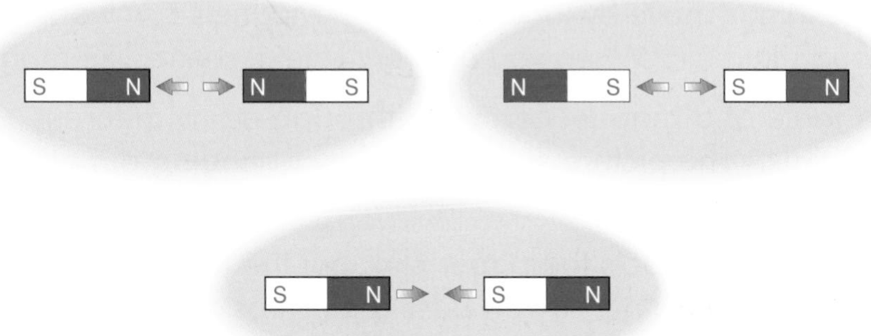

When two magnets are repelling each other, we draw the arrows pushing away from each other. The rule is:

- Two north poles repel each other. Two south poles repel each other.
- A north pole and a south pole attract each other.

We say: **Like poles repel, opposite poles attract!**

Magnet or magnetic material?

Start with two magnets and a piece of steel. The steel isn't a magnet.

- Show how the magnets can attract each other, and how they can repel each other. Where are the poles of the magnets?
- Now try one magnet with the piece of steel. Can you attract the steel? Can you repel it?
- If your teacher gave you another piece of steel, how could you decide if it was a magnet or just a piece of magnetic material?

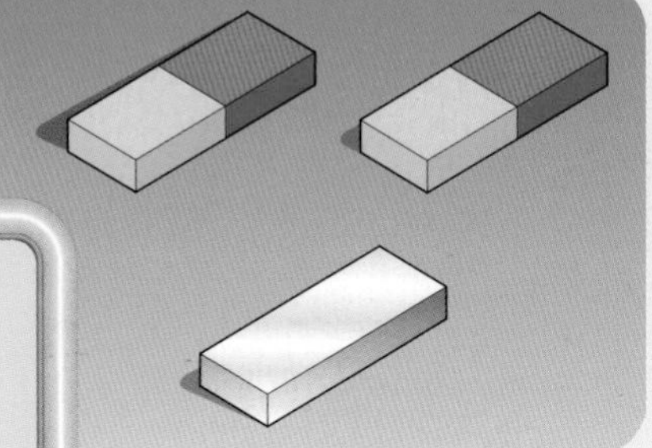

SUMMARY QUESTIONS

1 ☆ The table shows some magnetic materials and some non-magnetic materials, but they are all mixed up.
Copy the table, but put the different materials in the correct columns.

Magnetic materials	Non-magnetic materials
iron	wood
aluminium	iron oxide
water	steel

2 ☆☆ Copy and complete these sentences:
Two north magnetic poles will ***attract/repel*** each other.
A north magnetic pole will ***attract/repel*** a south pole.

3 ☆☆ The rule says 'Opposite poles attract'. What do we mean by *opposite poles*?

Key words

attract
magnetic material
pole
repel

Making and testing magnets

LEARN ABOUT
- making a magnet
- testing its strength

Through thin air

Small children find magnets very surprising. Usually, we make things move by touching them. Magnets can work through thin air. When you are very little, it seems like magic.

The force of a magnet can work through many different materials. The picture shows one way of finding out about this.

The magnet attracts the paper clip, but the thread stops them from touching. If you pass a piece of cardboard into the gap, the clip is still attracted. If you use a thin sheet of steel instead, the clip falls down. It is no longer attracted.

This shows that the magnetic force can pass through cardboard but not through steel.

Q1 Can the magnetic force pass through air?

Getting magnetised

As the north pole of the magnet moves away from the iron, it leaves a south pole behind

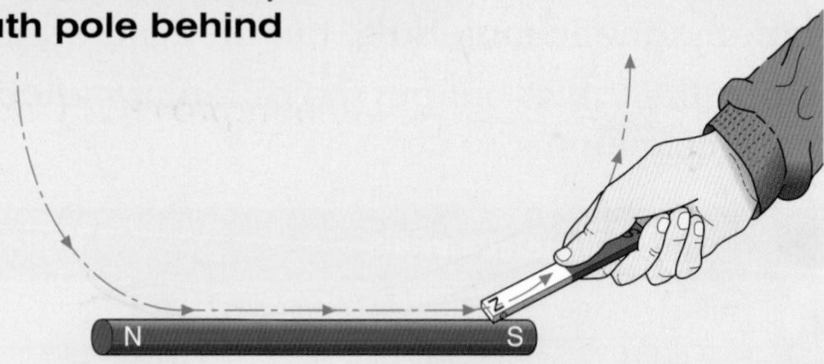

You can use one magnet to make another. Here's how to magnetise a piece of iron.

- Stroke the piece of iron from one end to the other, using the north pole of the magnet.
- Repeat this several times.
- Make sure you always stroke the iron in the *same* direction, using the *same* pole of the magnet.

Q2 What do you think will happen if you stroke the iron in the opposite direction? What will happen if you stroke it with the opposite pole of the magnet?

Testing the strength of a magnet

There are many ways to see how strong a magnet is. The pictures show three of them. You may be able to think of others.

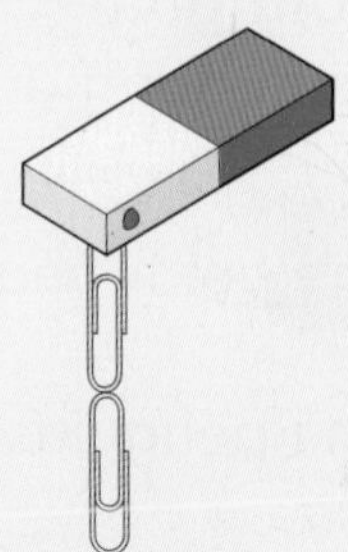

Hang paper clips end-to-end from the magnet.

How many will it hold?

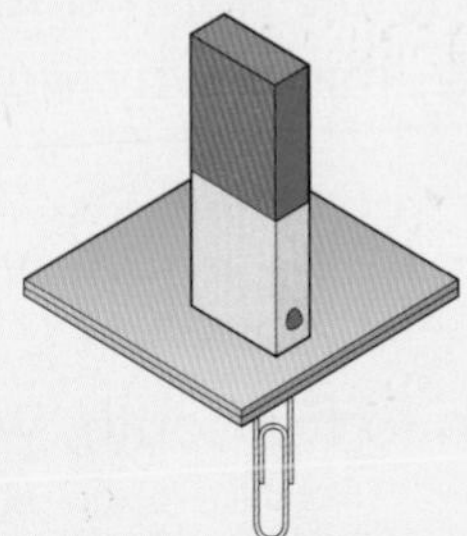

Put layers of cardboard between the magnet and the paper clip.

How thick is the cardboard when the paper clip won't stick on?

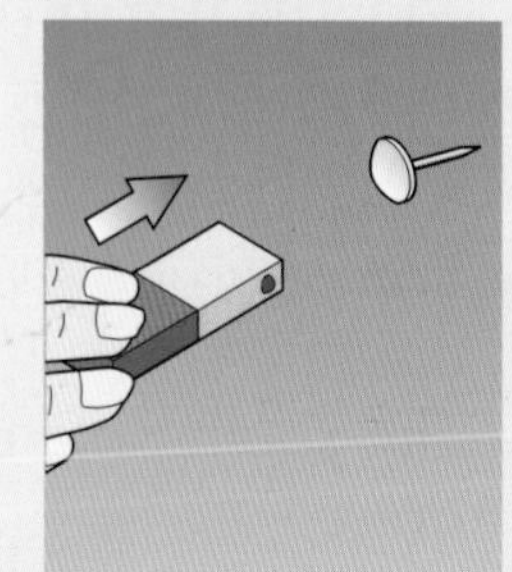

Push the magnet towards a pin.

When does the pin move?

- Try out each of these methods. Use them to compare some magnets – which magnet is the strongest? Which is the weakest?
- Then you have to decide – which is the best method for comparing magnets? Deciding which method is best is called **evaluating** them.
- Can your ideas help you to improve any of the methods?

SUMMARY QUESTIONS

1 ☆ Which type of material will a magnetic force *not* pass through?

2 ☆☆ Some 'copper' coins are made of a steel disc covered in copper. Explain why a magnet can pick up a coin like this.

3 ☆☆ Design a toy that makes use of magnets. The idea is that the toy should do something that will surprise a small child.

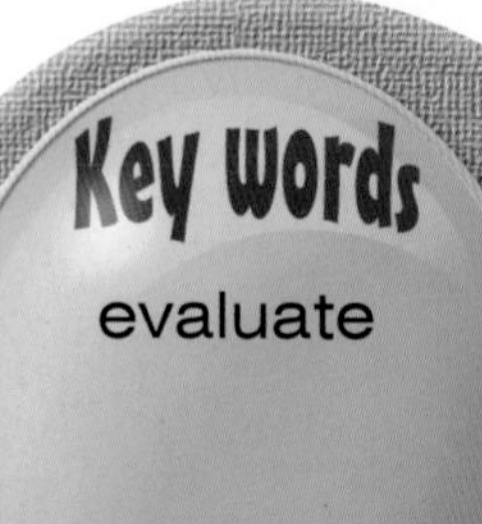

Key words

evaluate

8J3 Magnetic fields

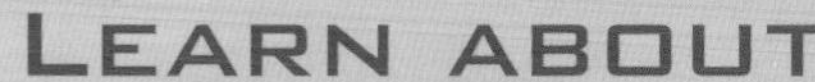

LEARN ABOUT
- magnetic fields
- using a compass

Compasses

The needle of a **compass** is a magnet. It is free to turn round. Its **north pole** points north and its **south pole** points south. Of course, this is why we call them north and south.

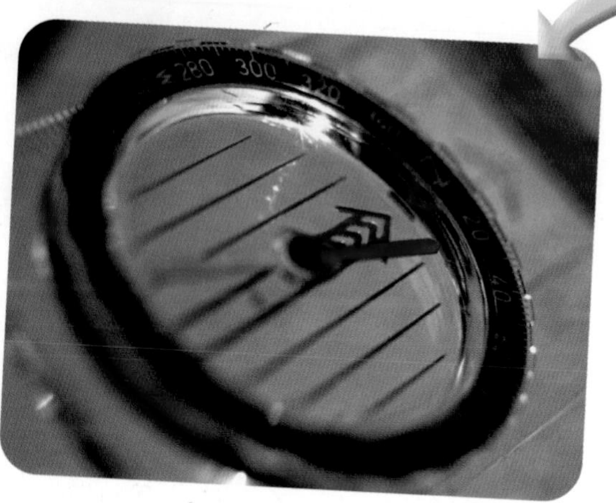

- The north pole points to the north, where the polar bears are.
- The south pole points to the south, where the penguins are.

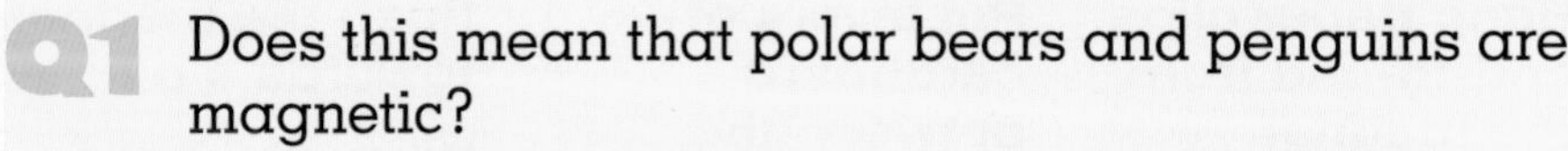

Q1 Does this mean that polar bears and penguins are magnetic?

You can use a compass to help you find your way around. Sailors have used compasses for centuries to help with navigation. When you are out of sight of land, it is useful to know which way is north.

- The north pole of the compass needle is attracted to the Earth's north pole.

Q2 Copy and complete this sentence:
The south pole of the compass needle is attracted to the Earth's . . .

Field lines

The force of a magnet is strongest near the poles. The further away you go, the weaker it gets.

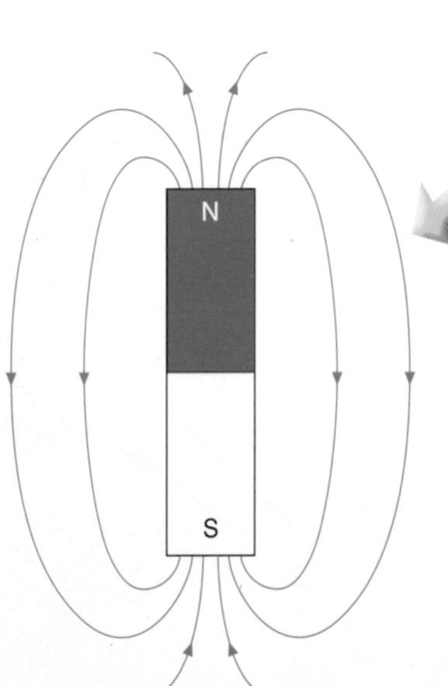

We say that the magnet is surrounded by a **magnetic field**.

To show the magnetic field around a magnet, we draw **magnetic field lines**. These come out of the north pole of a magnet and go round to the south pole.

The diagram shows that the lines are close together at the poles, where the field is strong. They are further apart where the field is weak.

Q3 How does the diagram show that the lines come out of the north pole?

Follow that field

You can use a compass to find out about the field around a magnet.

- Start with a diagram of a magnet, showing its field lines. Place a bar magnet in its correct position on the diagram.
- Put a plotting compass on the paper, near the magnet. Move it around. Does it always point straight towards the pole of the magnet?

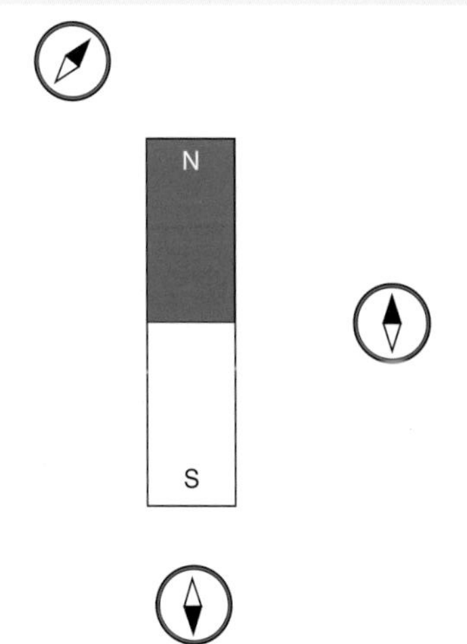

- Now slide the compass slowly along one of the field lines, from the north pole to the south pole. Observe carefully how the compass needle turns as you move it along.

Pigeons can detect the Earth's magnetic field. That's how racing pigeons can find their way home.

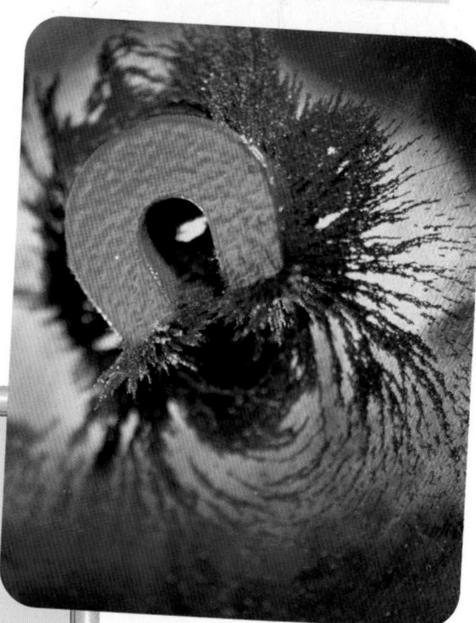

The iron filings help to show up the magnetic field around this horseshoe magnet

SUMMARY QUESTIONS

1 ☆ Copy and complete these sentences:

A compass has a needle which is a small . . .

The needle is free to turn around. The end which points north is its . . . . . .

2 ☆☆ Look at the photo of the horseshoe magnet. Where do you think its poles are? Draw a diagram to show your answer.

3 ☆☆☆ Look at the diagram of the magnetic field lines around two magnets.

a) Is pole X a north pole or a south pole? How do you know?

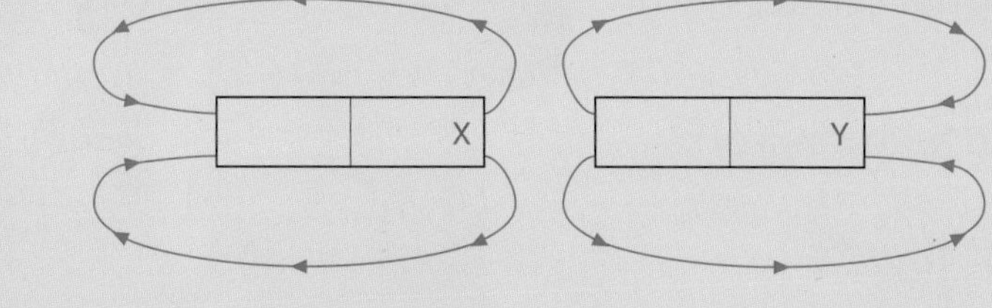

b) Is pole Y a north pole or a south pole? How do you know?

c) How can you tell from the field lines that the magnets are repelling each other?

Key words

compass
magnetic field
magnetic field line
north pole
south pole

Making an electromagnet

LEARN ABOUT
- making electromagnets
- changing the strength of an electromagnet

A magnet with a switch

An electromagnet at work in a steelworks, lifting iron

The photograph shows a very large magnet. It is being used to pick up scraps of iron. It will move the iron to where it is needed, then let it fall.

This is a magnet that can be switched on and off – it is an **electromagnet**. The operator switches on the electric current to the magnet, and it attracts the iron. He switches the current off, and the magnet no longer attracts the iron.

A bar magnet is not an electromagnet; it is a **permanent magnet**.

Q1 Why is an electromagnet better than a permanent magnet for lifting iron at a steelworks?

Making an electromagnet

You can make an electromagnet to experiment with.

- Wind a coil of insulated wire around a wooden rod. Connect the ends of the wire to a power supply.
- When your teacher has checked your circuit, switch on.
  a) Will your electromagnet attract a paper clip?
- Replace the wooden rod with an iron nail.
  b) What effect does this have?

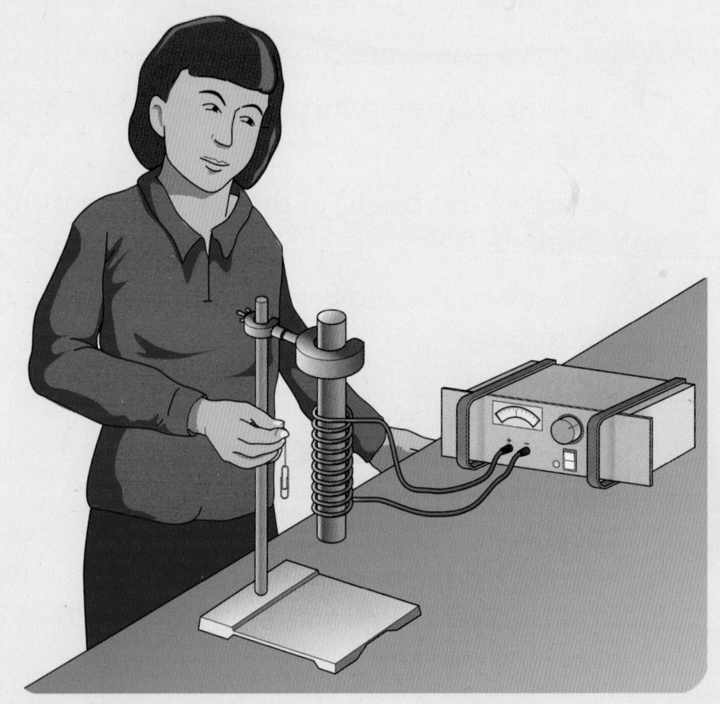

Inside an electromagnet

Every electromagnet is made from a coil of wire. To make the electromagnet work, an electric current must flow through the wire. When the current is switched off, the electromagnet stops working.

Most electromagnets also have a **core** inside the coil. In your experimental electromagnet, the iron nail was the core.

Q2 Suggest a reason why iron is a good material for a core, but wood is not.

Gruesome science

Eye surgeons use an electromagnet to pull metal splinters out of the eyes of patients who have been in car accidents.

Investigating an electromagnet

You have learnt how to make an electromagnet. Your task now is to discover how to make it stronger.

- Here are some things you could try:
  - Changing the current.
  - Using more wire.
  - Using two iron nails instead of one.
  - Pushing the coils of wire closer together.
- Decide which ideas you are going to test. How will you test the strength of the electromagnet?
- When you have planned your investigation, check your ideas with your teacher and carry out your plan.

1 ☆☆ Copy and complete the sentences, using words from the list below.

magnet **coil** **core** **current**

An electromagnet is made from a . . . of wire.

When an electric . . . flows through the wire, it becomes a . . .

It will be stronger if it has an iron . . . inside it.

2 ☆☆ What is the difference between a permanent magnet and an electromagnet?

Key words

core
electromagnet
permanent magnet

Explaining electromagnets

Learn about

- how electromagnets are used
- making an electromagnet stronger
- the magnetic field of an electromagnet

Using electromagnets

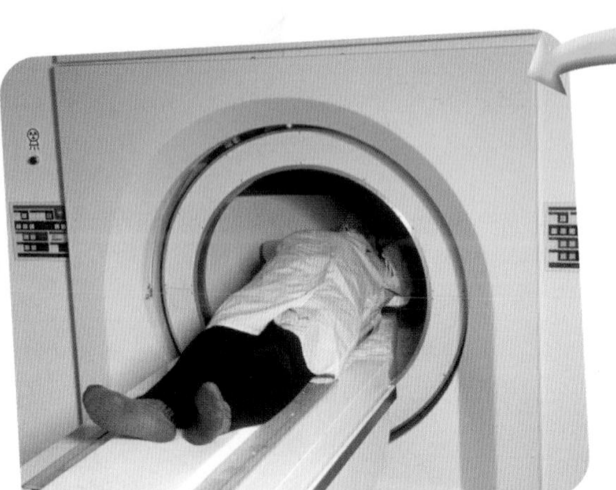

The photograph shows a patient having a scan in a hospital. He has to spend several minutes inside a giant electromagnet. He won't feel a thing!

Electromagnets are also used to sort rubbish. When a dustcart empties its load onto a conveyor belt, an electromagnet is used to pick up all the steel cans.

Q1 Will the electromagnet pick up aluminium cans?

Sorting metals

You can make a model system for sorting metals using an electromagnet. Start by making an electromagnet.

- Wind a coil of wire around an iron nail.
- Connect your coil up to a battery or power supply. (Check with your teacher before switching on.)
- Mix up some small objects – paper clips, coins, pieces of plastic and aluminium. Use your electromagnet to sort out the steel objects.

A stronger magnet

The hospital electromagnet in the photo is very strong. So is the scrapyard electromagnet on page 168. Engineers need to know how to make strong electromagnets.

There are several ways to make an electromagnet stronger. You can:

- Wind more turns of wire.
- Squash the turns of wire more closely together.
- Make a bigger current flow.
- Add an iron **core**.

You probably investigated some of these on page 169.

Remember! The electromagnet is only **magnetised** when it is switched on and the current flows.

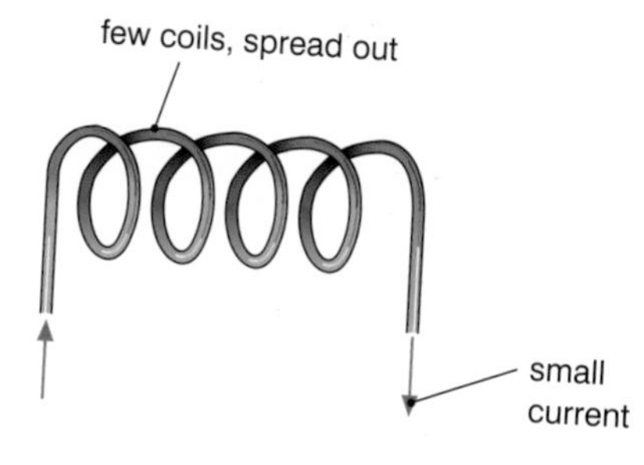

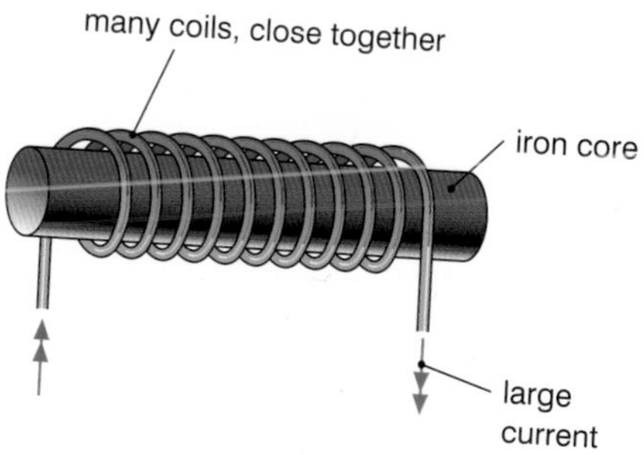

Q2 How can you make a bigger current flow?

The field of an electromagnet

Use a plotting compass to investigate the magnetic field around an electromagnet.

- Hold a compass close to the electromagnet. Move it around. Which way does it point?
- Try to answer these questions:
  a) Does an electromagnet have poles like a bar magnet?
  b) What happens if you swap over the connections to the power supply?

SUMMARY QUESTIONS

1 ☆ Copy and complete the sentence below.

You can make an electromagnet stronger by increasing the c... flowing through it, or by adding an iron c...

2 ☆☆ Make a list of different uses for electromagnets. (Start by looking at pages 168–171.) List as many different uses as you can.

Key words

core
magnetised

The Earth's magnetism

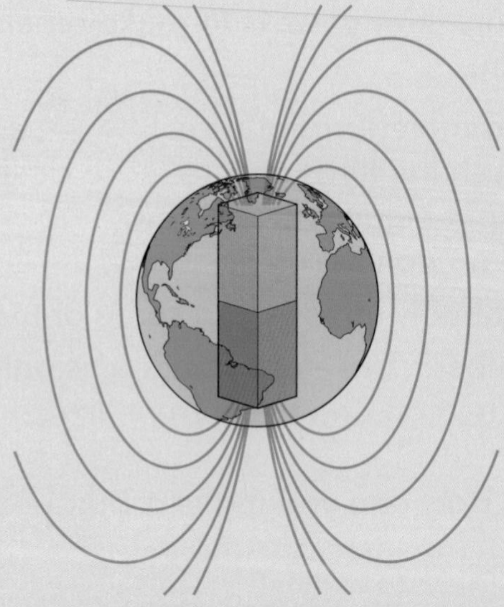

Getting around

Two thousand five hundred years ago, people living in China discovered a type of rock called **lodestone**, which is a natural magnet. (It contains iron oxide.) To make a compass, they put a piece of lodestone on a cork that was floating in a dish of water. It would turn towards the south. That was important, because many Chinese ships sailed south to trade.

By 1000 AD, the Chinese had discovered how to make magnetic compass needles by stroking steel wire with a piece of lodestone.

European sailors learned about compasses from Chinese sailors, but they didn't really understand how they worked. For a long time, people thought that a magnetic compass needle was attracted to the Pole Star, the star which can be seen due north in the sky.

In the 16th century, William Gilbert, an English doctor, was interested in magnets because they seemed to have magical properties. He realised why compasses behave as they do. The Earth is itself a giant magnet.

The Earth has a magnetic field like the field of a bar magnet. That is why sailors can use a compass to find their way around.

This picture is from William Gilbert's book about magnetism, published in 1600. It shows a blacksmith hammering an iron rod to magnetise it.

Today, satellites orbit the Earth, measuring its magnetic field. Scientists **publish** their ideas about the Earth's field in **scientific journals**, so that anyone can read them. A thousand years ago, people knew little about the scientific ideas of people in another part of the world. That's why it was possible for the Chinese to know about compasses and the Earth's magnetism for centuries before Europeans discovered it for themselves.

These are the four Cluster satellites which monitor the Earth's magnetic field. They warn us of magnetic storms from the Sun, which might affect our electricity supply.

- Magnetic materials are those which are attracted by a magnet.
- To test a magnet, see if it is repelled by another magnet.
- Opposite poles attract, like poles repel.
- Around a magnet is its magnetic field.
- We draw magnetic field lines to represent a magnetic field.
- An electromagnet is a coil of wire with a current flowing in it.
- More current, more turns of wire and an iron core make a stronger electromagnet.

DANGER! AVOID THESE COMMON ERRORS

Don't get confused about the Earth's magnetism. It's nothing to do with gravity.

- The Earth is a massive object, and its gravity attracts anything. The force of its attraction is what we call 'weight'.
- The Earth is also a giant magnet. Magnets will only attract magnetic materials.

So it isn't magnetism that makes us stick to the Earth, but gravity.

Key words

lodestone
publish
scientific journals

UNIT REVIEW

REVIEW QUESTIONS

Understanding and applying concepts

1 The diagrams show pairs of magnets. Think about how their poles are attracting and repelling each other.

Copy the diagrams. Add an arrow to each pole to show the force acting on it.

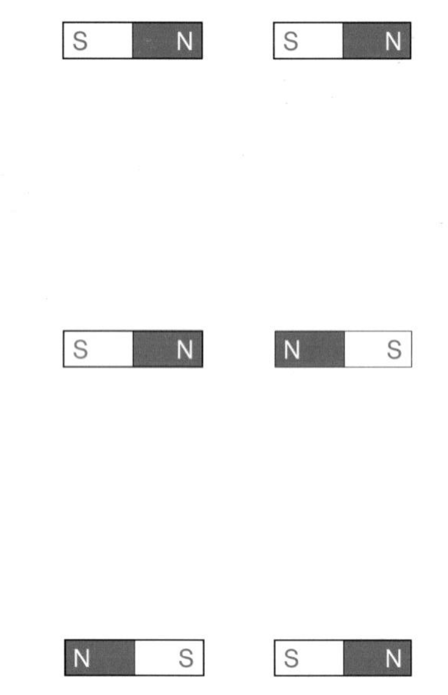

2 Pip made an electromagnet by winding ten turns of wire onto a wooden rod. She connected up to a power supply and switched on.

Which of these things would make the electromagnet stronger? Which would make it weaker? Which would have no effect?

- Winding ten more turns of wire (in the same direction as before).
- Replacing the wooden rod with a plastic core.
- Reducing the voltage of the power supply.

Ways with words

3 You have been studying magnetism – everything to do with magnets and magnetic fields. You will have used several words that sound very similar – don't get them confused!

Can you explain the difference between *magnetic* and *magnetised*? For example, what is the difference between saying that iron is a magnetic material, and that a piece of iron is magnetised?

Making more of maths

4 A graph can help to show a relationship between two quantities that you have measured.

Look at the three graph shapes, and decide which one would help to show each of these relationships:

- **a** The more turns of wire on an electromagnet, the greater its strength.
- **b** As you increase the current through an electromagnet, its strength increases.
- **c** As you push one south pole towards another south pole, the force between them increases.

For each example, copy the graph and label the x and *y* axes with the quantities each represents.

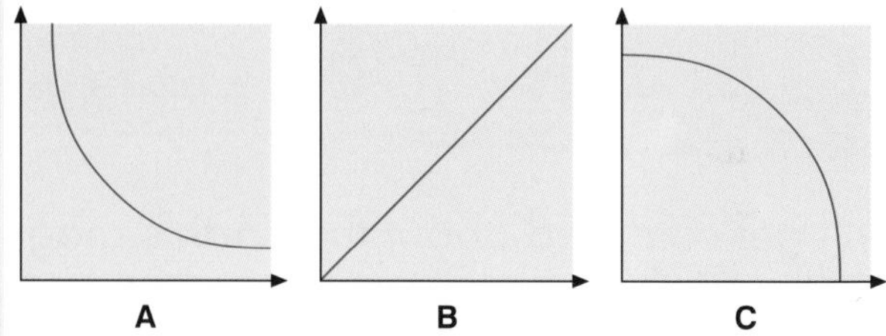

Thinking skills

5 Some paper clips are coloured. They are made from steel with a coloured plastic covering. You can attract one with a magnet, without even touching it.

Which *four* of the following statements do we need to use to explain this?

- There is a magnetic field around a magnet.
- Like poles repel each other.
- Magnetic force can pass through plastic.
- Magnetic force cannot pass through steel.
- A magnet has two poles, north and south.
- Steel is a magnetic material.
- A magnet can attract an object made from a magnetic material.

SAT-STYLE QUESTIONS

1 Pete was investigating a steel bar magnet. His teacher gave him a second steel bar. The magnet attracted the steel bar.

a What does this tell you about steel? (2)

Pete wrapped the magnet in a piece of cloth, and then brought it close to the steel bar.

b Would the magnet still attract the bar? Explain your answer. (2)

Pete's teacher asked him to find out if the second steel bar was a magnet.

c How could Pete do this? Explain your idea clearly. (2)

Then the teacher gave him some steel paper clips. Pete put the magnet into the paper clips.

d What would you expect to happen? (1)

2 Molly made a coil of wire, which she connected up to a power supply and a switch to make an electromagnet. She used an iron rod inside the coil, as a core.

a Explain why Molly put a core in her electromagnet. (1)

b Molly held a compass close to her electromagnet. When she switched the power supply on, the compass needle turned round and pointed at the end of the coil. What would happen if she turned the power supply off again? (1)

c Where are the poles of Molly's electromagnet? (1)

d If Molly repeated the experiment using a wooden rod instead of an iron one, what difference would she observe? (2)

3 Benson has been experimenting with three bar magnets. He put them in a line, as shown in the drawing:

He found that magnet B was attracted by magnet A, but was repelled by magnet C.

a Copy the diagram, and add arrows to show:
- the magnetic force on magnet A.
- the two magnetic forces on magnet B.
- the magnetic force on magnet C. (4)

In the diagram, the north pole of magnet A is marked with a dot.

b On your diagram, label the north and south poles of each magnet. (2)

Benson turned magnet B round the other way.

c Was magnet B attracted or repelled by magnet A? (1)

d Was magnet B attracted or repelled by magnet C? (1)

Key words

Unscramble these:
cemating
grantmecleeto
menparent
doloneets
spamsoc

8K
Light

Coming soon

Never buy a cheap laser!

What's it all about?

Our eyes are important to us. They gather the light that allows us to see the world around us. Roughly 80% of the information that comes into our brains comes from our eyes. If our eyes don't work well, our other senses try to take over.

Our eyes can tell us lots of things about what we are looking at. What colour is it? Does it have straight edges? Is it smooth and shiny or rough and dull? Is it transparent or does it block light? Does it have a shadow?

Young children, and people who don't think scientifically, think that our eyes can just do this. But if you are prepared to think like a scientist, you can understand how the light entering our eyes can tell us all this information about the world out there.

What do you remember?

You already know about:

- how shadows are formed.
- how light is reflected by shiny surfaces.
- how we see things.

1 What is formed when light is blocked?

curtains an eclipse
a reflection a shadow

2 Which word describes an object that makes its own light?

black luminous
non-luminous the Sun

3 When you look at a shiny surface, you see . . .

a bright light
a reflection
a shadow
straight through

4 You see things when light enters:

the room
the window
your brain
your eyes

Seeing the light

QUESTIONS

Look around you. Do you feel as if your eyes are like searchlights, scanning the room? Perhaps you have seen the eyes of animals at night, seeming to glow in the dark as you drive by.

You already know about how we see things.

a) How do we see luminous objects?

b) How do we see non-luminous objects?

You can see your eyes if you look in a mirror.

c) Can you draw a diagram to explain this?

How light travels

LEARN ABOUT
- light rays
- the speed of light

Laser light

You may have seen a laser light show at a pop concert or in the theatre. A **laser** is a useful **source** of light because it gives a narrow, bright **beam**.

A beam of light from a laser being used to monitor pollution near an American city. The more dust there is in the air, the more the beam shows up.

The photo shows another use for lasers – monitoring pollution. We can see the laser beam because the air is polluted with gas and dust. If the air were clean, the laser light would not show up.

The photo shows an important thing about light – it travels in **straight lines**. You would be very surprised if the laser light in the photograph went round in a circle.

Q1 Where else have you seen straight beams of light like this?

Lines of light

Try out some simple activities with light. For each one, try to say why 'light travels in straight lines' is part of the explanation.

- Take a length of rubber tubing. Try to look through it, from one end to the other.
- Make a pinhole in the middle of each of two pieces of paper. Can you line them up so that you can see light through them?
- Make the light from a ray box travel along the edge of a ruler.
- Use a piece of wood to block half the light from a ray box. Does the shadow have a straight edge?
- Reflect the beam of light from a ray box off a mirror. Does the beam remain straight?

Light travels at a speed of 300 000 000 metres per second (m/s).

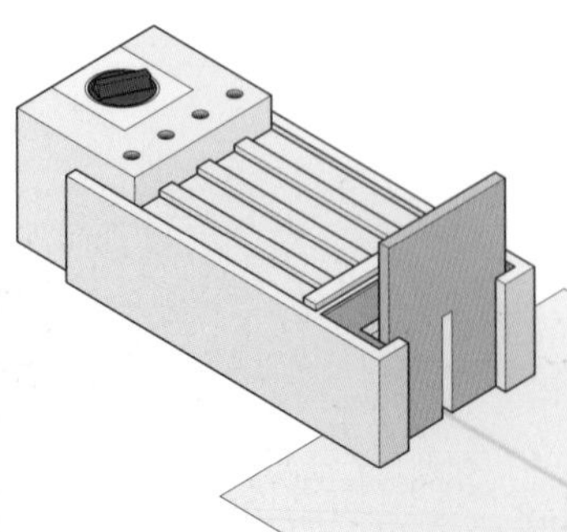

A ray box produces a narrow beam of light. You'll find out how to use one in this unit.

Seeing the light

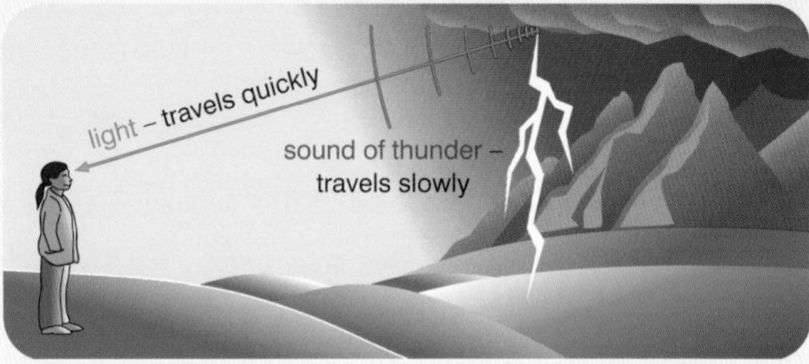

Here's an odd thing you may have noticed. You see a flash of lightning, and you hear the rumble of thunder a few seconds later. This happens because light travels much faster than sound. They set off towards you at the same time, but the light of the flash gets to you first, before the sound of the thunder.

Here's how to work out how far away the storm is:

- When you see the lightning flash, start counting in seconds.
- One second – two seconds – three seconds – four seconds . . .
- Stop when you hear the thunder.
- If you counted three seconds, the storm is 1 kilometre away. If you counted six seconds, the storm is 2 kilometres away.

Q2 If the storm is 3 kilometres away, how many seconds will you count?

As fast as can be

Astronauts have visited the Moon. It took them several days to get there, and several days to get back. Light travels much faster than a spaceship. It takes light less than a second and a half to travel from the Moon to the Earth.

The Sun is much farther away than the Moon. It takes light over 8 minutes to get here from the Sun. And the next star is so distant that it takes light four years to reach us here on Earth.

For all we know, the Sun may have stopped shining 7 minutes ago. In one minute from now, it will go very dark!

SUMMARY QUESTIONS

1 ☆ Copy and complete the sentences, using words from the list below.

quickly **straight lines** **ray box**

Light travels in . . . . . .

Light travels very . . .

In the lab, we use a . . . . . . to make a beam of light.

2 ☆☆ As you are driving along, you come to a road tunnel. You cannot see daylight at the other end. What does this tell you about the tunnel?

3 ☆☆☆ If you watch a hockey match or a cricket match, you may notice this: you see someone hit the ball, then, a fraction of a second later, you hear the ball being hit. Can you explain why you don't see and hear the hit at the same time?

Key words

beam
laser
source
straight lines

Passing through

LEARN ABOUT
- how light is transmitted, reflected and absorbed

Seeing through glass

We look through windows every day, but we don't usually think about the glass they are made of. Glass is great for windows because it is stiff and strong, and it lets light through. We say that glass **transmits** light. It is **transparent**.

There are different types of glass. Some glass is frosted, so that some light is transmitted, but you cannot get a clear picture of what's on the other side. A material like this is called **translucent**.

Q1 If you write on one side of a sheet of paper and then hold it up to the light, you may be able to read the writing from the other side. Is paper transparent or translucent?

Transmitting light

- How good is glass? Does it let through all of the light that falls on it?
- The picture shows one way of testing this. Put an electronic light meter on the bench near the window. Put a piece of glass over the sensor. Does the reading change?
- Investigate some other pieces of transparent and translucent materials. How much of the light gets through?

Reflections

Shop windows can work like giant mirrors. That's because the glass **reflects** some of the light that falls on it.

Absorption

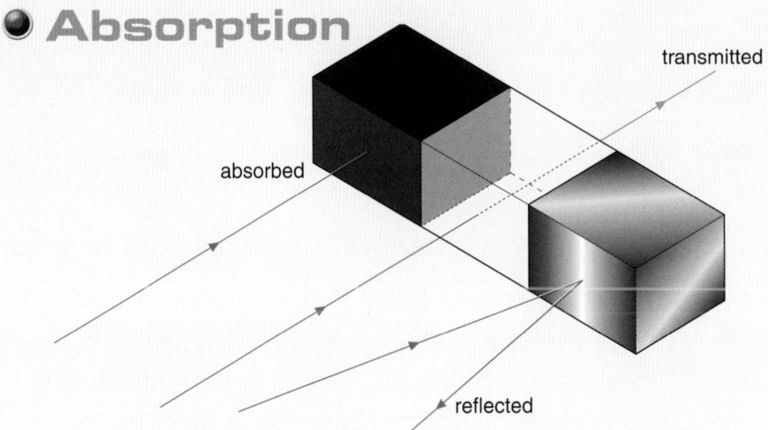

Think about a dull, black object. It doesn't let light through, so we describe it as **opaque**. It doesn't reflect light either. The light that falls on a dull black object disappears – it has been **absorbed**.

So there are three things that can happen when light falls on something:

- it can pass straight through – that's **transmission**.
- it can bounce off it – that's **reflection**.
- it disappears – that's **absorption**.

Q2 How could you find out which materials are best at absorbing light? (Think about how you could use a light sensor for this.)

Reflecting light

- Extend your study of what happens when light hits different materials. Can you use a light sensor to detect reflected light?
- Does a mirror reflect 100% of the light that falls on it? What about other materials, such as aluminium foil, white paper and coloured paper?

SUMMARY QUESTIONS

1 ☆ Look at this list of materials:

aluminium foil **water** **black paper**
glass **a mirror** **soil**

Which of these are:

a) good at transmitting light?
b) good at reflecting light?
c) good at absorbing light?

2 ☆☆ Copy the table and complete the first column using words from the list

absorption **reflection** **transmission**

	Light bouncing off the surface of an object.
	Light passing through an object.
	What happens to light which isn't reflected or transmitted.

Key words

absorption
opaque
reflection
translucent
transmission
transparent

Seeing things

LEARN ABOUT

- how we see things
- drawing ray diagrams

The eyes of creatures which hunt at night have large pupils, to collect as much light as possible

Seeing in black and white

Look at your eye in a mirror. In the centre is the **pupil**. It is very black.

The pupil of your eye is the hole through which light enters. It lets light in, but none comes back out.

When light reaches the back of your eye, a tiny **image** is formed of what you are looking at. An image is like a tiny picture. Your brain receives messages about the image. What goes on inside your brain is much harder to explain!

Q1 Does the pupil absorb, reflect or transmit light?

Believing about seeing

What do you do when you want to see something? You move your eyes around so that the light from the thing you want to look at will enter your pupils. The drawing shows this, using **rays** of light.

- We see a **luminous** object because rays travel directly from the object into our eyes.
- We see a **non-luminous** object because it reflects rays of light, and they enter our eyes.

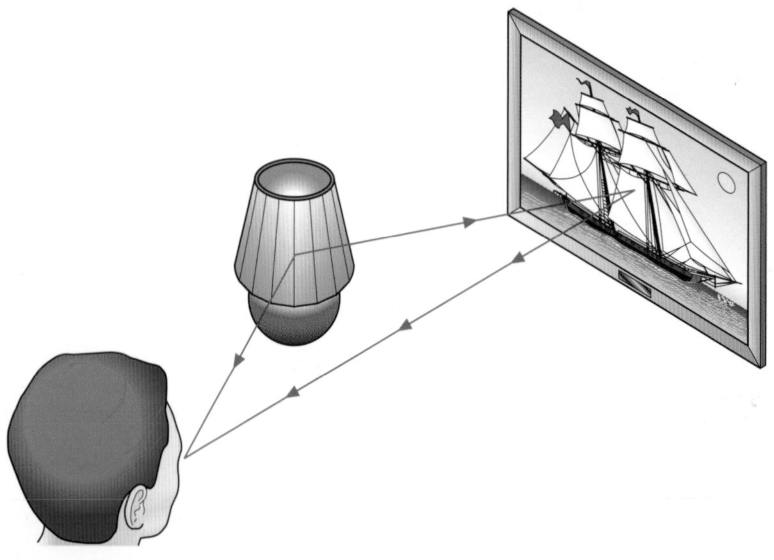

ICT CHALLENGE

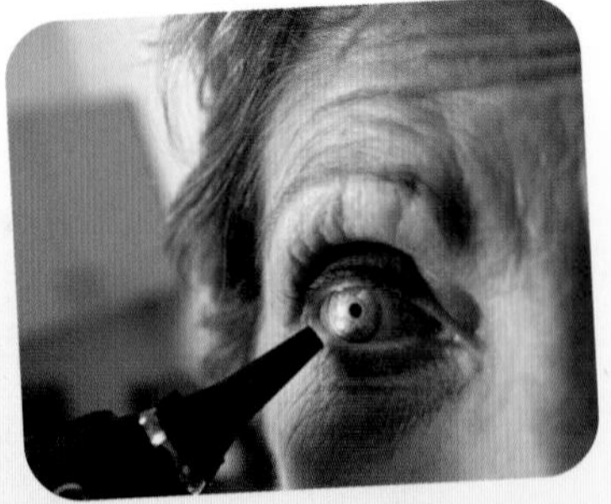

Search the Internet or a CD-ROM encyclopaedia to find out what an optician looks for during an eye examination.

Drawing rays of light

The picture on the opposite page shows how we see things. It shows the rays that tell the story of how we see the light bulb and the ship:

- One ray travels straight from the light bulb to the eye.
- One ray travels from the light bulb and reflects off the ship to the eye.

These tell us all we need to know. They make up a **ray diagram**.

Ray Diagram? Sounds like he should join the Scientifica crew!

Drawing rays of light

Use a ray box to make different patterns of light on a piece of paper.

- Make a single ray travel across the paper. Use a pencil to mark three dots along the ray. Use your ruler to draw a line through the dots, showing where the ray went.
- Put a mirror in the path of the ray. See how the mirror reflects the ray. Change the angle of the mirror and watch how the reflected ray changes.
- Mark the position of the mirror by drawing a line along the back of it. Mark the position of the ray before and after it has been reflected, and draw the ray.
- Adjust your ray box so that it makes three rays. Make them reflect off the mirror. What pattern do you see?

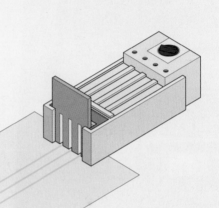

SUMMARY QUESTIONS

1 ☆ Which word means the picture that is formed at the back of your eye?

diagram **image** **pupil** **retina**

2 ☆☆ Copy these sentences, choosing the correct words from each pair:

A book is a ***luminous/non-luminous*** object.

A television screen is a ***luminous/non-luminous*** object.

3 ☆☆☆ Draw two ray diagrams:

- to show how, on a sunny day, you can read a book.
- to show how you can see a TV programme.

Key words

image
luminous
non-luminous
pupil
ray
ray diagram

Mirrors

LEARN ABOUT
- how mirrors reflect light
- how images are formed
- predicting where reflected rays go

Back-to-front

Why does an ambulance have this on the front?

AMBULANCE (mirror writing)

A driver in front will see this in his rear-view mirror, and it will appear the right way round. An image in a mirror (a reflection) is **inverted**.

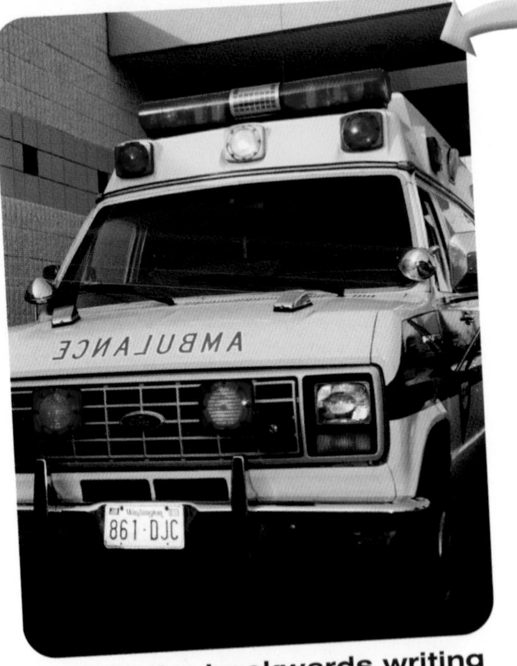

Look at the backwards writing on the front of this ambulance. Could we have printed this photo the wrong way round? Can you tell?

Q1 If you look at yourself in a mirror and wave your right hand, which hand does your reflection wave?

Flatter than paper

Mirrors are special. They are excellent reflectors of light.

A sheet of white paper reflects light, too. That's why it's white. However, there is a difference – you can't see a reflection of yourself in a sheet of paper.

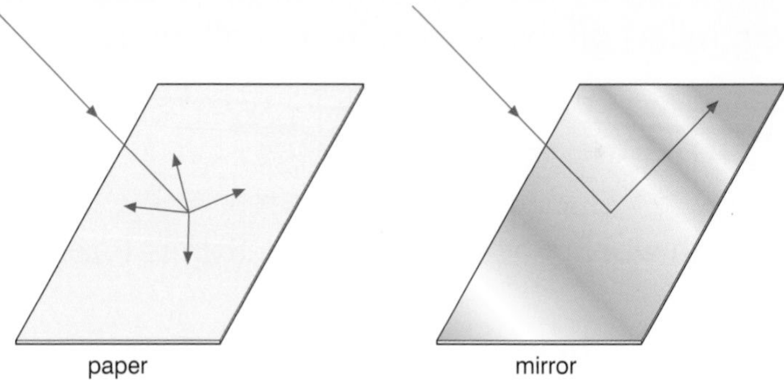

The diagrams show the difference.

- White paper has a rough surface. It reflects light in all directions.
- A mirror has a very smooth surface. A ray of light bounces off it without spreading out.

A ray of light bounces off a mirror at the same angle as it strikes it.

Reflecting rays

You can investigate how light rays are reflected. Shine a ray of light from a ray box at a small mirror.

- Mark the ray before it is reflected.
- Mark the ray after it is reflected.
- Mark the position of the mirror's reflecting surface.
  a) What angles will you measure and record?
  b) What will you alter?
- Present your results as a graph.
  c) What pattern does it show?

mirror

Modelling light

Snooker balls bounce off the side of the table just like light off a mirror. Players use this idea when they are working out where a ball will go.

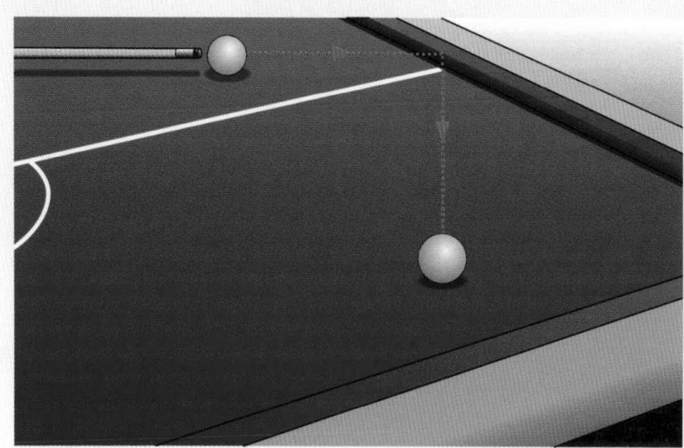

So, in some ways, light behaves like snooker balls.

- Light travels in straight lines, and so do snooker balls.
- Light and snooker balls show the same pattern when they reflect.

We can say that snooker balls are a **model** for the way light behaves.

SUMMARY QUESTIONS

1 ☆ Which word describes a back-to-front image?

2 ☆☆ Look at the diagrams which show rays of light reflecting off mirrors. Which ones show correctly how light is reflected by a mirror?

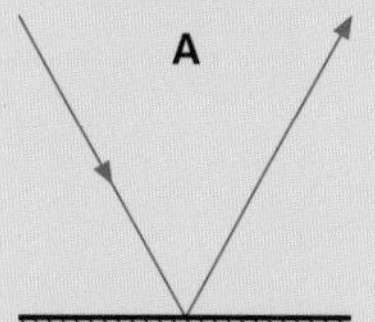

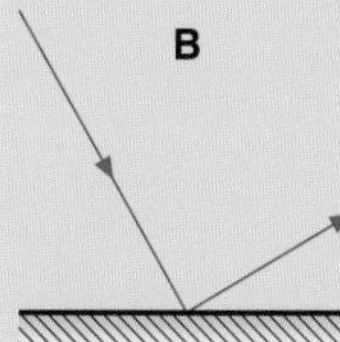

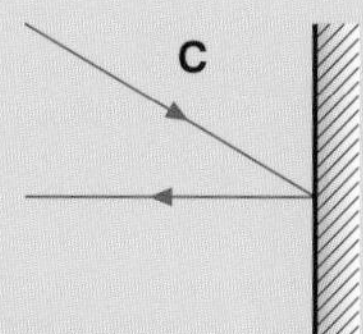

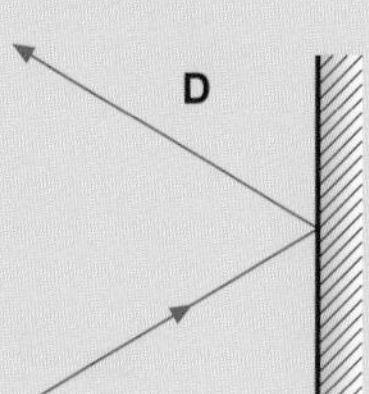

3 ☆☆ Set up two mirrors at right angles, as shown.
Look at yourself in this double mirror.
Try winking your right eye.
What do you notice? Try to explain what you see.

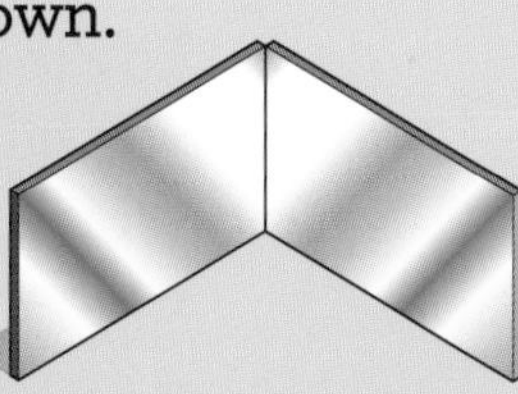

Key words
inverted
model

Refracting light

LEARN ABOUT
- bending light rays
- making a spectrum

A trick of the light

You can see lots of weird effects when light travels through something transparent, like glass or water. Fill a glass tumbler with water and look at the world through it. Everything becomes distorted. It makes you glad that you're not a goldfish in a bowl.

You have learned that light travels in straight lines. Mirrors make light rays change direction. Now you can find out another way of making light rays bend – by making them pass through a glass block.

Changing direction

- Use a ray box and a glass block. Place the block as shown, and shine a ray of light through it. Turn the block to different angles.

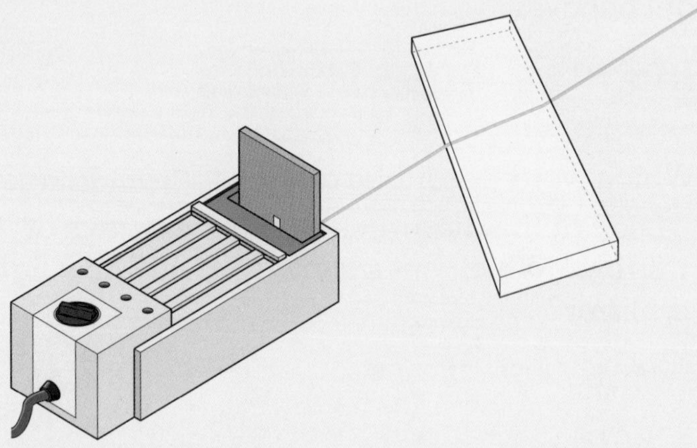

- The ray of light changes direction; this is called **refraction**.
- Lay the block down flat, and draw around it. Mark the ray before it goes into the block, and after it comes out. Now remove the block and draw in the complete path of the ray.
- Try again with the block at a different angle.

Bending one way, bending the other way

A ray of light doesn't change direction when it is travelling inside glass. It only changes direction when it goes in, and when it comes out.

When it goes in, it bends one way. When it comes out, it bends the other way.

Q1 When the ray of light comes out of the glass block, is it back on its original path?

Colours from nowhere

If you look at a beautiful diamond in a ring, you may notice that the diamond sparkles with different colours. The diamond is colourless. So where do these wonderful colours come from?

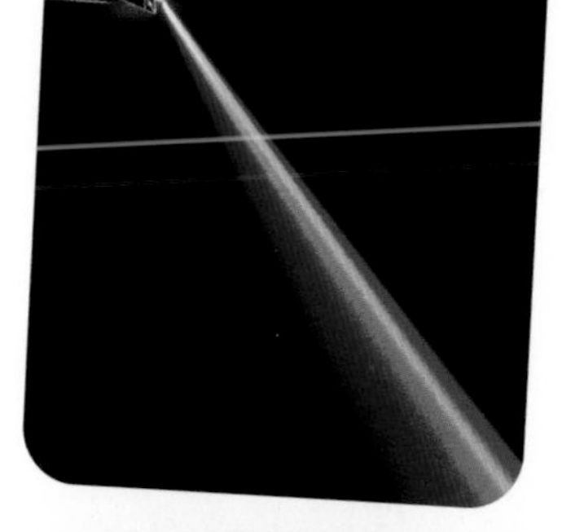

It's refraction again. You may have noticed that when you shone a ray of light into a glass block it split up into different colours. These are the colours of the rainbow:

red orange yellow green blue indigo violet

When light is split up like this, we say that a **spectrum** has been formed.

Looking at a spectrum

- Use a triangular block (a **prism**) to split a ray of white light into a spectrum. Which colour of light is refracted (bent) the most?

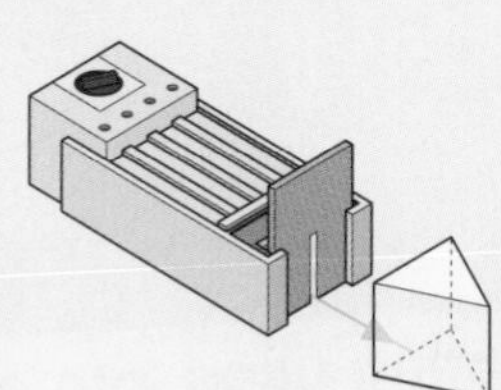

SUMMARY QUESTIONS

1 ☆ A ray of light changes direction when it goes into glass. This is called

a prism reflection refraction a spectrum

2 ☆☆ Which of these diagrams shows correctly how a ray of light is refracted by a glass block?

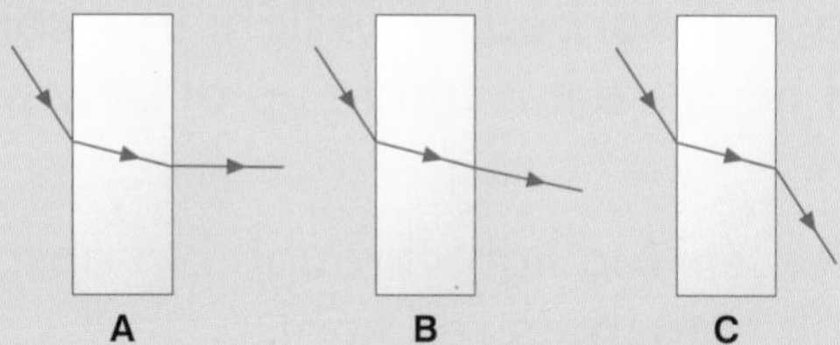

3 ☆ **a)** Which colours are at the two ends of the spectrum?
b) Which colour comes between orange and green?

Key words

prism
refraction
spectrum

Changing colours

LEARN ABOUT
- coloured filters
- transmitting, reflecting, and absorbing colours

Shades of colour

If it's a bright day, you may wear sunglasses. The lenses may be coloured, and that can make everything you see change colour. How does that happen?

It's better to say that the 'lenses' are **filters**. A filter is a device that lets some things through but stops others. So what does a coloured filter let through? Find out with the activity that follows.

Filtering light

- Look through some coloured filters at a white light. What colour is the light that comes through each one?
- Now try shining a ray of light through each coloured filter. What colour is the light when it falls on white paper?
- Try putting two filters together. Why does the light get dimmer when you use more filters?

Stage lighting uses lots of coloured filters

Absorbing and transmitting colours

White light is made up of all of the colours of the spectrum. When you shine it through a coloured filter, some of the colours are **absorbed**. The light that comes through is coloured because it is made up of only part of the spectrum.

A red filter lets red light through but absorbs all the other colours. It **transmits** red light.

Q1 Does a red filter absorb or transmit blue light? Does a blue filter absorb or transmit red light?

Supermarkets have special lighting to make the fruit and vegetables look bright and colourful.

Seeing true colours

When choosing new clothes, you may have taken them to the door of the shop to see what they look like in daylight, when white light falls on them. The lighting in the shop may be yellowish, so the clothes don't show their true colours.

- A red object looks red when white light falls on it, because it reflects only red light – it absorbs all the other colours.
- If you shine green light on a red object, it will look black. It absorbs the green light. There is no red light for it to reflect.

To work out what colours will be seen, first decide what colours of light are being shone on an object. Then decide which colours will be **absorbed**, and which will be **reflected**.

A red tomato with white light shining on it

A red tomato with red light shining on it

A red tomato with green light shining on it

Coloured views

- Try shining different colours of light, including white light, onto different objects.
- Now repeat the experiment, but look through a coloured filter. Can you discover any surprising effects?
- Try drawing a multicoloured picture with felt pens, and then look at it through filters. Can you make a game or puzzle using these ideas?

These spectacles have filters of different colours. What might they be used for?

SUMMARY QUESTIONS

1 ☆ Which word from the list means the same as 'lets through'?

absorbs **filters** **reflects** **transmits**

2 ☆ Copy these sentences, choosing the correct words:

A red filter transmits ***red/blue*** light.

A red filter absorbs ***red/blue*** light.

3 ☆☆ What colour will a blue book appear if you shine these different colours of light on it?

white **blue** **red**

Key words

absorb
filter
reflect
transmit

Using science today

Have you ever seen a laser light show at a concert? A laser is an unusual source of light. It is different from a light bulb in two ways:

- its light comes out in a narrow beam
- its light is of just one colour.

If you shine a laser beam through a prism, it won't be split up into a spectrum because there is just one colour there.

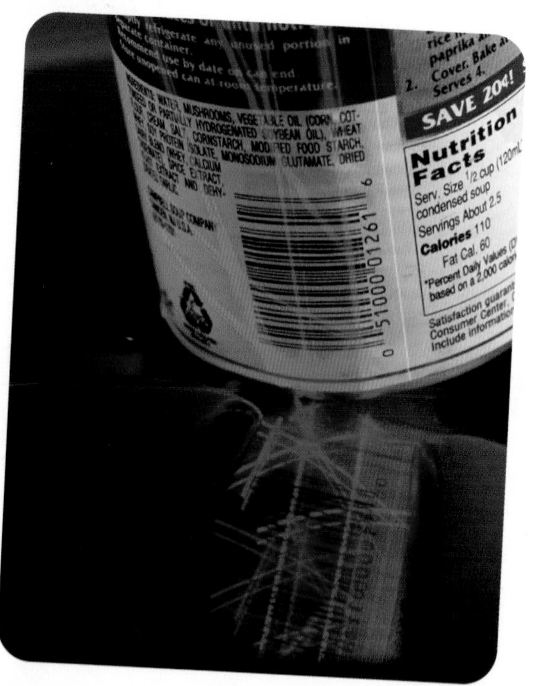

Supermarket check-outs use lasers in two ways. One is in the bar-code reader – you may have noticed the bright red light that reflects off shiny objects as they are scanned.

The other laser is used to stop the moving belt as your purchases are carried along it. At one side of the belt there is a small hole. A beam of laser light shines through this, across the belt to a detector at the other side. When an item breaks the beam, the belt automatically stops.

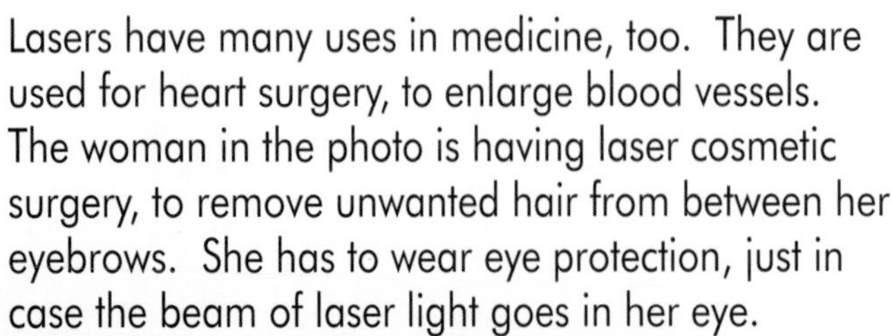

Lasers have many uses in medicine, too. They are used for heart surgery, to enlarge blood vessels. The woman in the photo is having laser cosmetic surgery, to remove unwanted hair from between her eyebrows. She has to wear eye protection, just in case the beam of laser light goes in her eye.

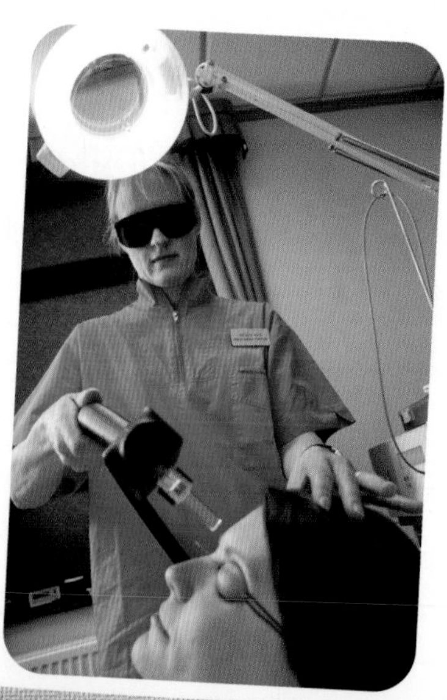

- Light travels very fast, in straight lines.
- Objects may reflect, absorb or transmit light.
- We see non-luminous objects when they reflect light into our eyes.
- A ray of light is refracted when it passes into or out of a transparent material.
- White light can be split up into a spectrum, showing all the colours it is made of.

DANGER! AVOID THESE COMMON ERRORS

It's easy to think that, when light passes through a coloured filter, some colour is *added to* the light, but that's wrong. White light is made up of all the colours of the spectrum. The filter *absorbs* some of these colours, leaving coloured rays of light.

In the same way, a red object doesn't add redness to the light. It looks red because it *reflects* red light and absorbs all of the other colours that fall on it.

Key words

laser
model
particles
prism
waves

UNIT REVIEW

REVIEW QUESTIONS

Understanding and applying concepts

1 **a** What colours make up the spectrum of white light? Give their names in the correct order, starting with *red*.

b Can you name any colours that are not in the spectrum?

2 Imagine that you are looking at the cover of a blue book.

a What colour will the book appear if you shine red light on it?

b What colour will the book appear if you shine blue light on it?

c What colour will the book appear if you shine white light on it, and look at it through a red filter?

Ways with words

3 Copy the table. Put a single word in each empty box. (Hint: the words all begin with re– and end with –tion.)

	Light changing direction when it bounces off something.
	Light changing direction when it travels into glass.

4 It is useful to remember the colours of the spectrum, in the right order. Some people just remember the name Roy G. Biv. Make up your own way of remembering them.

A rainbow shows all of the colours of the spectrum

5 Sometimes when we talk about a *reflection*, we mean 'what we see when we look in a mirror'. Give another word we could use for this. (Hint: it begins with 'i'.)

Making more of maths

6 Molly and Reese carried out an experiment on reflection. They shone a ray of light at a mirror (like the experiment on page 184). They altered the position of the mirror, and for each position they recorded two rays, as shown.

The diagram also shows the two angles, which their teacher asked them to measure. These are called the *angle of incidence* and the *angle of reflection*. The table shows their results.

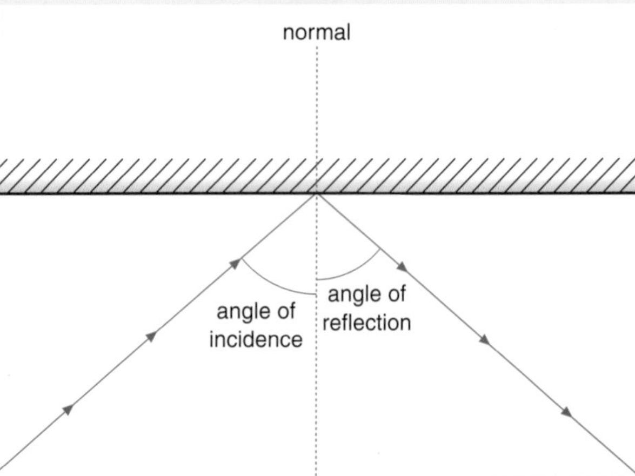

Draw a graph to show their results, and help them to decide: is the angle of reflection always equal to the angle of incidence? Why is drawing a graph a better way of looking at this data than simply using a table?

Angle of incidence	Angle of reflection
10°	10°
18°	20°
40°	39°
60°	61°
70°	72°

Thinking skills

7 Here is a list of words. They all have something to do with what happens when light hits an object.

Read the list, then draw a map or chart to show how you think the words might be connected to each other.

Be ready to explain your map to the rest of the class.

absorb reflect translucent transmit transparent opaque shadow

SAT-STYLE QUESTIONS

1 Reese shone a ray of white light at a prism, and saw a spectrum on a piece of white card.

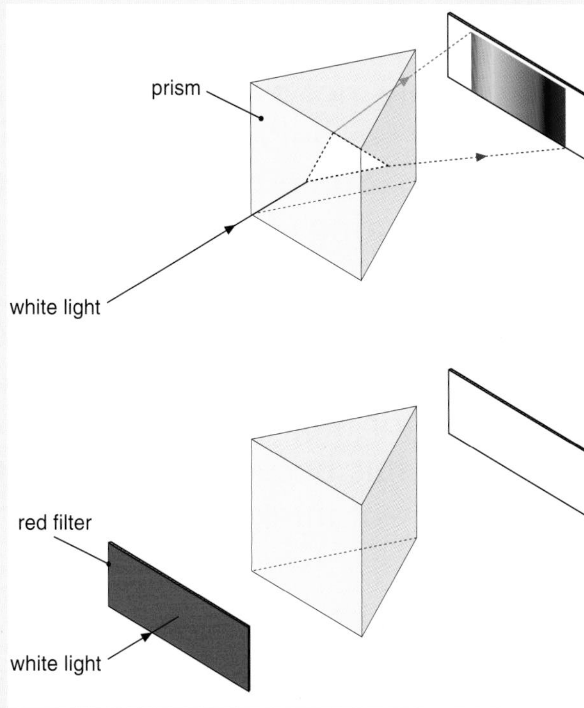

a She put a red filter in the path of the ray of light, as shown in the second diagram. Describe how the appearance of the spectrum would change. (1)

b She then put the filter between the prism and the white card. What would she see on the card? (1)

c Explain why Reese used a piece of *white* card in this experiment. (1)

2 The diagram shows a ray of light shining onto a flat mirror.

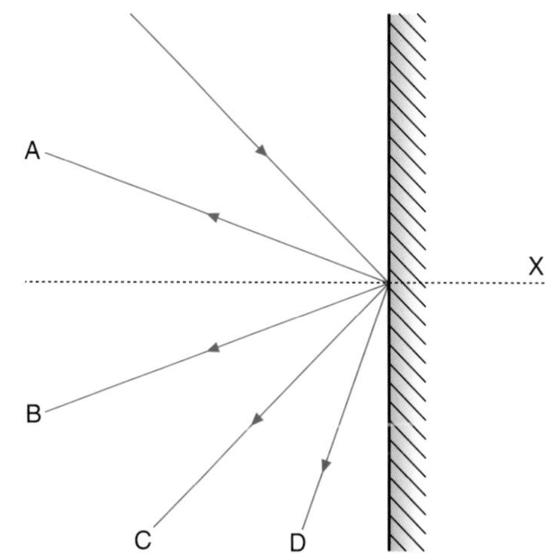

a Which of the rays (A, B, C or D) shows correctly the path of the ray after it has been reflected by the mirror? (1)

b Copy the diagram, and mark two angles which are equal. (1)

3 Benson is experimenting with a glass block. He shines a narrow ray of light at it. He tries different positions of the glass block.

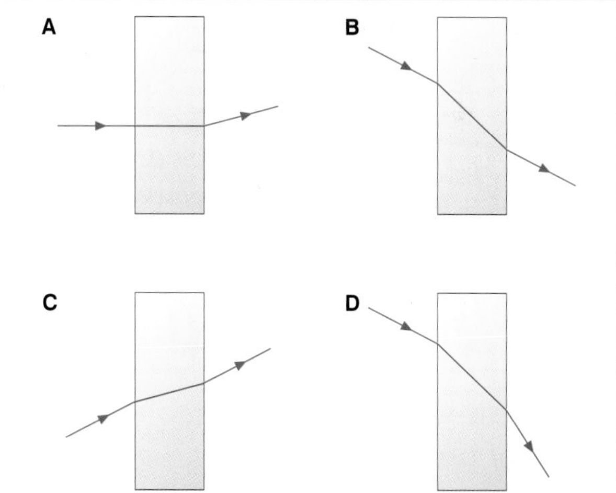

For each of the diagrams, say whether it shows correctly how the ray could have behaved. (4)

Key words

Unscramble these:
flecter
crafter
quepoa
clanternuts
marttins

8L

Sound and hearing

Coming soon

SCHOOL BUS
Yes, sound definitely does travel through the ground!

What's it all about?

Hearing is a remarkable sense. When you hear someone speak, you can guess all sorts of things about them – young or old, male or female, are they indoors or outdoors, and so on.

Unfortunately, not everyone has perfect hearing. As we get older, our hearing deteriorates. Some people are born with poor hearing, or they may be totally deaf.

Scientists and engineers have developed many ways of detecting and measuring sound, and for improving hearing. They can only do this because they have a scientific way of thinking about sound.

What do you remember?

You already know about:

- ways of producing sounds.
- sound travelling through different materials.
- the difference between pitch and loudness.
- changing the sound made by some musical instruments.

1 How do we detect sounds?
eyes ears nose mouth

2 Which makes the highest note?
dog elephant lion mouse

3 Which word means how high or low a note is?
height loudness pitch vibration

4 How does a source of sound move?
doesn't move
goes round and round
moves very slowly
vibrates

The Scientificalifragilistics

This really loud music is good exercise for your hearing.

Yes, afterwards your ears are too tired to hear faint sounds.

The harder I hit the drum, the higher the note.

TWANG!!!

If I tighten this a little more, I'll get really loud notes.

QUESTIONS

Making music together can be fun. Each instrument has a part to play, and each player must know how to make different notes.

a) How does the sound change if you hit a drum harder?

b) How many ways can you think of to change the note made by a guitar?

c) How do other instruments make different notes?

Musicians have to show some consideration for the people around them. Loud music can be annoying.

d) Can listening to loud music be hazardous, as well as annoying?

Changing sounds

LEARN ABOUT
- sounds and vibrations
- loudness and energy

Good vibrations

How do musicians make sounds? A guitarist strums on the strings. A violinist bows or plucks the strings. These things make the strings **vibrate**.

You may be able to see the strings of a guitar as they vibrate. They look blurred, because they only move a small amount, and they move very fast.

Sounds are made when things vibrate. When someone blows a trumpet, it is the air inside which vibrates, but you can't see that.

Q1 How does a drummer make a sound? Which part of the drum vibrates?

The vibrations of a tuning fork are almost too small to see, but they cause the water to fly everywhere

Loud and soft notes

Musicians have to be able to play loud notes and soft notes. To make a louder note, you have to put in more energy. You strum the strings harder, or blow harder. So the **loudness** of a sound tells you about its **energy**. A loud sound has more energy than a soft sound.

Q2 How does a drummer make a louder note? How does a pianist make a louder note?

Twang that ruler

- Press one end of a ruler onto the bench. Twang the other end. Watch the ruler vibrate and listen to the sound it makes.
- How does the loudness of the sound change as the vibrations die away? Use the idea of energy to explain what you observe.
- You can make different notes by changing the length that vibrates. How can you make high notes and low notes?

Care: Keep your feet away from heavy masses.

Getting in tune

Musicians have to be able to make high notes and low notes. How do they do this?

In the recording studio, the engineer has the job of making sure that all of the instruments are in tune with each other

- A guitarist or violinist makes the string shorter, or uses a string which is tighter or thinner.
- A trumpeter presses on the keys to get different notes.
- A drummer uses a smaller drum for higher notes.

We say that a high note has a high **pitch**. A low note has a low pitch.

Q3 Where are the high notes on a piano keyboard? Where are the low notes?

SUMMARY QUESTIONS

1 ☆ Which words tell you about the *pitch* of a sound? Which words tell you about its *loudness*?

high **loud** **low** **soft**

2 ☆☆ Match the instruments with the part that vibrates:

drum	strings
guitar	air inside tube
flute	skin

3 ☆☆☆ Look at the photo of the Japanese women playing musical instruments. Say as much as you can about how these instruments work.

Key words
energy
loudness
pitch
vibrate

Seeing sounds

8L2

LEARN ABOUT

- displaying sounds with an oscilloscope

On the screen

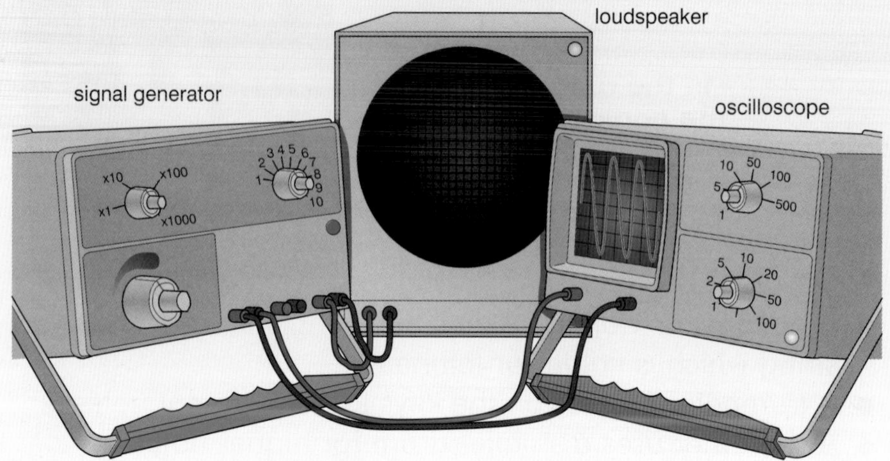

We can't see sounds; we hear them, with our ears. However, there is a way to make sounds visible, using some electronic equipment. Here's what you need:

- A **signal generator** makes high and low sounds. You can also change the loudness.
- A **loudspeaker** lets you hear the sounds from the signal generator.
- An **oscilloscope** lets you see a trace of the sound on its screen.

How the trace changes

A

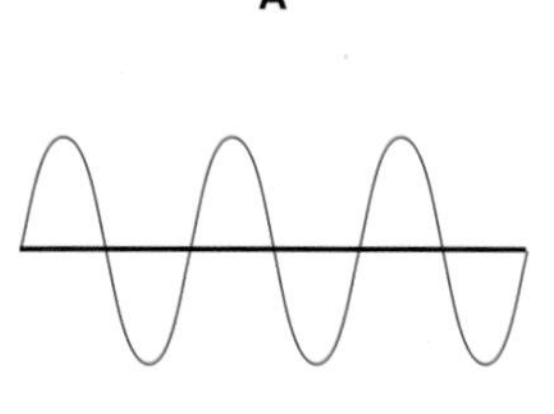

This is a soft sound – the trace doesn't go up and down very much

B

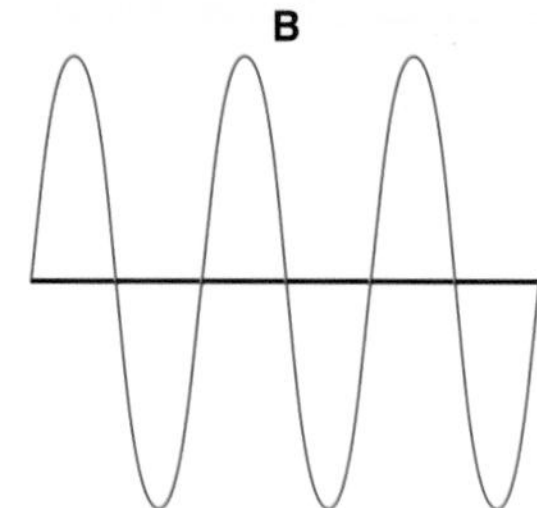

Now the sound is louder. The trace goes up and down more.

C

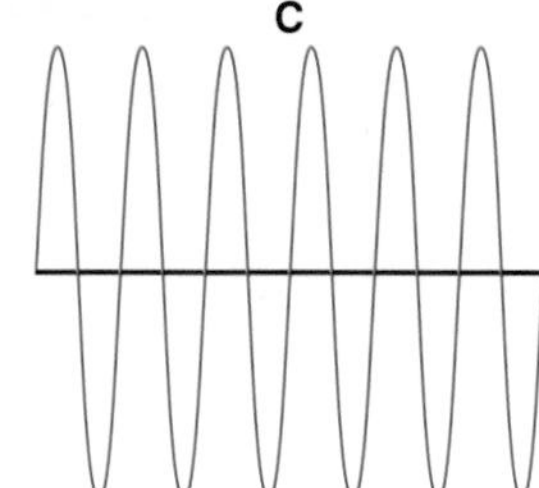

This note has a higher pitch. It vibrates up and down more often.

Q1 Which two traces have the same loudness? How can you tell?

Q2 Do the first two traces show a high note or a low note?

Making sense of sounds

- Watch how the trace on the screen changes as the sound gets louder and then softer. Describe how the trace changes. Can you waggle your finger up and down to show how the vibrations are changing?
- Watch how the trace on the screen changes as the sound gets higher and then lower. Waggle your finger to show the difference between a high note and a low note.

Capturing sounds

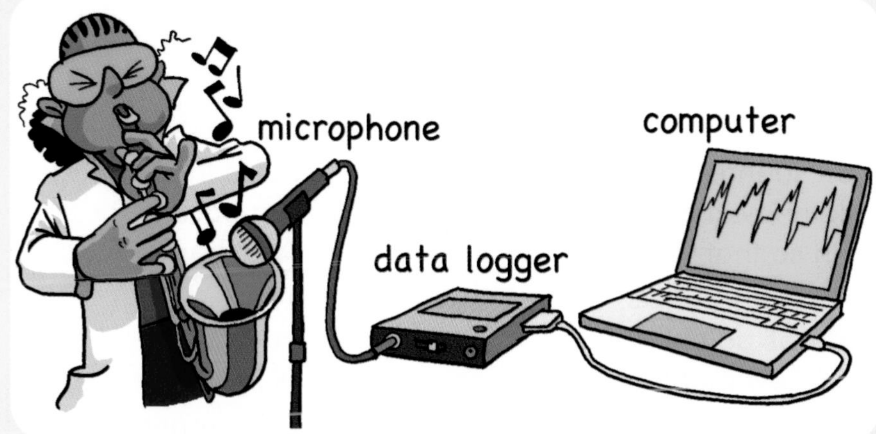

- If you connect a **microphone** to a data logger, you can record sounds and then look at them on a computer screen.
- Try things like clapping your hands, whistling and singing (preferably not all at the same time).
- You may be able to look at the patterns produced by different musical instruments. Do they look the same when they are playing the same note?

SUMMARY QUESTIONS

1 ☆ Look at the picture of the experiment at the top of the opposite page. Which piece of equipment vibrates to make the sounds we hear?

2 ☆☆ Look at the diagrams:

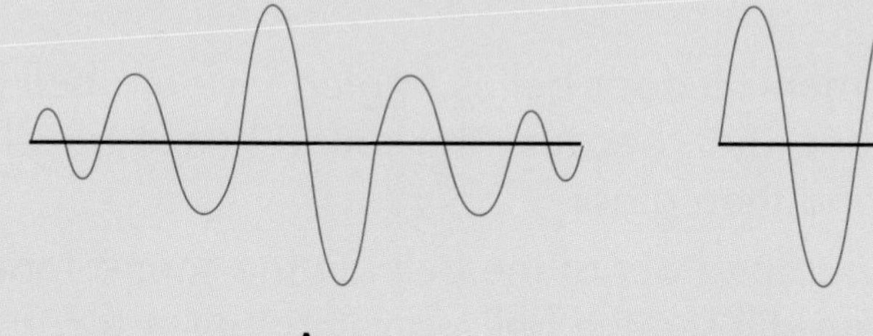

A

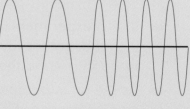

B

a) Which trace (A or B) shows a sound which gets louder and then softer?
b) Which trace (A or B) shows a sound which gets higher and higher?

Key words

loudspeaker
microphone
oscilloscope
signal generator

How sounds travel

LEARN ABOUT
- sound travelling through different materials
- the speed of sound

Solids, liquids, gases

Can sounds travel through water? Of course they can – just ask the next dolphin you meet. Or try lying back in the bath so that your ears are under water. Tap the side of the bath – you'll hear the sound.

Perhaps dolphins wonder if sounds can travel through air. We know that they can – that's how we usually hear things.

So sound can travel through a gas (air), and through a liquid (water). It can also travel through solids.

Dolphins and whales communicate under water using squeaks, grunts and other sounds

Q1 How could you show that sound travels through wood?

In space, no-one can hear the door bell

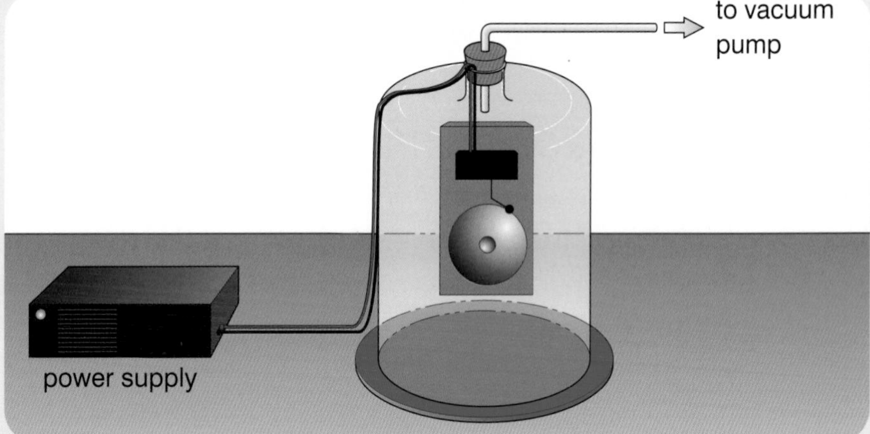

- In this experiment, a door bell is ringing inside a bell jar. It sounds rather faint, because the sound has to travel through air and then glass.
- As the air is pumped out of the bell jar, the sound fades away. You can still see the bell vibrating, but you can't hear it.
- When the air is pumped out, there is a **vacuum** in the jar. This experiment shows that sound cannot travel through a vacuum – there must be a material for it to pass through.

Q2 The Sun is a seething ball of hot gases. It must be very noisy, but we can't hear it. Explain why we can see the Sun, but we can't hear it.

The speed of sound

If you are ever locked up in a prison (or a boarding school), remember that you can communicate with the other inmates by tapping on the pipes. Put your ear to the pipes and you may hear someone else knocking. This shows that sound can travel easily through solids.

- Sounds travel quickly through the air.
- Sounds travel even faster through solids and liquids.

Vibrations spreading out

Sit next to a table. Tap the table gently. The sound of your tapping reaches your ear.

- When you tap the table, you make the table top vibrate.
- The vibrations spread out through the wood.
- They make the air nearby vibrate.
- The vibrations spread out through the air to reach your ears.

There's always got to be something to **vibrate**. It might be wood or water or air, or any other **material**.

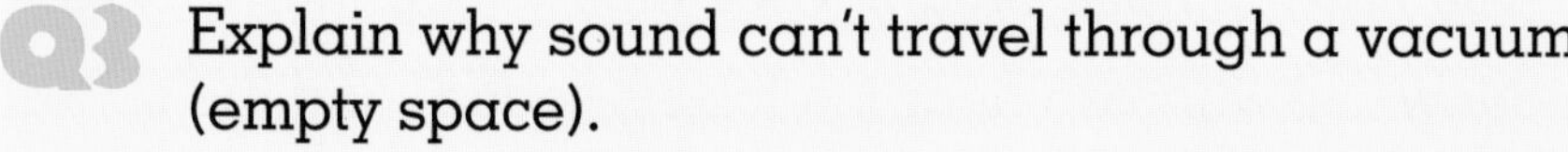

Q3 Explain why sound can't travel through a vacuum (empty space).

SUMMARY QUESTIONS

1 ☆☆ Can sounds travel through glass? Give some evidence. (Hint: look at the picture of the door bell experiment opposite.)

2 ☆☆ Put these in order, from slowest to fastest:

a snail **sound in air** **light** **an Olympic sprinter**

3 ☆☆ How could you show that sound can travel along a metal rod?

Key words

material
vacuum
vibrate

8L4 Hearing things

LEARN ABOUT
- range of hearing
- how ears work

What can you hear?

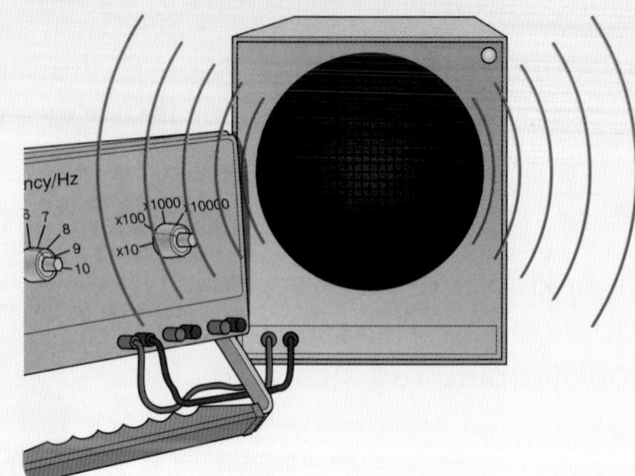

The signal generator will let you test your hearing. If it makes higher and higher sounds, eventually you will not be able to hear it.

Similarly, if the pitch gets lower and lower, the sound will eventually become inaudible. This usually happens at about 20 Hz (**hertz**) – that is, 20 vibrations per second.

Hearing test

- Devise a safe way of finding out which member of the class can hear the most high-pitched sound.
- Take care! Remember that people might try to cheat by claiming that they can hear a sound when they can't, so you need to build an anti-cheating method into your test.
- Now see who can hear the lowest sound, and the softest sound.

High and low

Children usually have a **range of hearing** from about 20 Hz to about 20 000 Hz (20 kilohertz). As you get older, it gets harder to hear high-pitched sounds. It also gets harder to hear faint sounds.

You can buy dog-whistles that we can't hear but which a dog will respond to. So dogs can hear higher notes than humans can.

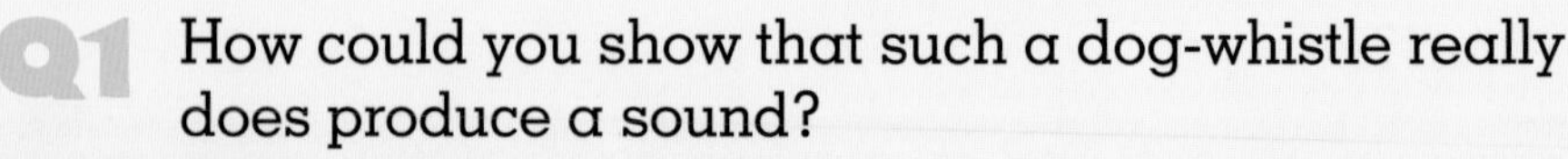

Q1 How could you show that such a dog-whistle really does produce a sound?

Elephants make very low sounds, which travel over long distances through the ground. They can hear sounds of much lower pitch than humans.

In your ear – how we hear

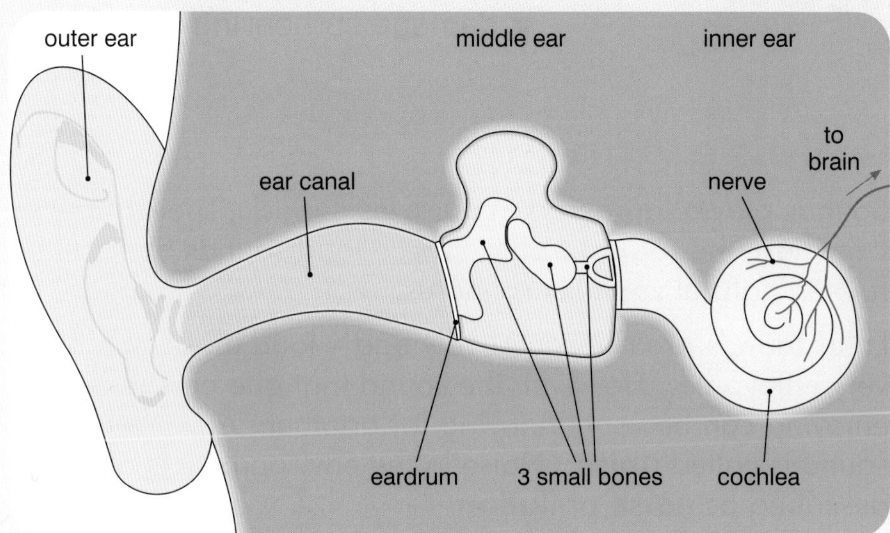

When a sound enters your ear, it pushes on your eardrum. Eventually a signal travels up the nerve into your brain.

The vibrations of sounds entering your ears travel as vibrations in the air. How does that end up as something in your brain?

- The vibrations of the air push back and forth on your **eardrum**.
- Your eardrum presses on the three small bones.
- These pass the vibrations on to the inner ear. A message is sent along the nerve to the brain.

Collecting sound

- Our ears are designed to collect sound. You can improve on nature by cupping your hands round your ears, so that they collect more sound.
- Better still, you can make big ear flaps. Test your hearing. Can you hear fainter sounds when you wear ear flaps?

SUMMARY QUESTIONS

1 ☆ Which of the following is *not* a bone in your ear?
anvil eardrum hammer stirrup

2 ☆☆ Name an animal which can hear *higher* sounds than people can.
Name an animal which can hear *lower* sounds than people can.

3 ☆☆ Put these in the order that they vibrate when a sound comes into your ear:
air in outer ear three small bones eardrum inner ear

4 ☆☆ Explain why it is dangerous to poke things into your ears.

Key words
eardrum
hertz
range of hearing

Noise pollution

LEARN ABOUT
- noise
- damage to hearing

Noise annoys

Sounds play a large part in our lives – music, speech on the television, the roar of traffic. These loud sounds blot out the fainter, natural sounds around us.

Loud sounds are not necessarily bad – loud music can be very enjoyable. However, the sound that one person is enjoying can be very annoying for another. Any unwanted sound is called **noise**. Noise in the environment is often described as **noise pollution**.

Could this be your idea of how to enjoy music?

Q1 Give some examples of sounds which are a pleasure for one person but which other people regard as noises.

Measuring noise

Sounds can be measured using a sound-level meter. This has a microphone, to detect the sounds, and a display which shows the sound level. The level of sound is usually measured in **decibels** (dB).

- 0 decibels – the faintest sound you can hear.
- 50 decibels – quiet conversation.
- 80 decibels – a door slamming.
- 110 decibels – a pneumatic drill.
- 130 decibels – the threshold of pain.

Q2 Guess how many decibels these score:
a) a watch ticking at a distance of 1 metre
b) loud conversation **c)** a loud car horn.

Gruesome science

Twenty per cent (20%) of people in the UK live in areas where traffic noise levels are above the accepted limit.

Noise harms

Noise isn't just annoying. It can be harmful.

- People who live in areas where there is a lot of noise – for example, from traffic or aircraft – may find it hard to sleep, and they can become stressed.
- People who work in noisy places need to wear ear protection. Better still, the noise level should be reduced.
- People who listen to music with the volume turned up high, especially through earphones or at concerts, can harm their ears.

This girl is having her hearing tested. The electronic box produces sounds – loud and soft, high and low – and the girl presses the button as she hears them.

The problem is that constant loud noise can damage your ears. You may not hear soft or high-pitched sounds. You may not notice it happening at the time, but the effects last a lifetime.

Q3 Describe how you would test someone's hearing to see if it had been damaged by noise. (The photo above may help.)

Sound insulation

Sound **insulation** makes use of materials that are good at absorbing sound. Thick curtains and carpets can help to absorb noise in a house.

- Devise a safe way of studying insulating materials. How can you compare different materials, to discover how good they are at absorbing sound?

SUMMARY QUESTIONS

1 ☆ Give a two-word phrase which means 'noise'.

2 ☆☆ List some examples of noise pollution which might damage people's hearing at home and at work.

3 ☆☆ Describe how you could use a sound-level meter to find out about noise levels near your school or home. Where would you expect it to be noisiest? Where would it be quietest?

4 ☆☆☆ People who live near a main road may have double-glazing fitted free of charge to reduce the noise. Find out other ways in which traffic noise can be reduced.

Key words

decibel
insulation
noise
noise pollution

Using science today

Ultrasound at work

Ultrasound is any sound which is too high-pitched for us to hear – more than 20 000 vibrations per second.

Ultrasound is now regularly used to scan expectant mothers, to show the developing baby in the womb. Ultrasound is passed into the mother's body, where it **reflects** off the baby. The reflected ultrasound is collected by a **detector**, and then analysed by a computer to produce an image of her baby.

Ultrasound scans have replaced X-rays, because X-rays were found to cause cancer in a small number of babies each year. As far as anyone can tell, ultrasound has no harmful side-effects.

There's another use of ultrasound in medicine. If you have kidney stones, they may be treated by directing a beam of ultrasound at them. This shatters them to a fine powder, which then comes out in the patient's urine.

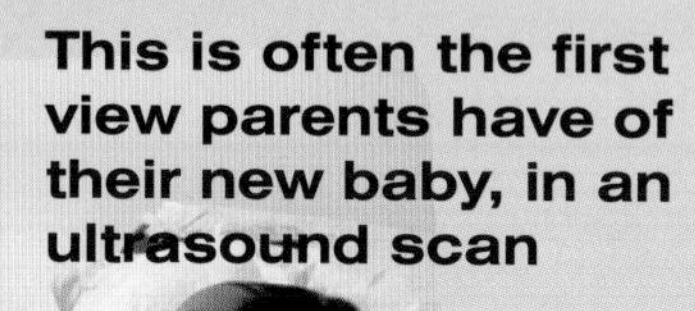

This is often the first view parents have of their new baby, in an ultrasound scan

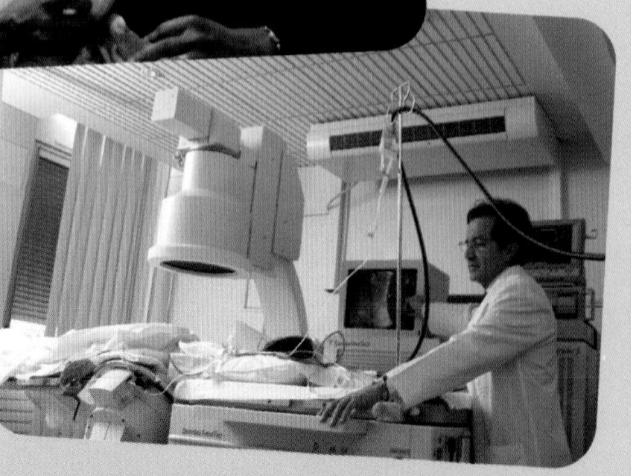

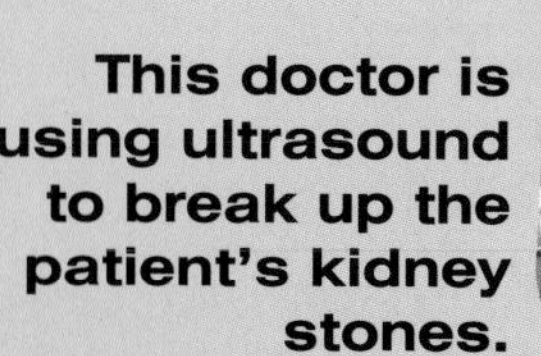

This doctor is using ultrasound to break up the patient's kidney stones.

Bats and ultrasound

You probably know that bats use ultrasound to find their way around in the dark. They emit high-pitched squeaks, which we cannot hear. Then they listen for the reflected sounds, so that they can build up a picture of their surroundings. They can distinguish between rough and smooth surfaces, and they can detect tiny insects which are their prey.

The frog-eating bat from Panama can eat as many as 40 frogs in a night. It simply listens for their croaks. It also knows how to distinguish between edible and poisonous frogs.

Some species of insect emit ultrasound to confuse any bats that may be after them. It's a real ultrasound arms race out there!

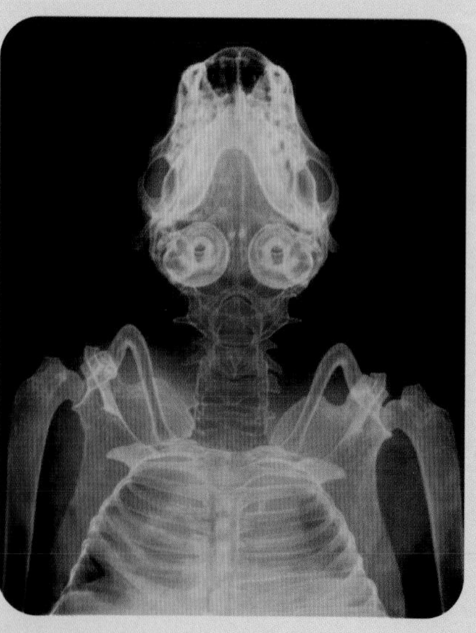

In this X-ray image, you can see the large, curled-up cochleas at the back of the bat's skull. These help it to detect very faint sounds.

THE HUSH CREW

Drum out of use

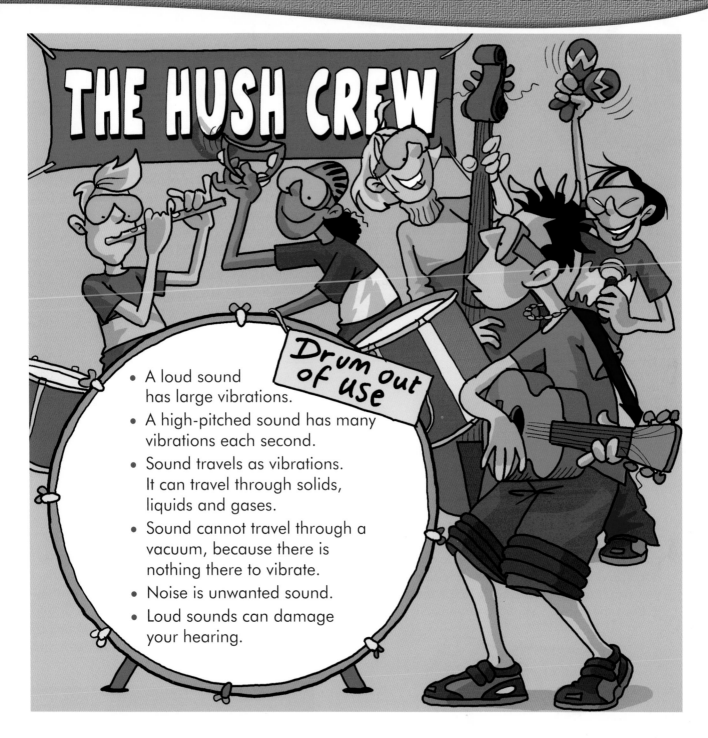

- A loud sound has large vibrations.
- A high-pitched sound has many vibrations each second.
- Sound travels as vibrations. It can travel through solids, liquids and gases.
- Sound cannot travel through a vacuum, because there is nothing there to vibrate.
- Noise is unwanted sound.
- Loud sounds can damage your hearing.

DANGER! AVOID THESE COMMON ERRORS

Don't get confused between 'high' sounds and 'loud' sounds. Sometimes we talk about turning the volume up high, but that makes the sound louder, not higher.

Remember that sound needs a material to travel through. There has to be something there to vibrate.

Key words

detector
reflect
ultrasound

UNIT REVIEW

REVIEW QUESTIONS

Understanding and applying concepts

1 Look at the three diagrams showing the traces of three sounds (A, B and C), as shown by an oscilloscope.

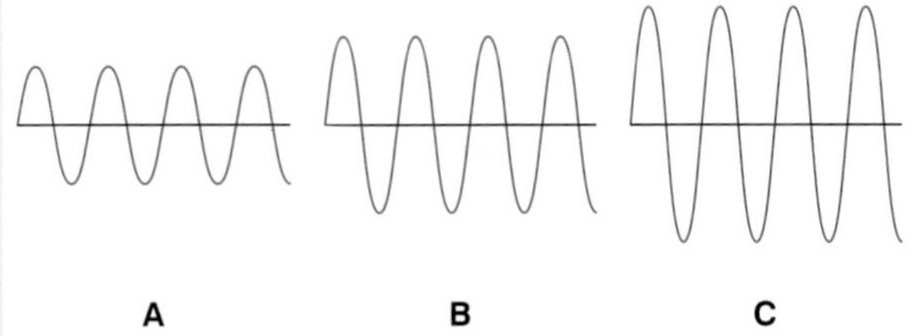

a How can you tell that the sounds get louder, from A to B to C?

b How can you tell that the sounds all have the same pitch?

2 The photograph shows a stethoscope. The doctor presses one end onto the patient's chest. The hollow tubes lead up to the doctor's ears. Explain in as much detail as you can how the stethoscope helps the doctor to hear the vibrations of the patient's heart.

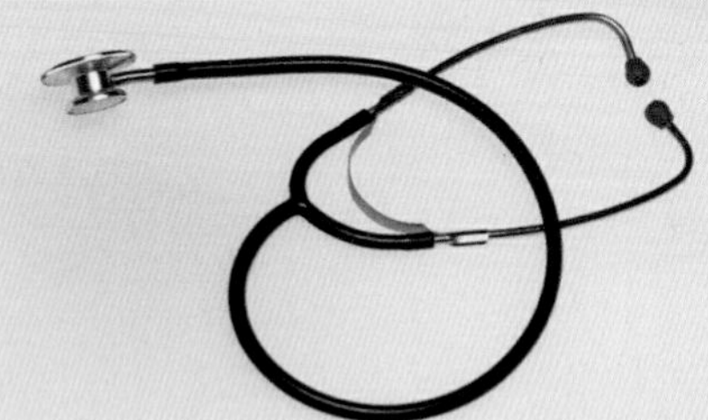

Ways with words

3 We talk about a sound having a 'high' pitch. The word 'high' usually describes how tall something is.

a Explain what it means to say that a sound has a high pitch or a low pitch.

b Suggest a way of remembering these meanings of the words 'high' and 'low'.

Making more of maths

4 A sound-level meter can be used to see how much noise there is. Here are some readings from around Scientifica High:

Playground at break	78 dB
Examination hall during practice SAT tests	44 dB
Dining hall	84 dB
Hall during band practice	98 dB
Corridor between lessons	60 dB
Science practical lesson	64 dB
CDT workshop, using machinery	84 dB

a Put these readings in order, from softest to loudest.

b Think of a way of presenting the readings as a graph or chart.

Thinking skills

5 Our senses help us to learn a lot about the world around us. Seeing and hearing are particularly important – these depend on light and sound.

Copy and complete the table, which compares light and sound. The first row has been done for you.

	Light	Sound
What are its sources?	Luminous objects	Vibrating objects
Can it travel through air?		
Can it travel through a vacuum?		
How fast is it?		
Can it be reflected?		
Can it be absorbed?		
How is it detected by people?		

Extension question

6 Pip was blowing her own trumpet into a microphone. The drawing shows the trace which appeared on the oscilloscope.

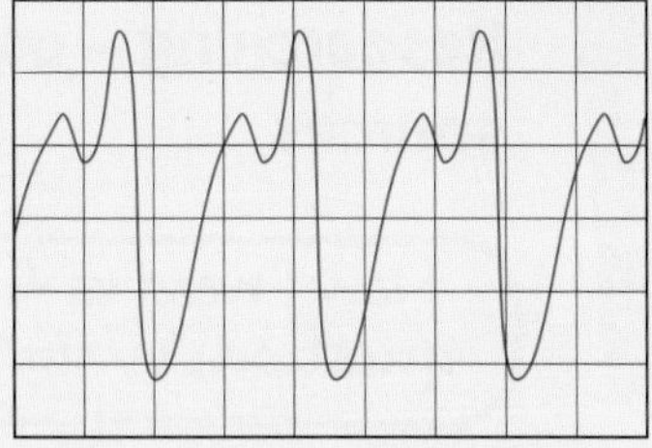

Describe how the particles of the air move when someone plays the trumpet. (You might find it easier to demonstrate this by waving your hand, rather than writing a description.)

How would the movement of the particles change if Pip played a higher note? Or a louder note?

SAT-STYLE QUESTIONS

1 Benson was investigating the different notes produced by his flute. He played it next to a microphone, which was connected to an oscilloscope. The diagrams show some of the traces he observed.

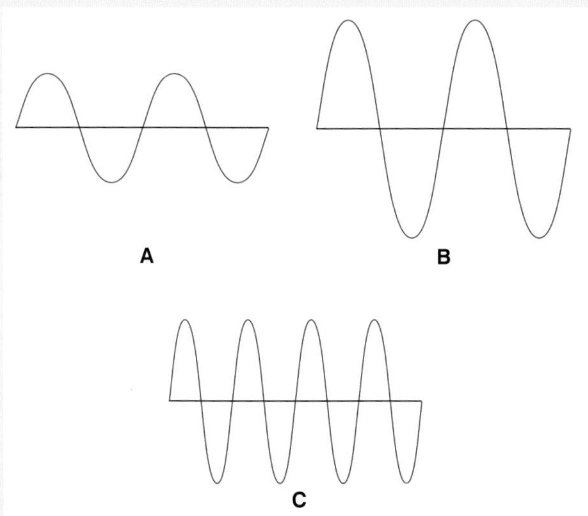

a Which diagram represents a loud, high-pitched note? (1)

b Which diagram represents a loud, low-pitched note? (1)

c Which diagram represents a soft, low-pitched note? (1)

2 Pip and Molly were investigating different materials, to see which was the best absorber of sound. Molly put squares of material over her ears, and Pip played her trumpet nearby. Molly judged which material let through the least sound.

a List *three* things which Molly and Pip should keep the same, for this to be a fair test. (3)

b Why would it be better to use a signal generator and a loudspeaker to produce the sound, rather than using a trumpet? (1)

3 Small children have to learn that it is dangerous to poke things into their ears, as this can damage their eardrum.

a Describe how the eardrum moves when a sound enters the ear. (1)

b How does its motion change if the sound gets louder? (1)

c How does its motion change if the pitch of the sound gets lower? (1)

Key words

Unscramble these:

chipt
earnigh
nudeloss
murdera
eosin

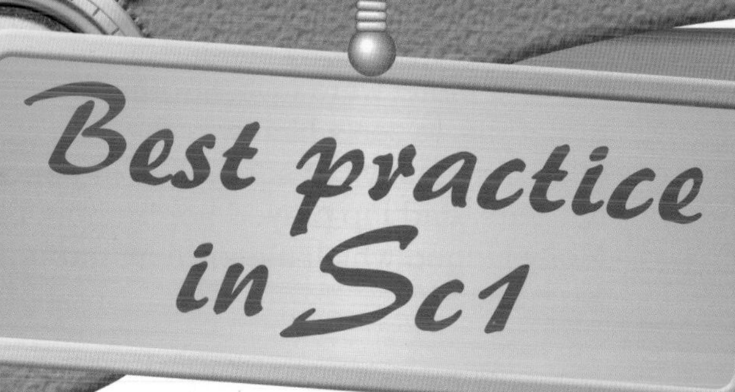

Best practice in Sc1

DIFFERENT TYPES OF ENQUIRY

Science is never boring... there are so many different ways to find the answers to scientific questions.

- Scientific enquiries (Sc1 activities) are all about finding the answers to questions.
- Here are some of the strategies you can use. The one you choose depends on the question you want to answer.

Observing and exploring

Just how many ladybirds can live on this rose bush and what do they eat?

- This is an example of a question that we could start to answer by observing and counting ladybirds.

Researching – using secondary sources

Now I need to find the answer to the question:'What's inside a ladybird?'
LADYBIRDS

- Mike can use reference material to find out the structure of a ladybird's body.

Fair testing – controlling variables

Sometimes we need to carry out a fair test to answer a question like 'What affects the pitch of a note made by a stretched string?'

- In some enquiries we can carefully control all the variables that might have an effect. We just vary the one under investigation, carrying out a fair test.
- So Molly might investigate the effect of the length of the string on pitch. In this case she would vary the length of the string. She would keep all other variables the same.
- This will show us how one variable (the length of the string) affects another variable (the pitch of the note).

Pattern seeking – surveys and correlation

Do the weeds we find in a field differ in different parts of the field?

- Sometimes we want to know how one variable affects another, but there may be lots of factors that we can't control. In these enquiries we need to increase the size of the sample. Then we can see any real patterns that come out of our data.

Identifying and classifying

What type of rock is this?
Here, use this key.

- Sometimes we want to identify things, such as plants, animals, rocks, compounds or stars. We can use a variety of methods to help us. For example, we might use keys, descriptions, chemical tests. At other times we might want to classify something to a particular group. For example, which group is this animal in?

Using models and analogies

I find sound much easier to understand now I can visualise a sound wave.
So can we use this model to explain about the amplitude and frequency of a note?

- We can use models to help investigate our questions. For example, in Year 7 you used a water pump to help explain how a battery works. In Year 8 we use molecular model kits to represent atoms and molecules.
- You can make predictions using a good model. The better a model, the more things it can help explain.

Using and evaluating a technique or design

Are you sure this circuit could work a set of traffic lights?

- In this type of enquiry you are solving a problem which might involve a sequence of steps. For example, you might be designing and making a burglar alarm.

Key words
- analogies
- classifying
- enquiry
- model
- variables

PLANNING HOW TO GATHER YOUR DATA

1. Reese and Pete are studying a pendulum. Their teacher asks them 'What affects how quickly a pendulum swings?'

2. First of all, they list all the variables that might affect the swinging pendulum. This is the start of planning their fair test.

Length of string, mass of the bob at the end, height you release it from... Er that's it I think.
What about the colour of the string...? Only joking!

3. Reese and Pete have now identified all the key variables in their investigation.

4.

What shall we investigate then?
The length of the string? Let's see how that affects how many swings it does in, say, 20 seconds.

5.

Right, let's sort out all the variables...

Planning a fair test.

We will change:
The independent variable.

The length of the string

We will measure its effect on:
The dependent variable.

The number of swings in 20 seconds

We will keep these things the same:
The control variables.

The mass of the bob

The height of release

You can use these questions below to help you plan and carry out fair tests.

Investigation planner

Have you thought about these?

1. What are you trying to find out?
2. a) What do you think (predict) will happen?
   b) Why do you think this will happen?
3. What are you going to change each time? This is your **independent variable**.
4. How can you judge the effect of changing your independent variable? What are you going to observe or measure each time? This is your **dependent variable.**
5. What will you keep the same each time to make it a fair test? These are your **control variables**.
6. How will you carry out your tests? How many values for your independent variable will you choose to test?
7. Is your plan safe? Could anything go wrong and somebody get hurt? (Check with your teacher.)
8. What equipment will you need?
9. How many readings will you need to take? Do you need to repeat tests?
10. What is the best way to show your results? A table? . . . and a bar chart? . . . or a line graph?

Questions

A group were investigating friction.

They wanted to see how the mass in a shoe affected the force needed to move the shoe.

- The title of their investigation was phrased as a question. What is the title of the investigation?
- What type of enquiry would answer their question?
- What was the independent variable in their investigation?
- What was the dependent variable?
- Which variables did they have to control?

RECORDING YOUR DATA

The story continues . . .

We'd better plan a table to put our results in.

Length of the string (cm)	Number of swings in 20 seconds			
	1st test	2nd test	3rd test	Mean

Key words

control variables
dependent variable
fair test
independent variable

Best practice in Sc1

1.

How many different lengths shall we investigate?
We need at least 5 different lengths to draw a graph from.

2.

Here we go then...

Length of the string (cm)	Number of swings in 20 seconds			
	1st test	2nd test	3rd test	Mean
10.0	32	33	31	32
20.1	23	22	21	22
30.0	17	19	18	18
39.8	16	17	15	16
50.0	14	14	14	14
60.2	12	14	13	13
80.1	11	11	11	11
100.0	10	10	10	10

3.

Now that we've done our testing, what shall we do with our data?
This can go on a line graph.

4.

Exactly, Pete. Then we can draw a line of best fit through our mean results... no 'dot-to-dot' now!

5.

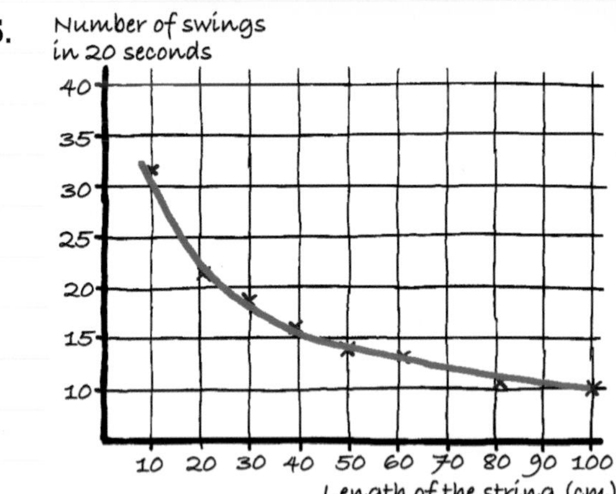

ANALYSING YOUR EVIDENCE

THE END IS NIGH!

- Having carried out your enquiry, you should try to answer your original question.
- You should also judge whether or not any predictions you made are supported by the evidence collected.
- Any patterns in your data should be explained using your science.

EVALUATING YOUR EVIDENCE

As you carry out your activity, and at the end, you should always think about the strength of your evidence:

- Can you draw a **valid** conclusion using the data collected?
- For example, you might choose a poor range for the 'Length of the string'.
- A narrow range of 10.0. 10.2, 10.4, 10.6, 10.8 and 11.0 cm might produce data that points to no pattern or only a slight **correlation** (link) between the length of string and the rate of swing.
- You need a wider set of values for the length of the string. Then you can get the data from which to draw a valid conclusion.
- Is your evidence **reliable**? If you, or somebody else, were to do the same investigation, would they come up with the same data?
- If they do, you have collected strong evidence for any conclusions you come to.
- This is why we carry out repeat readings in some investigations – to generate reliable data.
- Therefore, if you have large differences between your repeat readings, your data could be unreliable. You can't place much trust in your conclusions.
- How could you improve your enquiry? Write down any improvements you could make to collect better evidence.
- If you are doing a 'pattern seeking' enquiry, think about the size of the sample you chose. Was it large enough to be certain of your conclusions?

Ah-ha, the pattern is clear now.
Are you quite sure about that?

Questions

How would you tackle these questions? Choose from the types of enquiry described on the last two pages:

- How does temperature affect how quickly copper sulphate dissolves?
- What is the temperature on the surface of Jupiter?
- How can you make your own thermometer?
- What type of insect is this?
- Do men have a faster pulse rate than women?
- Why do metals expand when we heat them up?
- What happens when calcium metal is added to water?

Key words

analysing
conclusion
correlation
evaluating
reliable
valid

8A Food and digestion

8A2 Find out about vitamin A.

8A3 Visit the World Health Organisation's web site to find out about where in the world people are well fed, and where they don't get enough food.

8A5 People are encouraged to eat a low-fat diet for their health. Children need fatty acids from fat in their food to develop properly. Find out about essential fatty acids, and why we need them.

8A6 Washing powder enzymes digest food spilt on your clothes. Plan an experiment to find out how good enzyme washing powder is at removing food stains, such as tomato ketchup, gravy or blackcurrant drink.

8B Respiration

8B1 Some animals, such as glow worms, tropical fish and angler fish, use energy to make light. Find out about how one of these organisms uses light.

8B3 There is much less oxygen to breathe at the tops of very high mountains. How do mountaineers who climb mountains, like Mount Everest, or fighter pilots flying high in the air cope with a shortage of oxygen.

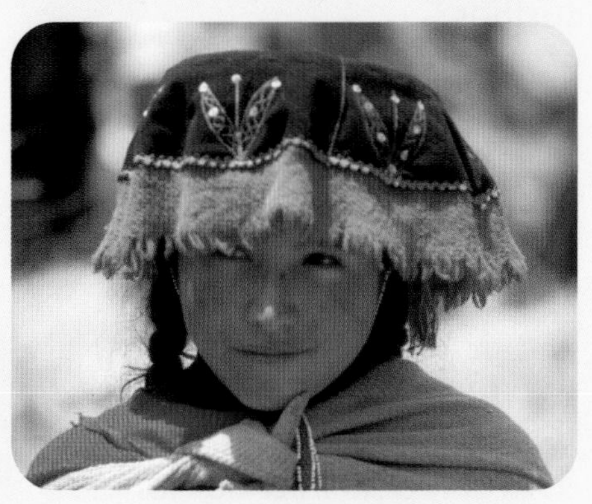

8B5 Find out about how fish get oxygen from water and release carbon dioxide.
Why do they die if the water in a river gets warm in the summer?

Key words

Research these new words:
emphysema
food additive
haemoglobin
heartbeat
vitamin D

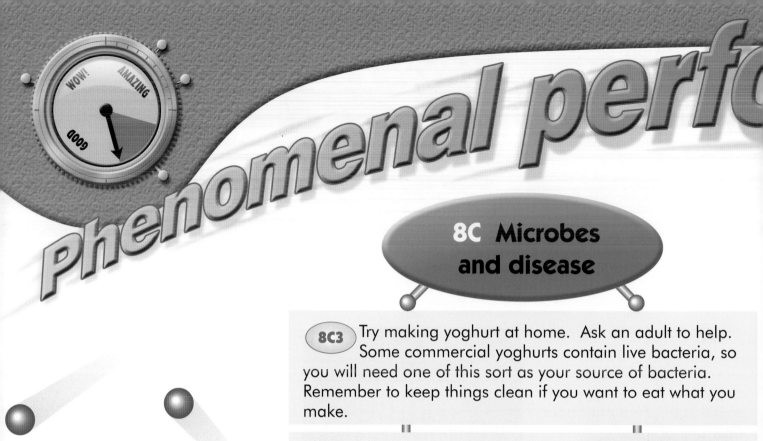

8C Microbes and disease

8C3 Try making yoghurt at home. Ask an adult to help. Some commercial yoghurts contain live bacteria, so you will need one of this sort as your source of bacteria. Remember to keep things clean if you want to eat what you make.

8C4 Look out for reports of outbreaks of infections such as 'flu, food poisoning, or cholera. What are health authorities doing to stop the disease spreading any further?

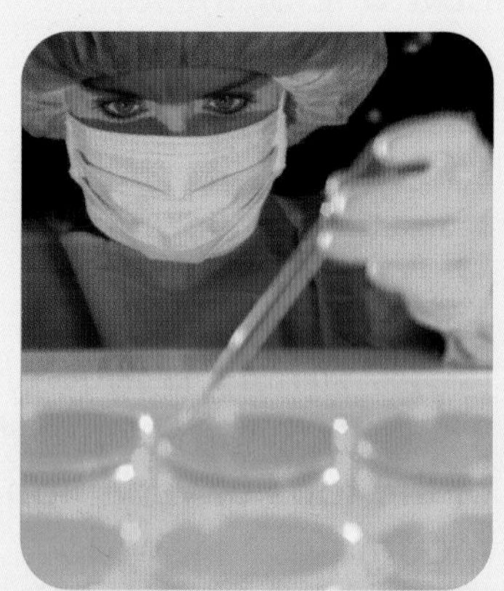

8C5 During the spring and summer the air is full of pollen. We breathe it in and it gets into our lungs. Some people are sensitive to pollen antigens and develop hay fever. Find out what happens in hay fever.

8C5 Find out about the bubonic plague in Europe in the Middle Ages.

8C7 Find out about the work of Joseph Lister who introduced the use of antiseptics into surgery.

8D Ecological relationships

8D2 Use the Internet to find out about bird ringing, and how the population of birds is monitored in the UK.

8D4 Lichen is a partnership between a fungus and an alga. Each provides something the other needs. Hermit crabs and sea anemones sometimes live in partnerships.
Research a partnership between two organisms.

8D4 Investigate how grey squirrels arrived in this country and how widely they are spread.

8D5 Plan making a model rock pool in your laboratory. You should think about how to keep the water cool if you want to keep British species as well as oxygenating the water.

a) How will you provide rock pool habitats such as crevices and sand to dig in?

b) Which species of animals and plants and how many would it be reasonable and humane to keep in your rock pool?

c) Will you need to feed your inhabitants or can your food web sustain itself?

Key words

Research these new words:
allergy
freshwater crayfish
limestone pavement
measles

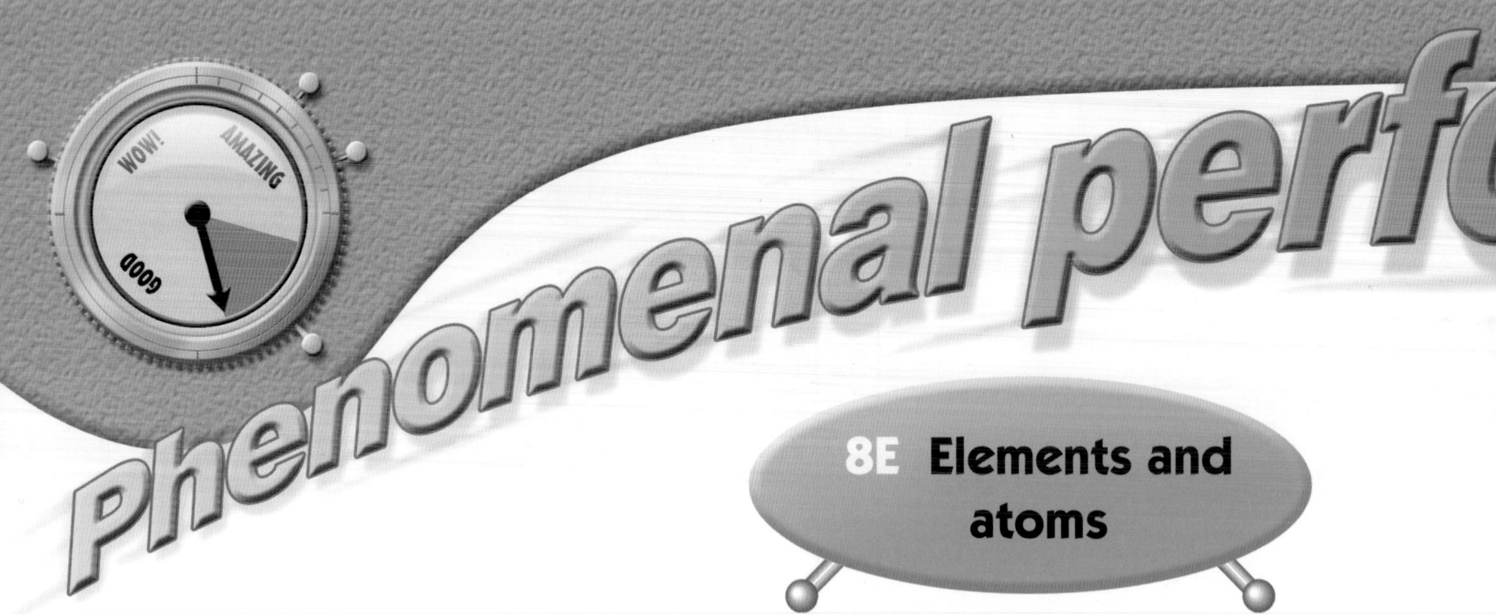

8E Elements and atoms

8E1 Imagine the chemical elements as the letters in the alphabet.

a) Use this model to explain why we have millions of 'non-elements' on Earth.

b) Water is a substance that is a 'non-element'. A particle of water contains twice as much hydrogen as oxygen. Using your model from part **a)**, how could you represent water?

8E2 **a)** Find six atoms (elements) whose symbols start with the letter 'C'. Write down two facts about each element.

b) The chemical symbol for lead is taken from its Latin name, plumbum.

i) What is the symbol for lead?

ii) Find out three other elements, not mentioned in 8E2, whose symbols come from their Latin names.

8E3 **a)** How many of the chemical elements are liquids at 20°C? Name them.

b) Work out roughly the percentage of elements that are metals.

c) Name one metalloid. What is special about its properties?

d) List five facts about the man who discovered the Periodic Table.

Dmitri Mendeleev

8E4 The chemical formula of insulin is $C_{254}H_{377}N_{65}O_{75}S_6$.

How many atoms are there in one molecule of insulin?

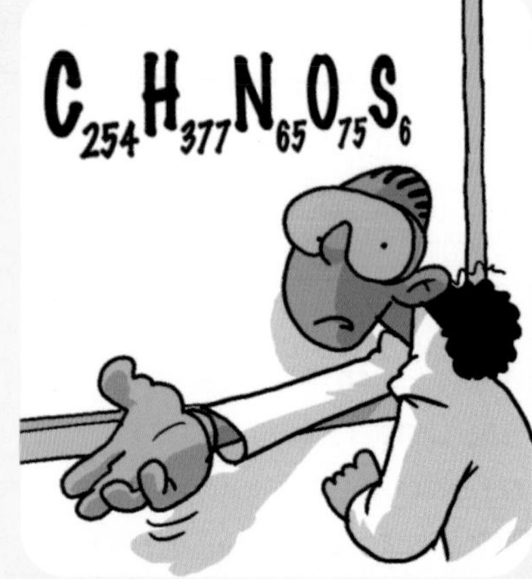

8E5 Draw a diagram to show how hydrogen (H_2) reacts with chlorine (Cl_2) to form hydrogen chloride (HCl).

8F Compounds and mixtures

8F1 Do some research to find out the differences between the following compounds and the elements that make them up:

a) potassium iodide **b)** silicon dioxide **c)** silver bromide.

8F2 We can think of the number of bonds an atom can form as its 'combining power'.

Hydrogen has a combining power of 1 (it can only form 1 bond).
Oxygen has a combining power of 2 (it can form two bonds).
So 1 oxygen atom can bond to 2 hydrogen atoms. Therefore the formula of hydrogen oxide, water, is H_2O.

Here is a table showing the combining powers of some atoms:

Element	Symbol	'Combining power'
hydrogen	H	1
nitrogen	N	3
chlorine	Cl	1

Using the 'combining powers' in the table, work out the formula of a compound formed between:

a) hydrogen and chlorine

b) nitrogen and hydrogen.

8F3 Think of some other mixtures that are emulsions, liquid foams, solid foams or sols. Write a list and say which type of mixture each product is.

8F4 Look at the temperature line drawn for bromine on page 100.
Now draw a temperature line for the element sodium.
Use your line to explain why sodium is in a different state to bromine at room temperature (20°C).

Key words

Research these new words:
atomic clocks
graphite
LCDs
UPAC
uranium

Phenomenal perfo

8G Rocks and weathering

Oil rig in the North Sea

8G1 Find out how the porosity of rock plays a part in the places where we find crude oil and natural gas.

8G2 Limestone regions are great for pot-holing. They often have underground caverns. Find out and explain how these are formed.

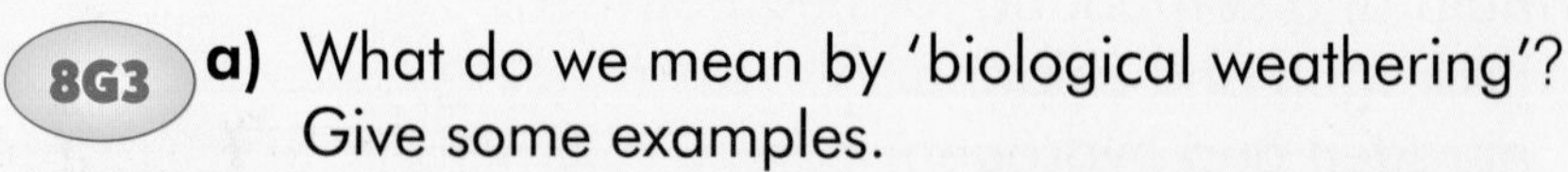

8G3 **a)** What do we mean by 'biological weathering'? Give some examples.

b) Why is biological weathering sometimes classified as physical weathering?

8G4 Describe how the energy associated with different stages of a river affects the processes of transportation, deposition and erosion.

8G6 Find out how fossils can help us understand more about the history of the Earth.

8H The rock cycle

8H1 Think of a situation from which a sedimentary rock with **a)** fine grains, and **b)** mixed grains, was formed.

8H2 Read this passage, then answer the question:

One theory suggests that sea levels were very high at the time when chalk was laid down. So there was not much land exposed. This meant there was little sediment carried to the sea by rivers. At present, similar deposits of sediment are only found at the bottom of oceans well away from land.

How does the passage explain the high proportion of calcium carbonate in chalk?

8H3 Draw a table showing sedimentary rocks in one column and the metamorphic rocks they form in the second column.

8H4 When an intrusion of magma cools down, the rate it cools differs the further you are from its edge.
How do you think this affects the crystals forming in an intrusion?
Draw a labelled diagram to show your ideas.

8H5 Describe how the rocks called obsidian and pumice were formed.

Obsidian

Pumice

Key words

Research these new words:
Giant's Causeway
Richter scale
metaquartzite
subduction

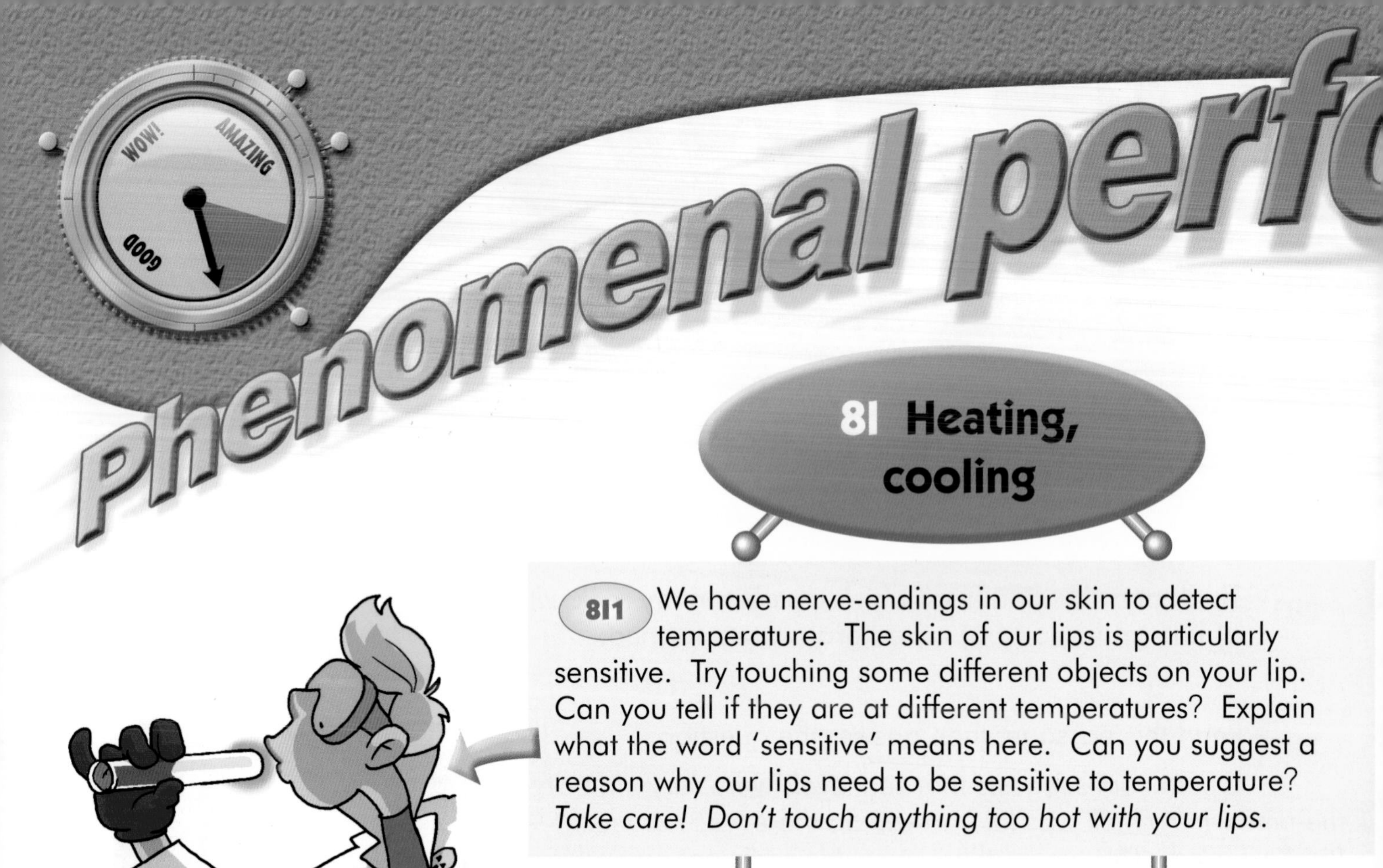

81 Heating, cooling

811 We have nerve-endings in our skin to detect temperature. The skin of our lips is particularly sensitive. Try touching some different objects on your lip. Can you tell if they are at different temperatures? Explain what the word 'sensitive' means here. Can you suggest a reason why our lips need to be sensitive to temperature? *Take care! Don't touch anything too hot with your lips.*

812 Draw a picture or a diagram of a room. Include some things that are hotter than the room – radiators, people, etc. – and things that are colder – the windows, perhaps. Add arrows to show how heat energy moves about in the room.

813 People and other animals live in the frozen Arctic. Find out how insulating materials make this possible.

815 People say, 'Hot air rises.'
You can explain this by thinking about the particles of the air. When air is heated, they move further apart. What happens to the density of the air? Will this air float upwards or sink downwards?

816 The Gulf Stream is a convection current. It brings warm water from the tropics to western Europe. Find a map of the Gulf Stream. How does it affect our climate? What would happen if it stopped flowing?

8J Magnets and electgromagnets

8J1 Find out which of the following metals are magnetic, and which are non-magnetic:

nickel lead cobalt tin

Add them to the correct columns of your table (Question 1, page 163).

8J2 You can magnetise a steel needle by stroking it with a bar magnet. It's possible to make a needle with south poles at both ends. It has to have two north poles near the middle. Try to make a magnet like this. How could you show where its poles are?

8J3 People use Ordnance Survey maps and a compass to find their way about in the countryside. Find an OS map, and look at the part where the symbols are explained. Is north exactly at the top of the map?
Find out how to place the compass correctly on the map to show the directions of different points around you.

8J4 Audio and video tapes are covered in tiny particles of magnetic material. Find out how electromagnets are used to magnetise these when music or a TV programme is recorded.
Do CD's use magnetism to store recordings?

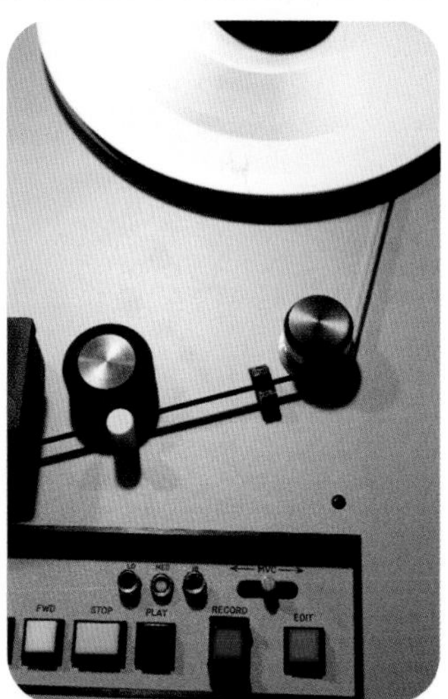

Magnetic recording makes use of electromagnets

8J5 The photo shows the inside of an electric doorbell. Which part is the electromagnet? Find out how a doorbell like this works.

Key words

Research these new words:
absolute zero
evaporation
ferrite

Phenomenal perfo

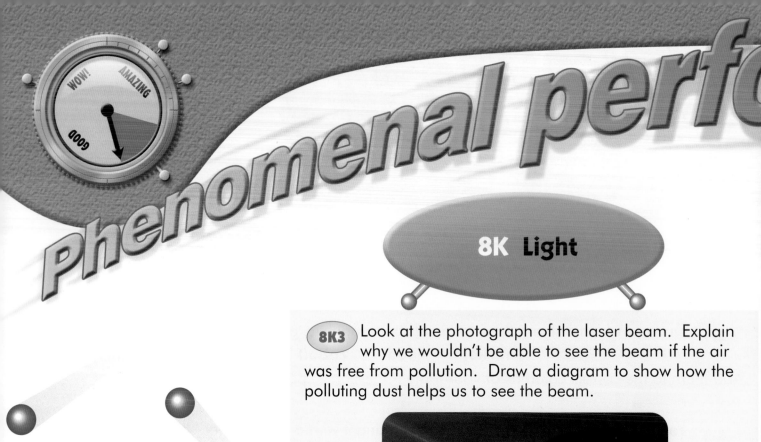

8K Light

8K3 Look at the photograph of the laser beam. Explain why we wouldn't be able to see the beam if the air was free from pollution. Draw a diagram to show how the polluting dust helps us to see the beam.

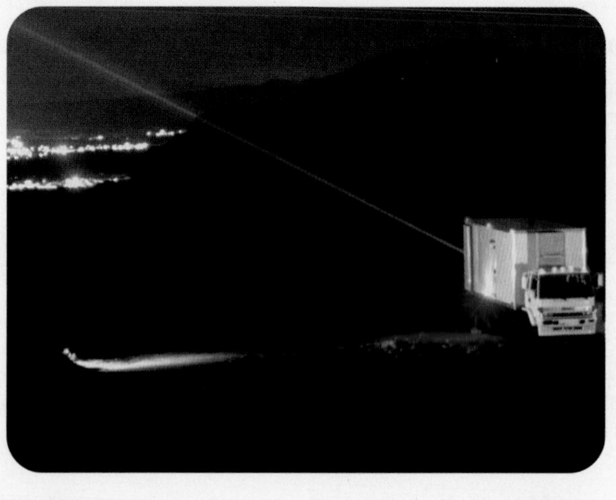

8K4 Explain why mirrors can be useful to these people: dentists, drivers, shopkeepers, astronomers.

8K5 Windows are made of flat sheets of glass. Some rooms, such as bathrooms, have windows with a different kind of glass. The thickness of this glass varies, so you can't see clearly through it. Use the idea of refraction to explain this.

8K6 Light isn't the only thing that can be filtered. List as many different kinds of filter as you can think of. Then research some more.

8L Sound and hearing

8L1 Draw a design for a musical toy for a child. Explain how they could use it to make sounds of different pitches and loudnesses.

8L3 Find out how double-glazing helps to reduce noise. (Hint: Find out what's between the two layers of glass.)

8L4 Some children can hear the squeaking of bats as they fly about at dusk. Older people may need to have the television turned up loud.

a) What does this tell you about how our hearing changes as we get older?

b) What advice would you give to a friend who listened to loud music with headphones a lot of the time? Do you think they would listen to you?

8L5 Imagine that you lived under the flight path of aircraft at an airport.

a) How could you try to cut out the noise of low-flying aircraft?

b) How would you react if the airport proposed to increase the number of aircraft landing and taking off at night?

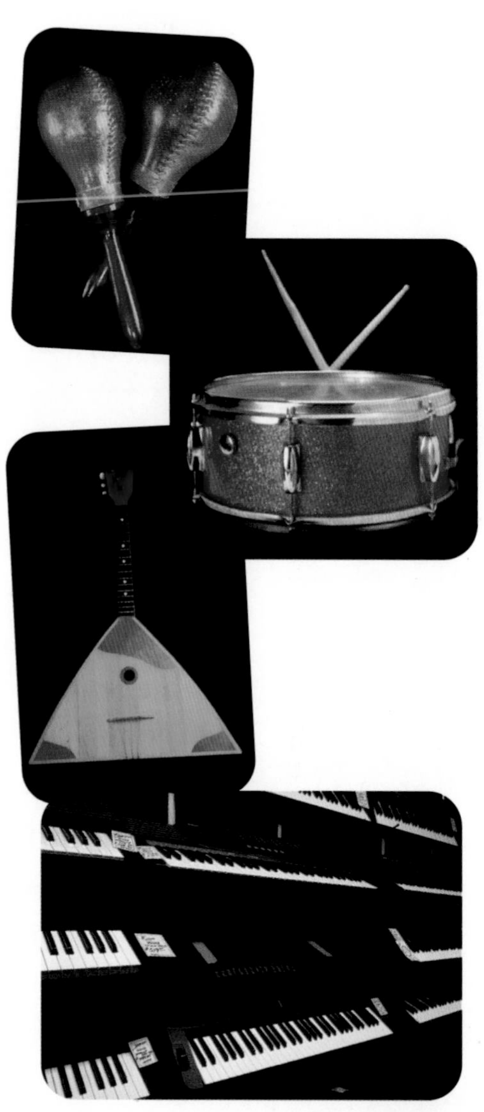

Key words

Research these new words:
fibre optics
focus
harmonics
reverberation
tinnitus

Glossary

absorption when something (e.g. light or sound) is absorbed, so that it no longer exists; taking substances into the body. **pp. 181, 188**

aerobic respiration uses oxygen to release energy from glucose. **p. 22**

alveolus an air sac in the lungs. **p. 30**

amino acid a substance made from digested protein. **p. 12**

amylase a digestive enzyme that breaks down starch. **pp. 12, 15**

antibiotic a substance that kills bacteria. **pp. 44, 52**

antibody a substance made by white blood cells against microbes. **p. 49**

antigen a marker on the outside of cells. **p. 49**

antiseptic a mild substance that kills micro-organisms in wounds. **p. 52**

artery a blood vessel that carries blood away from the heart. **p. 25**

arthropod an animal with a hard external skeleton and jointed legs. **p. 60**

atom the smallest particle of an element. **p. 80**

attract pull towards you with a force. **p. 163**

basalt an igneous rock made when molten rock cools quickly at or near the surface. **p. 133**

beam a wide ray of light. **p. 178**

boiling point the temperature at which a liquid becomes a gas. **pp. 100, 155**

bronchus the airway that leads from the trachea (wind-pipe) into a lung. **p. 29**

calcium a grey metallic element; a mineral we need for strong bones. **p. 6**

capillary a tiny blood vessel. It supplies cells with materials. It removes their wastes. **pp. 25, 26**

carbohydrate a type of nutrient used for energy. Includes starch and sugar. **p. 5**

Celsius scale the scientific scale of temperature. **p. 143**

cementation the process in which dissolved solids come out of solution to 'stick' bits of rock together. This helps to form sedimentary rock. **p. 126**

change of state a change from one state of matter to another. **p. 154**

circulatory system the system that sends blood round your body. **pp. 24, 34**

colony a group of bacteria growing on nutrient jelly. **p. 42**

compaction the process in which pressure builds up on sediment as layers are deposited on top. This helps form sedimentary rock. **p. 126**

composition details of the substances found in a material. **p. 97**

compound a substance made up of two or more different types of atom. **pp. 84, 95, 97**

conduction when heat energy travels through a solid material. **p. 152**

conserve save; don't waste; stop animals and plants dying out. **pp. 72, 152**

consumer an animal that eats plants or other animals. **p. 66**

contract get smaller; how muscles move body parts. **pp. 28, 148**

convection energy transfer by a hot liquid or gas as it flows. **pp. 151, 152**

convection current the circulation of a liquid or gas when hot material rises and cold material replaces it. **p. 150**

core a piece of iron or steel inside an electromagnet. **pp. 168, 171**

decibel (dB) the unit of loudness of a sound. **p. 205**

decomposer an organism that breaks down dead material. **pp. 60, 66**

deficiency disease an illness caused by not having enough of a nutrient. **p. 6**

degrees C (°C) the unit of temperature measurement. **p. 142**

denatured a denatured enzyme is changed by heat and cannot digest food. **p. 14**

diaphragm muscles used in breathing that separate your chest and your abdomen. **p. 28**

diet all the different foods we eat. **p. 8**

diffusion the tendency for particles to move about randomly, and to spread out and mix with each other. **p. 31**

Key words
on key people
Fleming
antibiotics
William Gilbert
magnetism

GLOSSARY

disinfectant	a powerful substance that kills micro-organisms. **p. 52**
eardrum	the first part of the ear to vibrate when a sound enters. **p. 203**
electromagnet	a magnet made from a coil of wire, operated by an electric current. **p. 168**
element	a substance made up of only one type of atom. **p. 79**
energy	the ability to make things happen. **p. 196**
enzyme	substance that breaks down foods to small nutrient molecules. **pp. 12, 14, 16, 44**
erosion	the wearing away of rocks as they come into contact with each other. **p. 115**
evaluate	consider how good an experimental method is. **p. 165**
exhale	to breathe out. **p. 28**
expand	get bigger. **p. 148**
faeces	undigested food and bacteria that pass out of your digestive system. **p. 11**
fatty acid	a substance made when fats are digested. **p. 12**
fermentation	using yeast or other microbes to make products such as alcohol. **p. 44**
fibre	indigestible material in food. **pp. 4, 11**
filter	a coloured material through which light can pass. **p. 188**
food web	a set of linked food chains in a habitat. **p. 66**
formula	the abbreviation that tells us the number of each type of atom in a molecule, e.g. H_2, CH_4, H_2O. **p. 85**
freezing point	the temperature at which a liquid becomes a solid. **p. 155**
gabbro	an igneous rock made up of large crystals. **p. 135**
glucose	a type of sugar. Cells use it in respiration. **pp. 12, 22**
gneiss	a metamorphic rock formed in the intense pressure and heat during mountain-building. **p. 130**
granite	an igneous rock made up of large crystals. **pp. 108, 111, 133, 135**
haemoglobin	the substance in red blood cells that carries oxygen. **p. 26**

heart an organ that pumps blood. **p. 25**

heat energy energy moving from a hotter place to a colder place. **p. 144**

hertz (Hz) the unit of frequency; 1 hertz = 1 vibration per second. **p. 202**

hydrochloric acid an acid you make in your stomach. **pp. 10, 15**

igneous rock types formed by solidifying molten rock. **p. 132**

image a picture of something, formed by light. **p. 182**

immune system defends us against infections. **p. 48**

immunisation giving someone a vaccine to protect them from an infection. **p. 50**

incubator keeps things at a warm temperature. **p. 43**

infectious disease a disease that can spread from one person to another. **p. 46**

inhale to breathe in. **p. 28**

insulation a material which prevents heat or sound energy from travelling. **pp. 153, 205**

invertebrate an animal that does not have an internal backbone. **p. 60**

inverted upside down, or left-right reversed. **p. 184**

iron a metallic element needed to make red blood cells. **p. 6**

lactic acid a substance made in cells by anaerobic respiration. **p. 27**

large intestine a section of your digestive system that removes water from undigested food remains. **p. 11**

laser a source of a narrow beam of light. **p. 178**

lipase an enzyme that digests fats. **p. 12**

loudness how loud or soft a sound is. **p. 196**

loudspeaker a scientific device used for making sounds. **p. 198**

luminous describes something that gives out light. **p. 182**

magnetic field the area around a magnet where it can affect magnetic materials. **p. 166**

Key words
on key people
Stephen Sparks
volcanoes
James Dewar
low temperatures

GLOSSARY

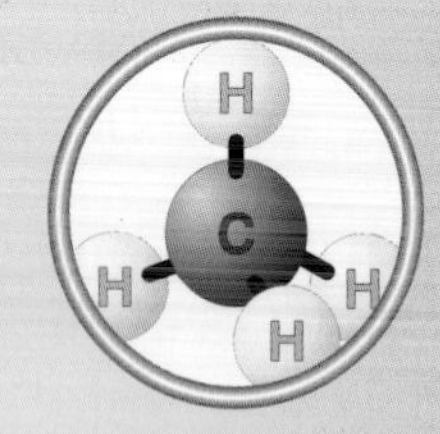

magnetic material	any material attracted by a magnet. **p. 162**
magnetised	turned into a magnet. **p. 170**
malnutrition	the result when you do not have the right balance of foods for your health. **p. 8**
melting point	the temperature at which a solid turns into a liquid. **p. 100**
metamorphic	rocks that have been changed by the action of heat and/or pressure. **p. 130**
microphone	a scientific instrument for collecting sounds. **p. 199**
mineral	a substance that plants and animals need to make their cells; a solid element or compound found naturally. **pp. 4, 6, 108**
mixture	two or more different substances mixed, but not chemically combined, together. **pp. 94, 97, 98**
model	a 'picture' constructed by scientists to help explain how things work. **p. 184**
molecule	groups of two or more atoms bonded together. **p. 84**
noise	unwanted sound. **p. 204**
noise pollution	unwanted sounds in the environment. **p. 204**
non-luminous	describes something that doesn't give out light. **p. 182**
north-seeking pole	the pole of a magnet which points north. **p. 166**
nutrient agar jelly	a food for growing bacteria. **p. 42**
nutrients	food molecules that are essential for our health. **p. 4**
obese	being so overweight that your health suffers. **p. 9**
opaque	describes a material that won't transmit light. **p. 181**
oscilloscope	a scientific instrument used for showing sounds. **p. 198**
pancreas	an organ that makes digestive enzymes. **p. 10**
particle model	a way of thinking about matter as made up of many tiny particles. **p. 149**
pasteurisation	treating milk to kill harmful bacteria. **p. 54**
pathogen	a micro-organism that causes infections. **p. 46**

penicillin	a type of antibiotic. **p. 52**
percentage cover	a way of measuring plants that grow in clumps. **p. 64**
Periodic Table	a table of the chemical elements in which similar elements line up in vertical columns. **p. 83**
permanent magnet	a magnet which doesn't require a current to make it work. **p. 168**
petri dish	a dish for growing bacteria. **p. 42**
pH	a measure of how acidic or alkaline a solution is. **p. 15**
pitch	how high or low a note sounds. **p. 196**
pole	where the magnetic force of a magnet is most concentrated. **p. 163**
pooter	a suction device for catching tiny animals. **p. 63**
population boom	the result of animals living and breeding successfully. **p. 68**
predator–prey relationship	changes in the population size of a predator and the prey it eats. **p. 69**
producer	a plant. It converts light energy into food energy. **p. 66**
proportion	the relative amount of a part present in the whole, usually shown as a fraction or percentage. **p. 97**
protease	an enzyme that digests protein. **pp. 12, 15**
protein	a nutrient that we need for growth. **p. 4**
pure	made of a single substance. **p. 101**
pyramid of numbers	this shows how many organisms there are at each step of a food chain. **p. 70**
quadrat	a piece of equipment for measuring the number of plants in an area. **p. 64**
radiation	when heat travels outwards from a hot object in the form of infra-red radiation. **pp. 150, 152**
random sampling	a way of gathering fair data about the plants and animals in an area. **p. 64**
ratio	the relative numbers of parts in a whole, e.g. each type of element in a compound. **p. 103**

Key words
on key people
Robert Boyle
gases
Isaac Newton
the spectrum

GLOSSARY

ray	a very thin beam of light. **p. 182**
ray diagram	a diagram to show where light travels. **p. 183**
red blood cells	cells in the blood that carry oxygen round the body. **p. 26**
reflect	bounce off a surface. **pp. 180, 189**
reflection	when light or sound bounces off a surface. **p. 181**
refraction	when light bends as it travels from one material into another. **p. 186**
repel	push away from you with a force. **p. 163**
respiration	releasing energy from glucose. **pp. 22, 27, 44, 70**
ribcage	the ribs and breastbone. **p. 28**
saliva	a digestive juice made in your mouth. **pp. 10, 15**
sampling	selecting small samples of something to measure. **p. 64**
schist	a metamorphic rock formed from mudstones and shale. **p. 130**
sediment	rock fragments that are deposited. **p. 115**
sedimentary	rock types formed from the compaction and cementation of sediment. **p. 127**
sensitive	able to sense small differences or changes. **pp. 142, 165**
signal generator	a scientific instrument used for making sounds of known frequencies. **pp. 198, 202**
slate	a metamorphic rock formed when mudstone or shale is subjected to high pressure. Its minerals line up in parallel layers. **p. 130**
source	where something (e.g. light) comes from. **p. 178**
south-seeking pole	the pole of a magnet which points south. **p. 166**
spectrum	when light has been split up into all the colours it is made from. **p. 187**
starch	a carbohydrate made by plants. **p. 4**
steel	a metal, made mostly of iron. **p. 162**
sterilise	to treat something so that there are no micro-organisms left alive. **p. 42**

symbol the abbreviation of the name of each chemical element, e.g. hydrogen = H, lead = Pb. **pp. 80, 85**

temperature a measure of how hot or cold something is. **p. 142**

thermal conductor a material that is good at conducting heat. **p. 146**

thermal insulator a material that is bad at conducting heat. **p. 146**

thermometer an instrument for measuring temperature. **p. 143**

trachea the airway leading from the back of the throat to the lungs. **p. 29**

transect in ecology, samples taken along a line. **p. 64**

translucent describes a material that lets light through but through which you can't see clearly. **p. 180**

transmission when light or sound is allowed to pass through a material the way micro-organisms spread from one person to another. **pp. 46, 181**

transmit allow light or sound to pass through. **pp. 180, 188**

transparent describes a material that lets light pass through. **p. 180**

transport the moving of rock fragments (by gravity, wind, rivers, sea or glaciers). **p. 114**

vaccination giving someone a vaccine to protect them from a disease. **p. 50**

vaccine a solution that contains fragments of micro-organisms. **p. 50**

vacuum empty space. **p. 200**

vein a blood vessel that conveys blood to the heart. **p. 25**

ventilation moving air in and out of your chest. **p. 28**

vibrate move back and forth at a regular rate. **pp. 196, 201**

villi tiny structures in the small intestine for absorbing nutrients. **p. 10**

vitamin a type of nutrient we need in small amounts. **pp. 4, 6**

weathering the breakdown of rocks in nature. **p. 110**

white blood cell a blood cell that protects against infections. **p. 48**

yeast a type of fungus. **pp. 44, 54**

Key words
on key people
Marie Curie
radium

ACKNOWLEDGEMENTS

Alamy Images: 14b, 112, 128t, 146t, 204; **Bettman/Corbis**: 220; **Brownie Harris/Corbis:** 132l; **Corel 7 (NT)** 106b, **Corel 18 (NT)** 67, **Corel 26 (NT)** 167t, **Corel 39 (NT)** 111 (both), 222r, **Corel 124 (NT)** 40t, **Corel 183 (NT)** 129t, **Corel 205 (NT)** 27, **Corel 244 (NT)** 66, **Corel 253 (NT)** 30, **Corel 375 (NT)** 188b, **Corel 406 (NT)** 124t, **Corel 416 (NT)** 8, **Corel 417 (NT)** 151b, **Corel 434 (NT)** 119t, **Corel 465 (NT)** 38b, **Corel 515 (NT):** 92t, **Corel 516 (NT)** 106t, **Corel 517 (NT)** 60b, **Corel 527 (NT)** 194, 227r (all 4), **Corel 541 (NT)** 44r, 54l, **Corel 559 (NT)** 217b, **Corel 587 (NT)** 223t, **Corel 604 (NT)** 227l, **Corel 620 (NT)** 219, **Corel 650 (NT)** 113, **Corel 669 (NT)** 14t, **Corel 759 (NT)** 50t, 170, **Corel 763 (NT)** 72m, 92b, **Corel 768 (NT)** 217t, **Corel 776 (NT)** 22; **Digital Stock 7 (NT)** 42br, **Digital Stock 12 (NT)** 26; **Digital Vision PB (NT)** 76b, **Digital Vision 1 (NT)** 168, **Digital Vision 2 (NT)** 4b, **Digital Vision 4 (NT)** 192, **Digital Vision 5 (NT)** 47m, 182t, **Digital Vision 6 (NT)** 140, **Digital Vision 11 (NT)** 20b, 20t, **Digital Vision 13 (NT)** 200, **Digital Vision 14 (NT)** 132r, 124b, **Digital Vision 15 (NT)** 222tl, **Digital Vision 17 (NT)** 4t, **Gerry Ellis and Michael Durham/Digital Vision LC (NT)** 58, 218b; **Dr B Booth/GSF Picture Library:** 116t, 116bl, 129b, **GSF Picture Library:** 127tr, 128b, 130b, 134l, 134r, **GSF/Rida/GSF Picture Library:** 127l; **Holt Studios:** 60t; **i100gc (NT)** 188t; **Illustazione Italiana/Mary Evans Picture Library:** 136; **Illustrated London News V2 (NT)** 54r; **Ingram ILV2CD5 (NT)** 16r; **Jeremy Woodhouse/Digital Vision WT (NT)** 202, 224; **Karl Ammann/Digital Vision AA (NT)** 151t; **Lawrie Ryan:** 82; **Mark Boulton/CEC:** 16l, 62, 143m, 146b, 162t, 189 (top3), 216l; **Milepost 92½:** 148; **Photodisc 4 (NT)** 225t, **Photodisc 6 (NT)** 64, 140, **Photodisc 18 (NT)** 182b, 184l, 208, **Photodisc 24 (NT)** 197b, 216r, **Photodisc 37 (NT)** 176, 189b, **Photodisc 40 (NT)** 206tl, **Photodisc 45 (NT)** 197t, **Photodisc 46 (NT)** 98l, **Photodisc 54 (NT)** 156b, 166, **Photodisc 67 (NT):** 2, **Photodisc 72 (NT)** 38t, 76t, 160, 167b, 218t; **Robert Eric/Corbis Sygma:** 190t; **Science Enhancement Programme:** 147; **Shout/ Rex Features:** 142; **Spectrum Colour Library**: 130t; **Science Photo Library:** 44l, 88l, 88r, 120r, 172l, **/CMS:** 33br, **/Eye Of Science:** 11, 33bl, **/Alfred Pasieka:** 12, **/Biophoto Associates:** 6, **/Dr Arthur Tucker:** 145, **/Jim Amos**: 156t, **/Kaj R Svensson**: 108r, 127br, **/St Bartholomew's Hospital:** 34, **/AJ Photo/Hop Americain:** 206bl, **/Andrew Lambert Photography:** 86, **/Andrew McClenaghan:** 42l, 52, **/Annabella Bluesky:** 205, **/BSIP Boucharlat:** 102r, **/BSIP Cardoso:** 143r, **/BSIP Chassenet:** 98r, **/BSIP, Laurent:** 43, **/Charles D Winters:** 108ml, **/Cordelia Molloy:** 102l, **/David Hardy:** 223l, **/Dave Roberts:** 206br, **/David Parker:** 109, 187, **/David Scharf:** 48tr; **/DavidTaylor:** 225b; **/Dirk Wiersma:** 133r, **/Dr Gary Gaugler:** 40b, **/Dr Linda Stannard, UCT:** 41, **/Dr P Marazzi:** 47t, **/E R Degginger:** 108tl, **/Eric Grave:** 40m, **/ESA:** 172r, **/George Bernard:** 133l , **/Gusto:** 72l, **/Hugh Turvey:** 143l, **/Los Alamos National Laboratory:** 178, 226, **/Martin Bond:** 33t, **/Martin Land:** 119b, **/Maximilian Stock Ltd:** 42tr, **/Merlin Tuttle:** 206tr, **/Michael Donne:** 190br; **/Pascal Goetgheluck:** 72r, **/Peter Menzel:** 48b, **/Richard Megna:** 162b, **/S Nagendra:** 50b, **/Science Pictures Ltd:** 47b, **/Sheila Terry:** 120l, 223bl, **/Simon Fraser:** 116r; **/Simon Fraser/RVI Newcastle-upon-Tyne** 32, **/Steve Allen:** 196, **/Tony McConnell:** 152r, 158, **Still Pictures/Tom Koene:** 9, **/Martin Bond:** 152l; **Stone/Getty Images:** 190l, **Taxi/Getty Images:** 150; **Tony Waltham Geophotos:** 222bl.

Picture research by Liz Savery and Stuart Sweatmore

Every effort has been made to trace all the copyright holders, but if any have been overlooked the publisher will be pleased to make the necessary arrangements at the first opportunity.